When Sex Goes to School

WARRING VIEWS ON SEX—

AND SEX EDUCATION—SINCE THE SIXTIES

When Sex Goes to School

WARRING VIEWS ON SEX—

AND SEX EDUCATION—SINCE THE SIXTIES

Kristin Luker

W. W. Norton & Company

NEW YORK · LONDON

For information about permission to reproduce selections from this book, write to
Permissions, W. W. Norton & Company, Inc., 500 Fifth Avenue, New York, NY 10110

Manufacturing by The Maple-Vail Book Manufacturing Group
Book design by Iris Weinstein
Production manager: Andrew Marasia

Library of Congress Cataloging-in-Publication Data

Luker, Kristin.
When sex goes to school ; warring views on sex—and sex education—
since the sixties / Kristin Luker. — 1st ed.
p. cm.
Includes bibliographical references and index.
ISBN-13: 978-0-393-06089-8 (hardcover)
ISBN-10: 0-393-06089-6 (hardcover)
1. Sex instruction—United States. 2. Sex educators—United States.
3. Sex customs—United States—History. I. Title.
HQ57.5.A3L84 2006
613.9071—dc22

2006006728

W. W. Norton & Company, Inc., 500 Fifth Avenue, New York, N.Y. 10110
www.wwnorton.com

W. W. Norton & Company Ltd., Castle House, 75/76 Wells Street, London W1T 3QT

1 2 3 4 5 6 7 8 9 0

We are all immigrants to the future, and our children are learning the language more quickly than we are.

— RIVER MALCOLM

Contents

Acknowledgments

Y̶ou'd think after spending years talking to people about sex, politics, and religion and then spending many more years writing about it, sitting down to write a brief thank-you to all of the people who made this book possible would be simple.

In fact, it's overwhelming. If it takes a village to raise a child, as the much-maligned African proverb puts it, then it takes a continent to write a book. Any book is the product not only of the actual flesh-and-blood people whose help and support make it a reality, but all of those other writers who have gone before and whose thoughts have shaped the way we think, not to mention the kind souls whose conversations sparked my thoughts.

I have spent so many years puzzling out what is going on with sex education that I have accumulated a much longer list of debts, intellectual and otherwise, than most people. If I even tried to begin to list all the people whose ideas, help, feedback, and moral support have made this book possible, this section would be far longer than the book itself. But let me try in however limited a way to say thank you to a few people and institutions whose help was unusually unstinting and prolonged.

First of all, I am most obviously indebted to those people who so kindly let me talk to them in homes, cafés, and diners all across the country. I have spent almost a third of my life now asking people what it is about sex education that got them out of their homes and into the streets, or at least into the school cafeterias where many of the meetings about sex education curricula take place. I am continually astonished—and grateful—for the willingness of people to share their most vulnerable selves when it comes to what they think young people should know about sex. Despite the air of confidence and surety that may come through in these interviews, no one believes in her heart that she has gotten in absolutely right when it comes to sex and children, especially if the children in question are her own. It's easy to talk about what schools and others ought to do or teach about sexuality, but it's another thing to share your thoughts—and your doubts—about what you are doing. That people were so open on both scores was a gift, and one I appreciate deeply.

Several institutions patiently supported the many years of fieldwork that yielded this book. In particular, the Guggenheim Foundation, the Spencer Foundation, the Ford Foundation, the Open Society Institute, and the National Endowment for the Humanities all supported the book financially and were remarkably patient with my requests for the infamous "no cost extensions," whereby scholars beg for just a little more time to finish the project.

I've been very lucky to be surrounded by provocative colleagues at the University of California, Berkeley, and the University of California, San Diego, as well as by colleagues I met during stays at Duke and Princeton. All of them have made this a much better book than it would be otherwise, and even if I can't thank them all personally, they will see their contributions if they look closely.

A number of outstanding undergraduate "project managers" helped keep this research effort afloat, and I owe them special thanks. Michelle Bebeau, Guadaloupe Bumatay, Michelle Davis, Lou Limon, Heather Ubelhor, and Elaine Villamin kept files straight, did research, checked interviews for accuracy, were unflaggingly energetic, and in Elaine's case found particularly innovative ways to maneuver around the bureaucracy. Special thanks are also due to Margo Rodriguez of the Jurisprudence and Social Policy Program of the University of California, Berkeley, who was able to soothe cranky computers more times than I can count and who has made recalcitrant files rise from the dead.

Outstanding graduate students helped too. Jody Foster, Chris Rhomberg, Arlene Stein, Rich Kaplan, Jon Pennington, and Laura Weide, among others, gave me much more intellectual excitement than I would have thought possible. John Pennington in particular was a data genius of the first order, and I am grateful.

Ruth Dixon, David Kirp, Jerome Karabel, Carole Joffe, Michele Lamont, Harriet Lerner, River Malcolm, Chandra Mukerji, Karen Paget, Deborah Rogoff, and Ruth Rosen all read the manuscript many more times than even the bonds of friendship and duty called for, and for that I am profoundly grateful.

Finally, the University of California has an innovative program designed by Terry Strathman, which places undergraduates in the offices of faculty members to become real partners in the research enterprise. I cannot thank all of them here, but their contributions are very much appreciated.

One of the very best things about writing a book is that it brings you into contact with new people, people you hope you can hold on to for a lifetime. I am immensely grateful for the help and support of my very special editor, Maria Guarnaschelli, who has been able to see to the heart of this book in ways that have been eye-opening even for me, the author. My agent, Victoria Pryor, has been everything a person could ever want in an agent and then some. She shares with Maria that rare capacity to be tough and supportive at the same time, and she had faith when mine was flagging. Liz Duvall was the kind of copy editor that you wish could just move in with you, knowing that everything you wrote would sound better. And my friend/writing coach/cheerleader and all-round-nice person, Jane-Anne Staw, already has many, many people who sing her praises for helping them make their books better than they would otherwise have been, and I feel honored to join their ranks.

No set of acknowledgments would be complete without a mention of the love and support of my family. Kelly, Jim, and Laurie kept me going from afar, and Jerry, Alex, and Sonya made sure that every time I opened my front door I found love and new energy. Edit and Uri Tulchinsky reminded me why scholarship matters and made it possible with their love and support. When people fight about the future of children and of families, I know from firsthand experience why they fight: because the stakes are so very high.

When Sex Goes to School

WARRING VIEWS ON SEX—

AND SEX EDUCATION—SINCE THE SIXTIES

Mrs. Boland, the Sexual Revolution, and Me

I was driving down a quiet, leafy street in a suburban East Coast town, cursing under my breath in that edited way people with children do. I was scheduled to talk to someone I will call Mrs. Boland, one of the main opponents of the new sex education curriculum being proposed for her son's middle school.[1] She had given me careful directions to her house, but the small town she lived in was nonchalant about posting street signs, as if to warn outsiders that we were not really welcome. After much aimless driving around and two stops at convenience stores, I finally pulled up in front of Mrs. Boland's tired-looking, somewhat faded stucco bungalow. I opened the waist-high chain-link gate, picked my way through the barren front yard, and found myself knocking on her door.

Although my wanderings had made me twenty minutes late for our interview, there was a long pause before a tiny, birdlike woman fluttering with nervous energy opened the door and ushered me into what was evidently Operations Central of the local opposition—a small, cluttered room filled with a fax machine, filing cabinets, and untidy piles of paper on every surface. There was something odd about the room, as if the furniture had been borrowed from another setting—a law office, perhaps—and squeezed into this small room, where it was weirdly out of scale. The chairs, the desk, and a sideboard were dark, ornate, and heavily carved, and together they made me think I should be speaking in low, hushed tones as we got ready to read the will or hear the last wishes of the deceased.

Mrs. Boland sat me down on a high-backed chair in front of her desk and sat herself behind it. The midday light streamed in through the window, keeping her face in shadows.

For reasons I couldn't quite articulate, I was anxious. Over the years I've come to terms with inviting myself into the homes of total strangers and asking them hard questions about touchy matters. (Ask me about the time when I tried to get a Mormon lawyer to tell me in detail why he didn't want his twelve-year-old son to know about masturbation.) But this interview was different: something about the atmosphere of the room, the way I had been placed so I could not see, and the massive desk made me feel both guilty and nervous.

I was in Mrs. Boland's living room on that beautiful fall day because I wanted to understand the fight over sex education and why it seems to be taking up a larger and larger part of American political life. What I already knew was that sex education, like abortion twenty years ago, was driving ordinary people into a level of political activism that was completely unprecedented for most of them. Mrs. Boland and women like her often worked the equivalent of full-time jobs to ensure that their values about sexuality would be taught in public schools. Perhaps it was this intensity that was putting me on edge.

I've never really found a good name for what it is that I do. I'm trained as a social scientist—a sociologist, to be exact—and when people ask me my area of expertise, I sound like a caricature of an academic, explaining that I study the social, political, and legal regulation of sexuality and reproduction. That description probably hints at the fact that I have appointments in both a sociology department and a law school, but it doesn't tell you much about what takes me to places like Mrs. Boland's living room.

Actually, the answer is easy. I'm attracted to topics on which everyone has an opinion, and a passionately held one at that. I go where people yell and scream and sometimes cry when I interview them. The more interesting question is why the opinions I feel most attracted to are the ones having to do with sex. I've studied and written about sex my whole scholarly career: about contraception and its use, about abortion, about teen pregnancy, and now about sex education.[2]

I think the answer is that men and women of a certain age have lived through a revolution as disorienting and historically important as any of the revolutions we routinely recognize as such. The American Revolution, the French, and the Russian, we're all taught in school, reshaped history so much that we can draw a clear line between the world before and what it was like after. The revolution at the heart of this book, the sexual revolution of the 1960s and 1970s, will in the end be as historic as any of these other revolutions, I think, and like them it will continue to reshape human life in profound ways for many, many years to come. That revolution questioned a whole set of assumptions about what were the right ways for men and women to relate to one another sexually, how sex was and should be related to maleness and femaleness, and how and where marriage and sex should coincide. The opening up of what had been taken-for-granted truths has changed the world. And that's why I write about sex.

Even though the sexual revolution has been officially declared over and done with many times, for many years, by many different observers, sometimes it seems to me that the fighting about it has never really ceased. In the 1970s we fought about abortion; in the 1980s, about whether teenagers needed parental consent to use contraception or to get an abortion. Now we are fighting about sex education and gay marriage, and just over the horizon are fights about emergency contraception (the "morning-after" pill) and whether pharmacists who think that unmarried sex is immoral can refuse to dispense it.

I believe that common themes tie all of these issues together and that sex education for young people is an excellent place to see what those themes are. I want to show you that fights about sex are also fights about gender, about power and trust and hierarchy, about human nature, and, not surprisingly, about what sex really is and what it means in human life. Even more deeply, fights about sex are fights about how we are to weigh our obligations to ourselves and others, issues that themselves are tied to our notions of what it means to be a man or a woman.

In short, the sexual revolution of the late 1960s and 1970s upended the world in which many of us grew up and significantly rearranged the way we thought about it. For some people, that was enormously liberating, opening new ways of being and new ways of life. For Mrs. Boland, the freedom of the 1960s and the loosening of rules and strictures that came with it quite literally ruined her life. And she is not alone, as I was to learn.

As I sat in Mrs. Boland's cluttered room that day, with its oddly outsized furniture, and the glare from the morning sun making her a shadowy presence behind her desk, I was ill at ease, jumpy, off stride. Then she began to speak.

Her voice was flat, depressed, drained of all emotion. She was opposed to sex education, she said, because her husband was a rapist; he had in fact raped their daughter, and she thought that sex education was at the root of it all. Not directly, of course, because he was well into his adult years before the kind of sex education Mrs. Boland objected to was being offered in the schools. Rather, she thought that sex education in its modern incarnation had had a baleful indirect effect on her husband. The way sex is taught nowadays, she said, takes the "thou shalt nots" out of it and validates personal preferences over right and wrong in sexual decision-making. It embodies and legitimates a morality based on selfish pleasure, and in her husband's case, the pleasure involved was the most selfish of all, that built on the pain of another person.

Though the connection may be obscure to others, for Mrs. Boland, the link between rape and sex education was all too real. The only way to keep people like her husband from harming others was to reestablish the rules that were overthrown in the 1960s, and sex education was the logical place to start. (When Mrs. Boland said "the sixties"—which she did often—her face contorted into a grimace of disgust.) She said that she opposed sex education unless it was taught in the context of morality, and for her the word "morality" was shorthand for the norms that once ruled American sexual behavior—that the only moral sex is between a man and a woman and within holy wedlock. Perhaps it was too late to save her daughter from men like her husband, she said, but most of her waking hours were spent trying to save the next generation.

As we spoke, I felt my world tip subtly off-balance. In Mrs. Boland's life, sex was a powerful and often destructive force of nature that could sweep otherwise reasonable men and women over their heads into something they could not control, try as they might. My own thinking over the years had been based on the assumption that sexuality was mostly benign, a source of pleasure rather than of danger and harm. It's not that I hadn't heard horror stories about sexual abuse and exploitation, but somehow I had always assumed that these examples were the exceptions, the disturbed acts of disturbed people, rather than at the heart of what sex was. What I was hearing from Mrs. Boland, backed up with terrible details, was the belief that sexuality, especially for men, was by its very nature destructive and needed to be contained. Mrs. Boland believed, and believed deeply, that the only way this powerful disruptive force could be controlled was to channel it into marriage and to marshal every resource—legal, moral, and emotional—to keep it there.

These two competing visions of sex—sex as pleasure versus sex as danger, sex as something that reasonable humans can handle versus sex as something that needs all the help it can get to keep from running amok—have long histories in American thinking. Even feminists have squabbled among themselves about which vision more accurately captures the basic nature of sex.[3]

But in the complicated world of values, interests are often intertwined with beliefs. When Mrs. Boland insisted that marriage was the only safe place for sex, she was reflecting not only the specifics of her own sad story but the social realities faced by more and more women. Increasingly, sex *is* becoming, if not the kind of dreadful danger that Mrs. Boland encountered, something that many women feel they do not own or control. That is not because they are increasingly likely to be victims in the way that Mrs. Boland had in mind, but because things that were commonplace in 1959—committed relationships, men who would marry women whom they made pregnant, men who would take responsibility for the children they fathered, even marriage itself—are becoming scarcer and scarcer.

In the wake of these changes, Mrs. Boland and the movement she represents are becoming more passionate and urgent every day. The sexual woes she pointed to are very real. But I suspect that what Mrs. Boland really wants is to turn back the clock sexually to 1959, and that just isn't going to happen. As the ancients remind us, you never step in the same river twice; once you have stepped in it, it is no longer the river it was before.

What I learned from Mrs. Boland's story was that sex can mean very different things to different people, and that those differences can be shaped by social circumstance. Although I did not know it at the time, my interview with Mrs. Boland set out the issues involved in the sex education debate with uncanny clarity. Is sex something for individuals to enjoy as they will, as long as they take proper precautions, or is it a powerful and unruly force that can be entered into only when it has been safely channeled into marriage? Will teaching young people to make sexual choices just give rise to more unhappiness, exploitation, and disaster of the kind Mrs. Boland encountered, or is human happiness best served by having sexual options? And how do issues from the sixties—the relationships between sex and gender, gender and what it means to have a life—shape how people think about these questions?

This book is my attempt to answer these questions by joining together two separate strands. One examines how the changes in women's as well as men's lives have shaped the ways we look at sex (and gender); the other shows what people engaged in the battles over sex education think and say about those changes. The story of the fight over sex education weaves together both of those strands, the sociology and the biography.

As a sociologist who has spent many years thinking about sex and society, I want to explore what has changed in our lives when it comes to sex, marriage, and gender over the last half-century. But that part of the story is necessarily somewhat abstract, dealing with statistics and large-scale social change. So I also want to make the story more intimate and real by showing how these big changes are playing out in the lives of individuals, people whose stories may not be as dramatic as Mrs. Boland's but who are grappling in different ways with sex and how to deal with it.

I should probably say at the outset that I'm not at all sure what the right answers are about what will best promote human happiness and fulfillment when it comes to sex, either for a society or for individuals. The more I talk to people about what they think, the more I come to see the world through their eyes. And the more I've explored the issues around sex and gender, the more I've come to see how complex these issues really are. I now know why Mrs. Boland can, in all good faith, feel that her husband's actions are rooted in modern sex education, and I hope that by the end of the book you will understand too.

On that note, come with me to the town of Shady Grove, where I began my fieldwork on what was driving the war over sex education.

CHAPTER ONE

Sex and Politics in American Life

Jenny Letterman is steamed. While picking up a few things for dinner at the local Stop & Shop, she happened to bump into her next-door neighbor. Jenny makes a point of trying to avoid this neighbor, because she's a gossip, the kind of person who knows exactly who has lost his job, who's sleeping with whom, and all the other big and small secrets in the town of Shady Grove. But this time the gossip was closer to home. Mrs. Busybody, glancing furtively around the aisles of the supermarket, confided that she had heard the local elementary school was in the process of setting up a new sex education program, one that would be given to all its students.

Now, Jenny loves Glenwood, the school where her son, Joshua, is enrolled, and she adores Ms. Vasquez, Josh's third-grade teacher, who was a certifiable saint when Josh was having troubles with multiplication. Josh now invites grownups to test him on his times tables, up to and including twelve times twelve, which Jenny thinks is nothing short of a miracle, given how difficult he found multiplication at the beginning of the year.

Still, sex is something pretty special for her. As a Christian, she believes it's a gift of the Creator, to be treated with respect, and she's not at all sure she wants her son thinking about it just yet. He's pretty young for his age, and eight-year-old boys can treat anything as smutty. Sex is a delicate and complex matter, and while she has complete confidence in the school and Ms. Vasquez, she thinks it would be too much like signing a blank check to turn over something as special as sex to them. More to the point, like Mrs. Boland, she is convinced that Glenwood cannot—or will not—teach morality along with the lessons of where babies come from.

Meanwhile, on the other side of town, Melanie Stevens is busy putting the final touches on the new human sexuality curriculum that riles Jenny so much. Melanie and the school nurse, Bethany Burt, have been working on this curriculum for months now and have spent many hours reading other curricula and discussing what they acknowledge is a volatile issue, even though Shady Grove is becoming more sophisticated as more and more families like Melanie's leave the city to embrace its small-town atmosphere.

Trained as a social worker before she decided to stay home full-time with her daughter, Devora, Melanie has been a little surprised by how upset she finds herself becoming when she talks to Bethany. Part of it is that she and Rob moved to Shady Grove to get away from all the ugliness and unhappiness of the city, and it disturbs her to hear Bethany's tales of pregnant seventh-graders, eighth-graders with their third case of gonorrhea, and ninth-graders having unwanted sex with their stepfathers. Devora is younger than those kids and, God willing, will never be exposed to those horrors firsthand. Melanie thinks forewarned is forearmed, and fourth grade is none too soon to start education in the facts of life. (She would actually prefer kindergarten as a starting point for sexuality education, she says, but she's not sure Shady Grove is ready for that.)

As part of the process of getting a sex education curriculum going, Melanie and Bethany have reached out to what they imagine to be the whole community of Shady Grove: parents, businesspeople, clergy, physicians, and others. Because they weren't born yesterday, as Bethany tells me, they have made extra-sure to invite people from all across the religious spectrum. Invitations went out to Temple Beth-El, to Saint Michael's, and to all the old-line churches that have been in Shady Grove since its founding. When it came to the churches that have sprung up in the past few years on the edges of town—the ones that Bethany tells me look more like motels than houses of worship—things got touchier. These evangelical and Pentecostal churches, she says, are "Christian," and the tone of her voice makes it clear that for her this is not a neutral description. Still, she contacted those churches too, and felt the glow of a job well done when she finally persuaded Reverend Smithers, the pastor of Calvary Christian Community Church, to come to meetings. Reverend Smithers, a bluff, hearty man with a winning manner, sings gospel in a way that brings to mind Anne Lamott's memorable phrase, "God gave the notes, he's just the channel."[1] He's also head of the largest of the new churches, and quite a catch for the committee. But unfortunately, Reverend Smithers never really seemed to feel at home with the group and finally begged off, pleading the press of other commitments.[2]

Anchored as they are in Shady Grove, Jenny and Melanie, Bethany and Reverend Smithers are part of something much bigger, a conflict brewing in small towns and large cities all over the country. Everybody involved knows the fight over sex education isn't confined to Shady Grove, of course. Melanie used to be a volunteer at the local Planned Parenthood office and called on her friends and acquaintances there when it came time to plan the "Family Life and Living" curriculum. The national offices of Planned Parenthood in New York helped by giving her guidelines for what a really good sex education course should cover, and so had the New York–based organization SIECUS (Sex Information and Education Council of the U.S.), which shared model curricula with her. When she became alarmed about how controversial sex education was becoming in a nearby town, Melanie was given the name of someone at People for the American Way, an advocacy group in Los Angeles that helps supporters of sex education and other liberal causes organize against the "right wing."

Jenny also found herself connected to large national organizations in remarkably short order. The week after she ran into her gossipy neighbor in the supermarket, she went to talk to her pastor at Calvary Christian—Reverend Smithers. He suggested that she call the local office of the Christian Coalition, and the person she talked to was incredibly helpful, giving her the names of people at the Family Research Council, Concerned Women for America, and the National Association of Christian Educators. The association even helped find her a psychiatrist who ended up testifying to the Shady Grove school board that exposure to sex during what Sigmund Freud called the latency period (usually defined as between age seven and puberty) was developmentally unsound.[3]

Despite the help that both Jenny and Melanie were able to get from national organizations, the fight over sex education is not yet generating the kind of big headlines that have been sparked by abortion and homosexuality, or even sexual harassment. But the battle is getting closer every day.

The same advocacy group that Melanie turned to for help, People for the American Way, reported almost five hundred controversies over sex education across the country in the early 1990s, and I suspect that this estimate is on the low end.[4] As both Melanie's and Jenny's experiences suggest, conflicts over sex education are increasingly on the agenda of major liberal and conservative organizations, both religious and secular. Conflicting views about sex education have also moved straight into the heart of partisan politics. Opposition to the kind of sex education that has been taught for the past thirty years is now officially part of the Republican national platform and many state Republican platforms as well.[5]

How did sex education, which has been surprisingly common for the better part of a century and which has enjoyed very high levels of public support for most of that time, come to be so controversial?[6] What is it about sex education that makes people so passionate about it? And what is it that translates that passion into politics at the national level?

Answering these questions took me almost twenty years and a little over one hundred interviews, not to mention countless hours spent in school board and committee meetings of various groups. On my journey, I interviewed people in four communities, taught myself the mostly unpublished history of sex education, and tried to follow the increasingly vociferous public debates that have begun to emerge on the airwaves and in magazines and newspapers.[7]

The interviews took place in communities I call Shady Grove (where Melanie and Jenny live), Las Colinas, Billingsley, and Lincoln Township. Each came to me in a different way, and each illustrates something different about sex education in the United States these days.

Looking for communities that were in the midst of some sort of fight over sex education, I first discovered Shady Grove, a once-rural town on the West Coast that is rapidly becoming a bedroom community for an urban center more than an hour's drive away. Old and new coexisted uneasily in Shady Grove; its small-town provincialism tucked uncomfortably beside its new, worldly, suburban self. Alfalfa fields were slowly giving way to tract developments, but when the wind blew the right way, you could still smell the earthy, sweet odor of the dairy farms that once dominated this community. Some children in Shady Grove attended the same elementary and high schools their parents had, sometimes even being taught by the same teachers, a rarity on the West Coast.

I spent more than four years in Shady Grove, talking to people more than once, chatting with the town's pharmacist, and sitting in the local café, which served hippies, sophisticates from the city, a contingent of Hell's Angels, and the occasional manure-spattered farmer in for his early morning latte. I've gone back several times in the intervening years to clarify points that came up as I pondered what people there had told me.

Next I spent a year in Billingsley, a small community in the South much like Shady Grove must have been in the 1950s. Still resolutely agrarian (tobacco remains a major crop in the fields surrounding town), the community, particularly the weathered, tumble-down tobacco sheds, sometimes looks like Dorothea Lange or Walker Evans photographs of the rural South in the 1930s. No one moves into Billingsley, and the old people lament that most

of the young people move out. Despite the fact that it too is only
an hour or so from a major urban center, it has remained very
much the small town for a very long time. I asked one Billingsley
resident if any "outsiders" were involved in the sex education
debate, and he named a woman who had moved to the community
as a child in 1952.

Not surprisingly, perhaps, it seemed to me that almost everyone I interviewed in Billingsley was an active member of a church,
although I did not know this when I chose it. The religion that
cast the longest shadow was Southern Baptist, but it was followed
closely by new nondenominational churches such as Reverend
Smithers's church in Shady Grove. Here I learned to ask a question that had rarely come up in Shady Grove, namely, "And what
does your pastor think of the sex education program in town?"
One's pastor, one's church, and one's denomination were all-
important social anchors in Billingsley, anchors that permitted
others to locate you within the social and geographical hierarchy.

To many people, Billingsley probably *is* the story of sex education, period. It's rural, its inhabitants are not highly educated,
and there is not a single Starbucks in the entire town, or at least
there wasn't during the year I did my fieldwork there. More
important, Billingsley is one of those towns where religion and
churches still structure much of social life. As many people I
interviewed will tell you, opposition to sex education is primarily
(and sometimes, to hear them talk about it, exclusively) religious
in nature. And not just any religion, but the kind of religion that
predominates in Billingsley—evangelical, and particularly fundamentalist, Protestantism.[8]

But as is so often the case, looking at the role of religion in people's views about sex education in this town made it clear that real
life is much more complicated than the stereotypes suggest. It is
absolutely the case that religion does play a role in the opposition
to sex education, but not in the clean, unambiguous way that most
people imagine. For example, religion also plays a role, albeit a

more limited one, in mobilizing support for sex education. Mostly, religion gives people a vocabulary, a cultural tool kit, with which to talk about the issues that sexuality raises, and a set of templates for understanding alternative visions of family life, not to mention the larger world.[9]

Although Billingsley was the epitome of a small, religious, tight-knit community in the rural South, it provided an astonishing variety of views on sex education. Deeply devout Southern Baptists as well as others who identified themselves as born-again Christians argued both sides of the issue, with some passionately in favor of full, comprehensive sex education and others equally passionately opposed. (The word "comprehensive" in the context of sex education has a special meaning, which we'll explore below.) Being devoutly religious and even, as they called themselves, "hard-shelled" Southern Baptists, or evangelicals, was not the end of the discussion when it came to how people felt about sex education.

After Billingsley I moved on to Lincoln Township, an affluent community in the Rust Belt East, where I spent almost two years. Although the larger area in which Lincoln finds itself is indeed part of the Rust Belt, and nearby urban areas in the state contain (in both senses of the word) some of the most desperate poverty in the country, you wouldn't know it from driving around Lincoln. A little over an hour's train ride from Lincoln lies a cosmopolitan city where you can hear people speaking languages from all over the globe. Lincoln's residents are part of that global elite; the more successful are driven into the city in limos, and the merely comfortable take the train.

The houses in Lincoln verge on being estates. The much prized and tastefully restored older homes date from the Revolutionary War or just after; the "newer" ones are stucco-and-stonework Tudors that housed an earlier Depression-era generation of successful entrepreneurs from the city. In Lincoln, unlike in the other three communities I studied, most of my research involved observing stormy school board meetings concerned with the proposed implementation of a new sex education curriculum and reading documents that the various committees in town had generated in support of or in opposition to that curriculum. Events unrelated to my fieldwork cut short my stay in Lincoln, so most of the interview material in this book comes from the three other sites, although I do occasionally draw on my interviews from Lincoln, as well as my ethnographies (observation of participants) there. Lincoln served mostly to assure me that the forces I was discovering in the West and the South, in rural and suburban communities, existed in an affluent and long-established community in the East as well.[10]

Well into the research in these three communities, I began to feel something was missing. I had ideas about what was helping to mobilize support for or opposition to sex education, but I needed to test them, and two of my three field sites were far from my base in the San Francisco Bay Area. Shady Grove, where I had begun my research, was closer to home, but the controversy over sex education was rapidly becoming a thing of the past.

So I sought out a new community, in a different part of the West Coast, to test out my ideas. Las Colinas, as I call it, is becoming incorporated into the sprawl of its larger urban neighbor and is, like Shady Grove, an erstwhile small town feeling the pressures of change. The new twist in Las Colinas was that the curriculum causing all the uproar was one from the fastest-growing part of sex education, something called "abstinence only." This kind of sex education, in stark contrast to more prevalent versions, teaches young people not to have sex at all rather than how to have sex safely. The paradox in Las Colinas was that the people protesting the curriculum were opposed because they wanted more *liberal* sex education. I've spent large chunks of the past five years there, and as with Shady Grove, I find myself going back on occasion to clarify something that was said.

At least part of the reason sex education is in the limelight these days is that almost everyone agrees American teenagers don't handle their sexuality very well. Myths to the contrary, American teenagers are no more likely to be sexually active than their peers in Europe, and they start having sex at roughly the same age, allowing for differences among the European countries.[11] Although the sexual *activities* of American teens are not so different from those of teens in the rest of the advanced industrial world, the *consequences* most surely are. Teen birth, abortion, and venereal disease rates are among the highest in the industrialized world.[12] More worrisome, about 20 percent of all AIDS cases in the United States are diagnosed among people in their twenties, and because of the long lag time between infection and symptoms, it is presumed that many of these people acquired the disease as teens.[13]

This litany, by the way, overlooks the fact that American adults don't handle their sexuality very well either, compared to citizens of other countries. Although most sex education programs don't pay much attention to adults (with the notable exception of AIDS prevention programs aimed at high-risk groups such as IV drug users and gay men), they probably should. Like teenagers, adult Americans get pregnant more often when they don't intend to, pass on more sexually transmitted diseases, and have higher abortion rates than almost any other adults in the industrialized world.[14]

Over the past three decades, a consensus about how to approach these problems slowly emerged among opinion leaders, experts, and the general public, and sex education was at the heart of this consensus. Between 1975 and 2005, as the nation confronted both a perceived crisis in teenage pregnancy and an AIDS crisis, sex education programs proliferated, based on the idea that young people needed more information to make better choices. By the 1990s, virtually all American teenagers had at least some exposure to sex education, and over that same period of time, everyone from the surgeon general of the United States, to the National Academy of Sciences, to the National Council of Governors, to most of the large philanthropic foundations, to the National

Council of Negro Women, and even to such groups as the Girls' Clubs and the Junior League endorsed more and better sex education as a way of curbing the toll that sex seemed to be taking on young lives. Remarkably enough, at one point, even both sides in the abortion conflict seemed to agree that more sex education was the answer, as such diverse groups as American Citizens Concerned for Life and the National Abortion Rights Action League (NARAL) signed on. State after state mandated either sex education or AIDS education, and in some cases, both.[15]

But as Jenny intuited that day in the Stop & Shop—and this is where the conflict arises—the kind of sex education that people were turning to in the 1970s and 1980s presumes that marriage is optional and happens later in an individual's sexual career and perhaps not at all. In short, it is based on a set of sexual values that grew out of the sexual revolution of the 1960s, values that many people have become increasingly bold in challenging. Although proponents of sex education often assume that only the facts, and such generally accepted values as not hurting yourself or others, are being taught, people like Jenny are as adamant as any deconstructionist that there is no such thing as "just the facts" when it comes to sex. Moreover, as she and Reverend Smithers sensed almost immediately, the value at the core of modern sex education—the idea that sex is defined by *how* you do it (carefully) rather than *where* you do it (in a marriage between a man and a woman)—is something worth fighting about.

When this study began, it was possible to use the shorthand terms "in favor of" and "opposed to" sex education and pretty much everyone involved knew what was meant. The people who favored sex education in the schools assumed that young people would have a range of sexual choices open to them and that the task of sex education was to teach them how to make good choices. People who favored such education preferred to have it offered to children early on (ideally, starting in kindergarten), as a cumulative program that went through all twelve grades, and to have it be a required rather than an elective part of the curriculum.[16] Proponents of sex education were also strong supporters of a curriculum that went beyond what they called the "plumbing" (basic anatomy and physiology) and into the complex issues of contraception and abortion, and perhaps some teaching to the effect that discrimination against homosexuals is an unacceptable form of intolerance. In general, advocates of sex education wanted a course that would help children come to understand and be comfortable with their own and others' sexuality and give them a way of thinking through the complex set of moral issues that the many sexual choices in front of them entailed.

In contrast, when this study began, people who opposed sex education in the schools were rock-solid in their conviction that parents, not schools, should take on the task of teaching something as intimate and personal as sex. Many parents revealed that they were grudgingly willing to turn a blind eye to the kinds of sex education programs in public schools they themselves may have encountered—namely, a reasonably factual discussion of the mechanics of human sexual and reproductive anatomy and perhaps some discreet discussion of issues such as menstruation and nocturnal emissions. As far as they were concerned, these were matters of physiology, not values, and no child was likely to hear conflicting views about nocturnal emissions or the function of the fallopian tubes between home and school.

What these parents emphatically did not want was what the proponents of sex education have increasingly come to take for granted as the sine qua non of modern sex education: an open, nonjudgmental discussion of sexuality that helps young people become more adept decision-makers. From the point of view of people who opposed sex education, the "values" that children should hold were clear-cut. They firmly believed that hearing a discussion of values not congruent with the values taught at home is confusing at best and morally destructive at worst. If you were doing the right thing as a parent, they felt, then neither a child nor an adolescent faced any real decisions about sex until he or she was out of the home, and in the ideal case, not until the wedding night.

During the course of my twenty-year exploration of conflicts over sex education, American teenagers actually got *better* at handling their sexuality, and both kinds of sex education took the credit. Teenage birth, abortion, and pregnancy rates all dropped, because of two things that happened simultaneously.[17] First, teenagers became more likely to abstain from having sex than they had in the past. My calculations suggest that the probability that a female between fifteen and nineteen would be sexually active and not married went from approximately 29 percent in 1995 to 25 percent in 2002. In other words, almost half a million teens who would have been sexually active a few years ago now aren't.[18]

The other good news is that teens who are sexually active are far more likely than before to use contraception the first time they have sex. Using contraception the first time is often the most challenging time, since it means that one or both partners must plan ahead rather than act on impulse, so increases in this measure are especially heartening. Although the numbers are small, it looks like teenage girls more than doubled their likelihood of being on the pill the first time they had sex (from roughly 8 percent to roughly 17 percent) between 1988 and 2001, and teens using a condom the first time they had sex soared from half to two out of three.[19]

Jenny Letterman isn't impressed by these figures. She likes her school and she likes her son's teacher, Ms. Vasquez. She thinks of herself as pretty open, and in a few years, when Josh gets past what she views as the "squirmy" stage, he'll probably take one of the sex-segregated sex education classes that Pastor Smithers offers at Calvary Christian. She just doesn't want sex ed offered in the school to kids his age, and she especially doesn't want the kind of sex education that will help him "clarify" his "values."

This really annoys Melanie Stevens. She suspects Jenny, whom she knows from soccer league, is a lot more uptight about sex than she seems to be. But what really bothers her is how Jenny apparently wants to keep all of the children of Shady Grove away from sex education, not just Josh. For heaven's sake, Melanie says, trying to keep the annoyance out of her voice, if Jenny thinks the home is the right place to teach about sex, why can't she just opt out and let Josh go to the library when the other fourth-graders talk about where baby chicks come from?

What Melanie doesn't understand is that this suggestion enrages Jenny almost as much as Jenny's reluctance to opt out infuriates Melanie. Although Jenny's feeling that home is the best place to teach about sex obscures more complicated feelings, it's a deeply held value nonetheless. If people come to expect the school to teach about sex, then what's the point of having a family? she asks me rhetorically, waving her hands in the air. For her, sex education in the schools is just what is wrong with America: impersonal institutions are increasingly taking the role families ought to be taking and are, in her opinion, shirking. When the fight about sex education at Glenwood started, Jenny thought she was just pointing out the obvious when she argued that no teacher, not even one as talented as Ms. Vasquez, could know as much about each child as that child's parents did, and parents should be the ones to decide when and what to teach that child about sex.

Jenny has other, purely practical reasons for opposing the opt-out strategy: she thinks her son will feel weird and different going to the library when everyone else stays behind. But where she finds herself at a loss for words is in talking about the big picture—about why this whole issue raises such troubling feelings.

Part of what is being fought about here, although neither Jenny nor Melanie is very good at articulating it, is an issue that emerged with the sexual revolution of the 1960s: the relationship of sex to marriage. Melanie, for example, thinks marriage is a wonderful thing, and she tells me that Rob is the best thing that ever happened to her. She and Rob married in their late thirties, and both of them had had intimate relationships with other people before

that. Although Melanie skips over some of the details, it is evident
when we talk that she expects her daughter, Devora, to follow
much the same route. Melanie would prefer Devora not to be sexually active in high school, but it's clear that she takes for granted
that Devora will experiment sexually before she gets married, and
that her deepest hope is that Devora, like Melanie herself, will have
a life and see the world before she settles down. She doesn't want
Devora to miss the pleasure and intimacy of sex while she's exploring herself and her horizons. One of Melanie's deep but unarticulated values is that Devora needs to have a wide range of experiences,
sexual, emotional, and other, before she can happily settle down into
a marriage without feeling trapped and resentful.[20]

Jenny would be horrified to hear this. For her marriage is the
only legitimate—and safe—place for sex to occur, particularly for
women. Her situation is a bit complicated, however, because she
is far less confident about her ability to control Josh's sexual experiences than she would be about controlling a daughter's. For the
record, she's ambivalent about whether male sexuality is inherently more unruly than female sexuality or whether our culture
makes boys that way. She is clear, though, that male sexuality is
very different from female sexuality and that daughters can only
lose by being sexually active before marriage. Virginity is a special
gift a young woman can give her husband, one that sets her apart
from all others. At the same time, Jenny believes that sexual experiences before marriage make both men and women "damaged
goods," hardened and jaded and closed off from the miracle of true
emotional and physical intimacy a happy marriage can bring.

Because marriage, and by extension ideas about maleness and
femaleness, are at the heart of this discussion, proponents and
opponents just talk past each other in ways that infuriate everyone. Jenny says families should teach about sex and that Josh
would feel discriminated against if he had to go to the library.
Melanie says that while she knows that people like Jenny are
doing a fine job of teaching about sex, the same can't be said of all

the parents in Shady Grove. She doesn't really address the point about how kids like Josh would feel, because she doesn't understand why Jenny can't just live and let live.

Jenny can't just live and let live because marriage, one of the most cherished institutions in her life, is being devalued in the classroom. When she and I talk, she echoes Mrs. Boland, arguing that because of the Supreme Court, schools can't and won't teach morality. (She's referring here to *Engel v. Vitale*, the famous—or, from the point of view of Jenny and her friends, infamous— "prayer in the schools" case.)[21] As she sees it, a cherished American institution, the public school, has become so oversensitive in its wish not to favor one religion over another that it has become actively antireligion. And, although for her, religion and morality are not exactly synonymous, she is convinced that any institution so nervous about anything that looks like the "establishment" of religion is not going to take on the complex job of bolstering marriage by telling students sex is wrong unless people are married. This is the nub of the problem for her, although articulating it is difficult. One thing that Jenny knows, and knows wholeheartedly, is that if information about sex is given without the framework of a moral code, then sex becomes something casual, merely physical, less than it is and less than it can be. In a metaphor that comes up over and over again, Jenny says that providing information without moral direction is like showing teenagers the car keys, telling them all of the mechanics of driving, and then being surprised when they take the car out for a joyride.

As Jenny herself found, arguing that sex education should be taught by families, not schools, became an increasingly untenable position over time. The twin threats of AIDS and teen pregnancy simply eroded the argument. In one school board meeting called to discuss the proposed sex education curriculum in Shady Grove, Melanie addressed the crowd by saying—with a glance in Jenny's direction—that while she trusted the ability of concerned parents to teach their children at home, they were in no position to vouch

for the abilities of other parents in town, including single mothers, recent immigrants from other countries whose English was
poor, the depressed, and the apathetic poor. Her voice shaking
with emotion, Melanie told the people sitting on hard metal
chairs in the Glenwood elementary school lunchroom that if only
one child in the community was to be ignorant about sex, "all of
our precious, beautiful children are at risk of death."[22]

This argument put people like Jenny on the defensive. While
they could and did argue that they were entirely capable of teaching their own children everything they needed to know about sex,
few were foolhardy enough to argue that parents in general were
doing a good job. Consequently, in recent years the fight across
the nation has shifted, becoming less and less about *whether* sex
education will take place in the schools and more and more about
what kind of sex education it will be. Grudgingly conceding that
most schools have to teach something about sex in this era of
AIDS and out-of-wedlock babies, Jenny and people like her have
increasingly become proponents of "abstinence-only" sex education, in contrast to Melanie's kind of sex education, which is now
being called "comprehensive."[23]

As a result, abstinence education is an increasingly large part of
what "sex education" has come to mean. In 1999, almost one of
every four secondary school teachers of sex education reported that
they taught "abstinence" education, and 40 percent of all teachers
(including those teaching "comprehensive" sex education) thought
that abstaining from sexual activity was the most important message they were trying to convey.[24]

Although there is almost as wide a variety of abstinence-only
sex education programs as there is of the comprehensive kind, in
general abstinence education teaches that marriage is the only
acceptable place for sex, that contraception can and often does fail,
and that abortions can and do leave lasting emotional effects on
people. It also teaches the kinds of values that Jenny would second
in a heartbeat: that the best kind of sex comes when you are emo-

tionally, spiritually, and physically in tune with your partner and that this kind of union can happen only when people have committed themselves in a marriage.

To its opponents, this kind of teaching is "fear-based" and inflates the rates of contraceptive failure and the psychological after-effects of abortion while overstating the effectiveness of abstinence education, all in the service of promoting the ideal of no sex before marriage. For the moment, it is important to realize that as far as the people most involved in the debate are concerned, the values are more important than the facts.

Jenny insists on abstinence unless people are married—not only for Josh but for all the children of Shady Grove—but not because she dreads or dislikes sex. Quite the contrary. As far as she can tell, sex in all its majesty and mystery is more at risk from the kind of sex education program that Melanie has in mind than from the values she'd like to see surrounding any discussion about it. Although she can never quite get anyone on Melanie's side to listen, she's militant about sex and inflexible in her commitment to sex only within marriage not because she's antisex but because she thinks sex needs to be protected. Powerful forces are trying to turn sex into something trivial, into just another form of recreation, and she regards people like Melanie as part of the problem, not part of the solution.

As Jenny points out to anyone who will listen, when she was growing up no one had heard of abortion, of teenagers becoming infertile for life thanks to sexually transmitted diseases like pelvic inflammatory disease, or of people dying from the consequences of a "gay lifestyle." (When Jenny talks about this, her fingers sketch the quotation marks around the words.) The daily newspapers didn't carry stories about affluent teenagers who murdered their babies at the senior prom, and child sexual abuse existed only in the minds of the twisted few. When she was a girl, there were far fewer sex education classes, true, but there were also far fewer of the sexual troubles that recent education about sexuality has been designed to remedy. She, for one, thinks there may well be a connection, but it's not the one Melanie points to. While Melanie thinks that our sexual problems as a society are the result of young people not having enough information about sex, Jenny thinks it's just the opposite—our sexual problems are due to *too much* information. In fact, Jenny's slogan, and the slogan of all the parents in Shady Grove who join her in opposing sex education, is exactly that: Melanie's curriculum is "too much, too soon."

Melanie's view is that no sex before marriage is both unrealistic and unwholesome. She expects Devora to travel, get an education, and have a satisfying job before she is "ready" for marriage. (I spent years trying to decode the word "ready," because it contains an ocean of hopes and values.) And the thought that Devora would deprive herself of sexually and emotionally satisfying relationships until she settles down in her late thirties (the age that Melanie and Rob tied the knot) worries and saddens her.

These conflicts about the meanings of sex and marriage are taking place in and being shaped by a world that is very different from the one that Jenny and Melanie grew up in, and although they sense that this is the case, they are hard put to make the link between their own experiences and the larger world in which they find themselves.

What I know as a sociologist, in part because I have spent so many years talking with people like Melanie and Jenny, is that sex and love and marriage have undergone revolutionary shifts in just a few decades. In the years before Jenny and Melanie were coming of age, girls did not have sex with boys unless they were deeply in love. (Only bad girls were "promiscuous.") Sex was risky, true, but not in the same ways that it is today. In those more innocent days, sex meant pregnancy and with it the dismal possibility that the boy involved might deny paternity or simply leave town. But often enough, in the face of pressure from families, the community, and perhaps their own sense of what was right, boys married the girls they had "knocked up." In fact, during the 1950s, about

70 percent of white women pregnant out of wedlock got married before the baby was born.[25]

With the legalization of contraception in 1964 and the legalization of abortion nine years later, that world disappeared. What was once taken for granted about sex and pregnancy and marriage came undone. Now that pregnancy is a choice rather than a fate, the traditional understandings between men and women about what sex and marriage mean have undergone radical shifts.

For some women, the advent of contraception and abortion was liberating, permitting them to invest in themselves in new ways and to dream of being equal to men. For other women, however— for women who were less interested in higher education and careers and for whom marriage and a family were the main route to happiness and satisfaction—the sexual revolution and all it represented reduced their overall well-being by loosening men's ties to marriage and family. Now that sex is no longer a scarce resource and men don't have to promise marriage in order to get it, premarital pregnancy is no longer a way to chivvy a reluctant male to the altar, and single motherhood, and with it female poverty, are on the rise.

These realities shape the values that people like Melanie and Jenny bring to bear when they think about sex today. In the nineteenth century, Sigmund Freud famously thought that life was sex in disguise. A joke, a pun, a slip of the tongue, a symptom, were all silent expressions of forbidden wishes in nineteenth-century Vienna, and the forbidden was very often the sexual. By looking at sex and sex education today, I want to argue the other side of that equation: that sex is life in disguise. When Americans talk about sex, we are simultaneously and covertly talking about all the things going on in our world outside of the bedroom. Gender, power, conflict, cooperation, religion, culture, class, the future, and even (bear with me) the global economy are there, as I hope to show you.

CHAPTER TWO

The Birth of Sex Education

In order to understand how Jenny and Melanie got where they are, you have to know that the sexual revolution they are fighting over was the second such revolution in the twentieth century. The first one, which some people think was the only real one, took place not in the love-bead and tie-dyed sixties but in the opening years of the 1900s, and it gave rise to the values that were overthrown in the 1960s—values that many people now see as timeless. Not coincidentally, this first sexual revolution gave birth to sex education as we know it today.

Whether they are aware of it or not, Melanie and Jenny feel passionate about this issue because revolutions in the sexual realm, as in the political one, spawn both winners and losers, and each woman is engaged in a war of ideas (and programs) designed to validate views about sexuality that support her own views of sex, and therefore of gender. Part of the contest—the part Jenny is most involved in—is about undoing some of the changes that happened in the 1960s, but the main part is an attempt to determine the direction in which sex will change next and what sex and gender will mean to coming generations.

So Melanie and Jenny are fighting about sex because they care passionately about all the things that sex is connected to and is a symbol of—marriage and families; relationships between men and women and between parents and children; and the life of the family and the life of the market.

Which brings us to sex education and its history. Sex education was invented in the midst of the first sexual revolution, in the Progressive era, between 1880 and 1920.[1] It was conceived, so to speak, in 1913 in a luxurious red dining room in a mansion on New York's Fifth Avenue owned by one Grace Hoadley

Dodge. Miss Dodge (as she probably insisted on being called) had gathered into her dining room a Who's Who of people who called themselves "the reform element," at a time when reformers were busier, more effective, and more self-confident than ever before.[2]

Among the dozen or so people at Miss Dodge's home were the recently retired president of Harvard, at least one millionaire, a woman minister who had helped found both the Women's Peace Party and the NAACP, a luminary in the reform of women's prisons, two outstanding physicians, and at least two prominent lawyers.[3] In a surprisingly modern turn of phrase, one of the women described the group as an "interlocking directorate," and recounting the story many years later, that woman, Anna Garlin Spencer, remembered, "As Grace Dodge in her practical way said, 'If we are on everything, why don't we all come together and be on one thing?' And so we did."[4]

It took almost two years for that "one thing" to become a reality, but after months of planning, these men and women met to announce the founding of the American Social Hygiene Association (ASHA), the first group ever to champion sex education.[5] Charmingly enough, they resolved to announce the birth of their new organization on Valentine's Day.

The association chose to call itself a "social hygiene" organization because both parts of that term had special resonance for its members. For Progressives, "hygiene" was a magical word that encompassed health in all its dimensions: social, mental, spiritual, and physical. It brought to mind not only the task of educating young people about sex but the equally important job of making sure they were spared the tenements that housed so many poor people in American cities, ensuring they had clean water and pure milk to drink, playgrounds for "wholesome" activities, and that their lungs would never know the ravages of tuberculosis, which had ended the lives of so many of their parents and siblings.

The word "social" was special too—for these new "social hygien-ists," it was a euphemism for sex (as in the "social diseases," mean-ing the venereal diseases), but it also marked the fact that for them, the proper use of sexuality was intimately related to all the dimensions of "hygiene" that they cared so much about.

The biographies of the people in that red dining room on fash-ionable Fifth Avenue indicate just how important managing sex was to these active, prominent, and well-bred men and women at the turn of the century. One of the physicians present, Thomas Hepburn (uncle of Katharine Hepburn), later explained how he enlisted Harvard president Charles Eliot, a Boston Brahmin and perhaps the most prominent and respected educator of his time, in the cause of sex education. As Dr. Hepburn tells the story, when he arrived unannounced and unknown in Eliot's Cambridge office, Eliot received him graciously and listened to him with great interest. At the end of the conversation, Eliot made a dra-matic gesture. Pointing to a stamped and sealed envelope on his desk, he confided to Hepburn that President Woodrow Wilson had asked him to serve as the American ambassador to the Court of St. James's and that the letter on the desk contained Eliot's acceptance. But having listened carefully to Dr. Hepburn over the course of the afternoon, he had concluded that "I think it is prob-ably my duty to accept your proposition and lend my influence in forwarding education in this unusual field of thought." With that, Eliot tore the letter to bits and tossed it into a wastebasket.[6]

To modern eyes, the idea of a Harvard president turning down a prestigious ambassadorial appointment to run a group dedicated to sex education seems odd, to say the least. But the Progressives with a capital *P* were convinced that teaching people about sex was the surest and best way to make American society better in regard to a wide range of problems. Crucially, for them, "sex" meant all the ambiguities that a later wave of feminism would try to dissolve—what we call "sexuality" and what we call "gender" were inextricably intertwined for these men and women. They

believed that solving the baffling problems of a newly industrial-
izing society could be accomplished only by solving the dilemmas
confronting men and women both in and out of the bedroom. A
key part of their remarkable confidence in the face of this daunt-
ing task was their passionate conviction that they could bring
together the historically "male" values of the professions with the
historically "female" ones of morality and the family.[7] For the
women in particular—people like Grace Dodge, Anna Garlin
Spencer, and Martha Falconer, members in good standing of
"social housekeeping"—American life could be improved only
when women brought their skills as mothers and homemakers to
the wider canvas of society as a whole.[8]

Their message that Americans needed to be educated about sex
was remarkably persuasive. Early and generous financial support
came from people like John D. Rockefeller, Jr., heir to the Standard Oil fortune; Julius Rosenwald, the president of Sears, Roe-
buck; Mrs. E. H. Harriman, the wife of the railroad magnate;
Edward S. Harkness, also of Standard Oil; and Henry C. Frick,
formerly of Carnegie Steel, who each gave individual contributions of between $1,000 and $5,000 to the new organization, the
equivalent of between $15,000 and $75,000 in today's money.[9]

Not only the wealthy but the public-spirited as well supported
the call for sex education. The Young Men's Christian Association
and the Young Men's Hebrew Association both sought cooperation between their organizations and the American Social
Hygiene Association, while the Metropolitan Life Insurance
Company pledged $1,000 for the best pamphlet on sex hygiene.
The Children's Bureau, staffed with feminist comrades-in-arms of
the men and women of ASHA, worked with them to bring the
message of sex education to the General Federation of Women's
Clubs, the largest women's organization in the country, and from
there to a far-flung network of women's clubs who took the message to towns and cities across the country.[10] Within just a few
years, the National Congress of Parents and Teachers (the forerun-

ner of our modern PTA) had signed on to the cause, and by World War I, the federal government was teaching the message of social hygiene to draftees.[11]

What was it about sex at the turn of the twentieth century that made it seem so alarming? And why did the unprecedented idea of teaching people about sex recruit such talented partisans and such widespread support?[12]

Like sex educators today, these pioneers had their own answers to these questions. They pointed to the open and widely accepted prostitution in all big and many small cities in America.[13] Physicians in the group warned that the red-light districts and bordellos spread venereal diseases, most prominently syphilis, as terrifying to the Progressives as HIV/AIDS is to us.

For the women in Grace Dodge's dining room, the whole question of sex was surrounded by what they took to be dangerous and demeaning ideas—demeaning, that is, to women, and hence to men. And the only answer to the problems of prostitution, VD, and men's exploitation of women, they thought, was to educate Americans about the proper uses of sexuality.

Prostitution was just the most visible sign of what was wrong with American sex. For much of the nineteenth century, American cities had toyed with the idea of legalizing prostitution in the French manner, permitting licensed prostitutes to ply their trade in special districts as long as they were regularly inspected by physicians for signs of disease.[14] Social hygienists were opposed on two grounds. The physicians put forth a professional point of view: such policies were dangerously wrong-headed, giving both prostitutes and customers a false sense of security about VD. In contrast to earlier medical and popular views that venereal diseases were merely nuisances, forward-looking physicians of the kind gathered in Grace Dodge's dining room were well aware of just how pernicious these diseases really were. New research and new technologies, such as the Wasserman test, were demonstrating that everything from insanity to blindness in newborns to heart disease to the disabling "female problems" that consigned many women to lifelong pain and ill health were all complications of the venereal diseases.[15]

Women objected on even more visceral grounds. They believed that the social problems that they had come together to address all stemmed from a single source: the idea that because men and women are different, sexually and otherwise, they have different rights and obligations. For them, legalized and "tolerated" prostitution, as it was called, was the visible and noxious symbol of this double standard.[16]

When the social hygienists resolved to begin educating the American public about sex, they confronted a social order that called prostitution a "necessary evil" and took for granted the doctrine of "physical necessity"—the idea that if men could not have regular sex, their health would suffer.[17] Polite society looked the other way when men purchased sex, won it by subterfuge, or simply took it from their wives or other women, whether the women were willing or not. And because "honorable" women had to be protected from such imperious male sexuality, it made sense that there had to be a stigmatized class of women whose bodies could be used at the whim of men.[18]

For women reformers, prostitution and the double standard on which it was based institutionalized ideas about men, women, and sexuality that had to be challenged. As Lavinia Dock, a purity reformer turned social hygienist, put it tartly in 1910:

> The double standard tacitly permits men to indulge freely and unchecked in sexual irregularity without consequent loss of social standing, but it dooms the women who are necessarily involved in these irregularities to social ostracism and even to complete degradation.
>
> In order to justify immoral practices among themselves and to have a plausible explanation ready if criticism is offered, the doctrine of "physical necessity" has been invented for men by

themselves, and has even been fortified by the positive teachings of prominent medical men . . . The practical results of this
psychological jugglery have been, that, of two partners in one
and the same act, neither one of whom could execute this act
alone, and with whom, if the element of compulsion entered as
a complication, it could not possibly be present in the case of
the stronger partner,—men, the stronger, have remained free
from blame; women, the weaker have lived under a curse.[19]

That such an arrangement imperiled not only "bad" women
but *all* women was made clear by Anna Garlin Spencer, who
declared forcefully, "The ancient denial of full human equality to
womanhood has thus taken its stand in the last refuge of infamy,
the sex-slavery of a minority of outcaste women. Let no woman
think she is safe from ignominy, however praised and beloved,
while any other woman is bought and sold in the auction-mart
of vice! Let no man believe, however pure and upright his own
life may be, that he can wipe from his forehead the brand of
despotic class-morality while any other man buys and sells women
in sex-slavery!"[20]

This was a core belief of social hygiene—that no equality for
women could ever be achieved so long as the double standard held
sway. To the women and men of the social hygiene movement, the
"full human equality" of womanhood demanded a new model of
sexuality. And they were not alone. Stamping out the double
standard came to represent a whole new vision of women and
their emerging place in a new society. So potent was this symbol
that the members of the Maine Federation of Women's Clubs
voted to spend all their energies agitating for a single standard of
sexual behavior.[21]

So many women across the country found themselves involved
in getting rid of the double standard because American society
was in the midst of a genuine revolution, and unsettling changes
in sexuality—and gender—surrounded them on every side. In

fact, some scholars even argue that the period from roughly 1880 to 1920 saw the *only* real sexual revolution in American history, and that the cultural changes in sexuality during the 1960s and 1970s were mere aftershocks.[22]

Let's look at this first sexual revolution more closely, by examining the life of my own grandmother, a woman born in 1878, whose photograph on the wall of my study has kept me company as I have written this book. Taken on the last day of 1903, the photograph is a wedding portrait of Grandmother Wester, slim and erect, her chin firm, clutching a spray of flowers. When I knew her, she embodied Victorian propriety and Congregationalist piety. A chapel in the Congregationalist church in Eugene, Oregon, bears her family's name. When my father was growing up, she took her religion so seriously that he was not allowed to play with his dog on the Sabbath.

My father was not my grandmother's biological child. In a pattern that was common among white people until World War I, and that is still common among African Americans, my father was given to his more prosperous aunt and uncle to raise. The way my relatives tell it, my childless grandmother adopted my father because she thought he was very bright and should go to college, something he would never be able to do if left with his family of tenant farmers.

A family story about the wedding portrait claims that my grandmother's dress was shipped in from the East with great fanfare but didn't arrive until the day of the wedding. There was no time to iron the dress, taken wrinkled from the box before the wedding party posed for pictures. All the female relatives assured my grandmother that the wrinkles wouldn't show, but they did. Almost a century later, the outlines of the long-ago box are still etched on the dress, and the pain of that fact shows on my grandmother's face.

Now I know another drama lies behind the portrait, something besides a wrinkled dress to account for Grandmother Wester's firm chin and grim expression. Told to me almost seventy years later by my great-aunt, the story is that my grandmother was pregnant when she married my grandfather, but the child was born prematurely and died soon after birth (whether this was a genuine premature birth or simply a story told to keep up the family honor, I do not know). Something about the birth and its consequences—a hysterectomy, perhaps?—made my grandmother unable to have more children and to decide to adopt her nephew, my father.

I can only guess at what this woman, whom I never knew very well, thought and felt about the intimate choices she made over a century ago. But what I do know—what the history of sex (and sex education) in her time has taught me—is that her generation was caught in the middle of one of the historic shifts in what sex means. My grandmother's generation, like Melanie's and Jenny's and mine, was born into a world of one set of sexual values and came of sexual age in another. In 1878, when Grandmother Wester was born, sexuality and all that surrounded it was dominated by the role of reproduction; when she married in 1903, sex was becoming a source of intimacy rather than babies.

The last two decades of the nineteenth century and the first two decades of the twentieth were very much like our own: a period of empire, technological change, mass immigration, changing economies, and a new sense of what it meant to be an American. Within this forty-year period, give or take a few years, the frontier closed, putting an end to the option of moving west to find a new life.[23] America became a significant industrial power in the global economy for the first time, and the first billion-dollar corporation was spawned on these shores.[24] By 1910, immigration to the United States totaled more than 13 million people, out of a total population of 92 million; immigrants from southern and eastern Europe (culturally distinct from those who styled themselves "native" Americans) had surged from less than 20 percent of all immigrants in the 1870s to the majority.[25] Railroads and telegraphs united the sprawling country, making it seem as if the world were shrinking, as regional communities became more and more integrated in a new, national sense of self.[26]

All of these changes affected how people experienced their intimate lives. In almost any arena related to personal life—marriage, divorce, relations between the sexes, birth patterns, the raising of children—Americans like my grandmother were confronted by a world where the landscape was almost unrecognizably different from what it had been just decades earlier.

Marriage seemed to be on the decline. More and more people, especially of the "best sort"—which for the kinds of people who wrote the hand-wringing jeremiads meant upper-class, native-born white men and women—began to postpone marriage, and many refused to marry at all. If this were not bad enough for those worried observers, a new wave of feminism was encouraging upper-middle-class women to aspire to careers and to turn their backs on family life, or so it seemed. All over America, women began to organize to get the vote, to enter the workforce, and to question men's and women's roles.[27]

Along with the decline in marriage came a decline in family size among those who did marry, as urbanization, industrialization, rising levels of education, and the failure of the farming economy all took their toll on the large families of the past. The large farm family, as enshrined in early twentieth-century nostalgia as the male-breadwinner family was to be at the end, was no more. Between 1800 and 1900, the size of the average American family dropped by half, from almost seven children to a little over three.[28]

The decline in the birthrate was variously blamed on higher education for women, feminism, bicycle-riding, and even the use of sewing machines by women (these activities were thought to be particularly hard on the womb), but it was obvious that white native-born women were just not doing their duty when it came to being fruitful and multiplying, especially compared to the female immigrants. The resulting panic, termed "race suicide" by none other than Theodore Roosevelt, became a much-repeated obsession among cultural observers.[29] In 1902, before joining the cause of social hygiene, President Eliot of Harvard noted that Harvard graduates—then, as now, often thought to be the best and the brightest—were raising such small families that they were failing utterly to replace themselves, presumably leaving their ranks to be filled by immigrants and the lower classes.[30]

If later and fewer marriages and smaller families were not bad enough, the divorce rate skyrocketed in the first years of the new century, and once again the trend seemed most visible among the well-to-do. The ratio of divorces to marriages went up by a third between 1880 and 1900 and almost doubled between 1910 and 1920. Although low by current standards, these increases were alarming to people who had seen divorces soar in just one generation.[31]

And then, closer to home in a story about the birth of sex education, Americans discovered a new group of strangers in their very midst, a group that the psychologist G. Stanley Hall christened "adolescents" in 1904.[32] The fact that we had no name for these young people until Hall coined it illustrates that Americans were coming to view their young in new ways. For much of the previous two centuries, the boundaries between childhood and adulthood were fluid and mostly economic in nature. Seventeenth- and early eighteenth-century children were put to work at six or seven, and full adulthood was typically measured by economic independence rather than age. Even as late as the 1850s, Harvard and Yale enrolled students as young as fourteen and as old as twenty-six, and writers of advice books aimed at "young men" assumed them to be somewhere between fourteen and twenty-one.[33]

Once named, however, these newly discovered adolescents gave adults plenty to worry about. Sexual revolutions are most visible in the young, so the discovery of adolescence was given a particularly sharp edge by the very different kinds of sexual behaviors emerging among young people. Working-class youth, "factory girls and boys," with money in their pockets and new places to spend it, such as skating rinks, amusement parks, dance halls, and roadhouses, alarmed middle-class observers.[34] Young people could mingle in these new public spaces without adult supervision, and sexual danger seemed everywhere. Such danger came in two forms, depending on whether a girl or a boy was the object of concern.

For boys, the path of sexual indulgence could lead away from the older virtues of thrift, self-discipline, and deferred gratification. Amos G. Warner, one of the most prominent reformers and social critics of the day, wrote in 1894:

> Careful observers believe [licentiousness] to be a more constant and fundamental cause of degeneration than intemperance . . . Personal acquaintance with railroad day laborers, and others of a similar class, convinces the writer that they are commonly kept from rising in the industrial scale by their sensuality, and that it is this and resulting degeneration that finally converts them into lazy vagabonds. The inherent uncleanness of their minds prevents them from rising above the rank of day laborers, and finally incapacitates them even for that position. It may also be suggested that the modern man has a stronger imagination than the man of a few hundred years ago, and that sensuality destroys him the more rapidly.[35]

Factory girls, no longer under the watchful eyes of parents, faced another kind of danger. By the 1880s, narratives of country girls seduced and abandoned by city slickers were being replaced by tales of working girls going out with young men who bought them dinner, took them to amusement parts or skating rinks, and then "ruined" them. Worse yet, some of the young women seemed actively to enjoy the process of ruination, entering into it enthusiastically. Once ruined, their only recourse—or so it was thought—was prostitution, starting the cycle of depravity all over again.[36]

Parts of the new industrial economy were even turning such ruin from callous sport to monstrous business. Offering jobs to

young women, unscrupulous entrepreneurs often enticed them
into another line of work entirely:

> The surroundings, business methods, and frauds pale into
> insignificance beside conscious deliberate immorality of many
> [employment bureaus] and the traps they set for their unwary
> and helpless victims. Of these the honest employer knows but
> little and the employee recalls many escapes. The bare fact is
> that while advertising honest work and furnishing it to some,
> many also degrade, debase, and ruin others and later cast them
> out moral and physical wrecks.[37]

Reformers were convinced that a combination of low wages,
independence from their parents, and new notions about sexuality put factory girls in danger as never before. As a trade union-
ist writing in 1915 put it, "We are demanding in the every-day
life of our working girls the stuff out of which heroes and martyrs
are made."[38]

Middle-class and affluent boys and girls worried adults just as
much, although in different ways. Coeducational high schools
became an increasing part of these young people's lives, and the
growth of coed universities meant that middle- and upper-middle-
class students spent a great deal of unchaperoned time together.[39]

Some of the same forces that put young working-class people at
risk affected middle- and upper-class young people too. "Dating"
came to take the place of "courting," as boys and girls went to the
skating rinks and dance halls and got to know each other without
the knowledge of parents and families. As in our own day, getting
ahead meant getting more education, and young people started
postponing marriage in order to finish their education and get a
start in life first.[40]

If working-class boys could become distracted from getting
ahead by "the inherent uncleanness of their minds," as Amos G.
Warner claimed, then middle- and upper-class boys could fail to

advance their careers (not to mention the future of civilization) by refusing to repress their sexual drive during that long period between puberty and marriage. Drawing on the newly popularized theories of Sigmund Freud, reformers argued that being sexual "too early" (then, as now, a code for being unmarried) derailed the delicate process of sublimation, the bedrock of modern "higher" civilization.[41] As G. Stanley Hall argued in the inaugural issue of the journal *Social Hygiene*:

> Tension repressed gives human nature much of all that is best in it and it is basal for everything, so that we must make no degree of concession whatever in the ideals of chastity for boys at this stage any more than we do for girls. Apart from the social stigma, there is now some reason to think that lapses from chastity for boys at this age are physiologically and biologically worse in their effect on the last, highest, and always most precarious stages of the psychophysical development of the individual. Hence we must never let down our ideals of purity, innocence, modesty which unfortunately we have to call virginal for male youth.[42]

Or as the Reverend Mabel MacCoy Irwin, a social hygienist and purity reformer, exulted about this kind of argument, "I rejoice that they have put the scientific facts under our feet on which we may stand, as we tell our message of chastity to a sin-sick world."[43]

Taken together, this relatively brief period at the turn of the twentieth century, when women's fashion went from long skirts that swept the floor to the short, short skirts of the flapper in less than a decade, gave plenty to worry about. What with immigration, dropping fertility rates, rising divorce rates, coeducation, women smoking, drinking, and "petting," and the visibility of "new woman" with her bobbed hair and brazen manners, few people doubted that a new world had come about.

For the social hygienists, young people seemed to be making a radical break with the recent past. As early as 1931, American historians were already looking back and painting this period as a "revolution in manners and morals," underlining the enormity of change in sexual behavior, particularly among women.[44] While no nationally representative data from this period exist, virtually all of the admittedly limited sources point in the same direction: the new equality between men and women, which feminists sought and social hygienists supported, was showing up in new patterns of sexual expression.

For example, Lewis Terman, the popularizer of the IQ test and an indefatigable researcher of the "intellectually gifted," found that premarital sex was becoming more common among the men and women he studied. Half of the men and only 13 percent of the women born before 1890 had been sexually active before marriage; 58 percent of the men and 26 percent of the women born between 1890 and 1900 had been; and 66 percent of the men and almost half of the women born between 1900 and 1909 had had sex before they were married.[45] The famous Kinsey studies found similar figures—14 percent of the women born before 1900 reported premarital sex by age twenty-five, compared to more than twice that number among women born after 1900.[46] Significantly, for both men and women in the Terman study, premarital sex was often (and for women, predominantly) with a fiancé or a fiancée. The Kinsey data show the same pattern.

The shifts in what people were doing were paralleled by shifts in what people were thinking. It was "sex o'clock" in America, one anonymous editorial worried; another author wrote of the "repeal of reticence."[47] These observers were on to something: between 1910 and 1914, articles in the public media on birth control, prostitution, sexual morals, and divorce became more numerous than ever before.[48] As the historian Beth Bailey has so convincingly shown, what was changing were *conventions*, assumptions about how men and women were to behave with each other, sexually and otherwise.[49]

When the early social hygienists looked around them, they saw that sex and procreation were becoming disconnected. One scolded in the inaugural issue of the flagship journal, *Social Hygiene* (1914), "Knowledge of popular methods of preventing conception is at present the possession of school children, and disgrace is easily covered in our rapidly shifting population. Social checks of the traditional type are breaking down."[50]

As the feminist physician and social hygienist Rachel Yarros noted, looking back on the period surrounding the Great War,

> Sex, among other things, has come into its own. It has been rediscovered, and there is remarkable frankness in the discussion of sex, as of marriage, monogamy, the family and birth control . . . The intelligent and independent youth of today has little respect for Puritan ideas or standards . . . Many young people believe in pre-marital sex experience. Even those who do not accept the free love doctrine, and who protest that they believe in marriage and expect to marry, argue that meanwhile they have a right to occasional indulgences. They do not see why society should object to this degree of freedom, provided there are not children. The demand for contraceptive information on the part of college students, male and female, and even of high-school pupils, is extraordinary, and would appall the complacent, conservative parents of those emancipated insurgents.[51]

The social hygienists were probably mistaken about how widespread the use of contraception was; very real social class and racial differences in the use of contraception persisted well into the 1960s, when the availability of the birth-control pill brought them to an end.[52] But the social hygienists were not mistaken in perceiving that sex was different from what it had been before middle- and upper-middle-class families came to believe that they could and should choose when to have children and how many to have.

This presented a problem. The disconnection of sex and procreation threatened to imperil marriage. If the whole point of marriage was no longer to be fruitful and multiply, what was to keep marriages together? As sex became untethered from procreation, men and women were rethinking what marriage was about, and the new sexual behaviors among working-class girls and boys, not to mention the boys and girls of their own class, made it clear that they were not the only ones thinking this way.

In the face of this shift, the social hygienists turned to education—teaching people not so much about sex as about marriage. They took for granted that their task was to educate Americans about "wholesome" sex, which for them meant wholesome sex within marriage. In fact, what they were really up to was recruiting sex to support a new model of marriage-as-intimacy, then emerging among the middle and upper classes.

Along with issuing dire warnings about the dangers of sex outside marriage, social hygienists also sought to improve the quality of sex within it. Setting in motion what would eventually become a whole world of information, specialists, and organizations, they were the first to try to do something about the quality of the sex life of (properly married) Americans.[53]

If sex within marriage was troubled or unsatisfying, the social hygienists were astute enough to observe, their warnings about sex outside marriage would be only minimally successful. They were keenly aware that continued reference to the "morbid" aspects of sexual disease and danger—aspects that they were compelled to mention in warning people away from "promiscuous" sex—could have the unintended consequence of making people queasy about sex in general, including married sex.[54] So social hygiene from the outset was committed to educating people simultaneously about the dangers of the wrong kind of sex and the pleasures of the right kind.

They proposed making sex within marriage better by educating men and women in a new vision of sexuality, one that revered women for their capacity (and perhaps their willingness, in the face of contraception) to give birth.[55] In this, the social hygienists were in tune with the larger culture, which sentimentalized motherhood. As the special committee on "The Matter and Methods of Sex Education" put it in 1912: "A knowledge of the marvelous processes by which life is perpetuated, from its lowest forms to its highest, impresses on the mind, more firmly than is possible in any other way, the sacredness of human reproduction and the direct consequences to future generations of wrong sexual conduct."[56] The key to this vision was the idea that sex and children were meant to bring husbands and wives together, that both sex and children cemented the husband-wife bond, a bond that had seemed so much in the nature of things before that no one had worried about how to sustain it.

Sex educators assumed that the "wholesome" sex adjustment they sought to encourage would lead to happier marriages, happier people, and declines in a wide range of social problems. Explaining the need for parents to educate themselves about sex in order to educate their children, the social hygienist Benjamin Gruenberg laid out in 1928 both the wide range of problems sex education was designed to remedy and the underlying logic of how it could accomplish so many goals:

> For many years it has become increasingly evident that with vast numbers of men and women the sex life is far from wholesome. The failure of so many marriages, one out of every nine or ten ending in divorce, and many of the others simply hiding their failure, indicates at least that young people have not been adequately prepared for married life or for the selection of a mate. Another lack in the education of youth is indicated by the fact that so many of the men and women one meets every day have one or another extreme attitude toward sex—that is, some are over-delicate, regarding the whole subject as beastly, vile or indecent; while others are actually beastly, and wallow in sex. Finally, a lack of suitable guidance and training is shown by the large amount of sexual perversion, by the large amounts of nervous disorder due to certain types of anxieties and wor-

ries, by the wide extent and far-reaching influence of prostitution, and by the wide distribution of the venereal diseases, with
all of the by-products of blindness, sterility, insanity, paralysis,
and defectiveness.

The failure to attain satisfactory use and control of sex on the
part of adults is paralleled and, in part, caused by the difficul-
ties and unsolved problems of adolescence and youth. Much of
the delinquency with which the courts and police have to deal
results from untrained and unguided impulses connected with
sex, even in cases that have no apparent relation to sex matters.
The large amount and steady increase of illegitimacy and widespread promiscuity in sex relations, quite apart from prostitution, indicates that young people have not acquired the
knowledge, ideals, and skill necessary for managing their affairs
to the best advantage. The morbid curiosity as well as the worries and fears concerning sex, prevalent among young people
and often standing in the way of marriage, and the large
amount of serious sex repression and of perversion, point
equally to the shortcomings in our training of youth.[57]

These bold new reformers dreamed of establishing a world of
gender and sexual equality, a world where the "single standard of
sex behavior" would replace the hated double standard. But this
was not the gender and sexual equality of the 1960s. The sexual
conduct of women, not men, was to be the template. Or as Anna
Garlin Spencer put it, in noting that "the leading moral and intellectual elite of both sexes declare for a single standard of morals in
sex-relationship." "What does that mean? Does it mean that
women shall grow careless, lax, and tolerant of vice, as men have
been?" Answering her own rhetorical challenge, she emphatically
concluded that this was not to be the case: "We may, therefore,
conclude that a single standard of morals in sex-relationship will
not mean a leveling down of women's ideals to those which men
have allowed to become embodied in the social evil. If not, then it

must mean a leveling up of men to the standards they have themselves exacted of the women to whom they entrusted the welfare
of their family life."[58]

What the social hygienists were doing behind the mantle of the
single standard was to assail not just the forms of male sexuality
but its very essence. The double standard was based on the idea
that male and female sexuality were fundamentally different,
which in turn suggested that men and women were different in
other ways as well. Men, in the vision that held sway in the world
the social hygienists inherited, had a basic, primitive sexuality
that constantly sought outlet, while women had a more civilized,
contingent sexuality that could be subordinated to the needs of
both family and society. So when social hygienists urged the single standard, telling young men that they should treat all women
as they would want their sisters to be treated, they were claiming
that male sexuality, like female sexuality, could and must be controlled. In place of the imperious, hotheaded, and hard-to-control
male sexuality of the previous century, the social hygienists proposed a tender, intimate, comradely, and feminized sexuality
modeled on existing notions of how women experienced their own
sexual drives.[59]

And that, in turn, brought its own set of cultural changes. In an
earlier era, people could joke about the relationship between sex
and pregnancy because it was so inevitable. But now, as sex and
pregnancy were coming to be separate social entities, the social
hygienists sought to make voluntary reproduction both a spiritual
and a public-spirited act.

Michel Foucault and others have made much of the fact that
social hygienists and other activists in the realm of sex denounced
the "conspiracy of silence" that surrounded it. To Foucault and his
followers, such claims are at best disingenuous, in that sexual
reformers proliferate "discourses" about sex while claiming that
silence surrounds it.[60] But a careful reading of the social hygienists suggests something quite different: that what they were chal-

lenging in the conspiracy of silence was a *male* view of sex and procreation, and what they were substituting was a *female* one. For example, Maurice Bigelow, one of the founders of social hygiene, noted that "expectant motherhood is commonly concealed as long as possible and all reference to the development of new life is usually accomplished with blushes and tones suggestive of great shame. Nothing sexual is commonly regarded as sacred. Love and marriage, motherhood and birth, are all freely selected as themes for sexual jests, many of them so vulgar that no printed dictionary supplies the necessary words."[61]

We see this shift in ideas about sex most clearly in the research of one of the few scholars who actually asked women about sex during this time. Clelia Mosher, a pioneering physician, interviewed women about sexuality and found, side by side, both the old attitudes of the nineteenth century and the new ones of the twentieth. The engagingly frank Dr. Mosher asked her subjects, forty-seven mostly upper-middle-class women both in the Midwest and in California, "What is the purpose of intercourse?" (In later versions of her questionnaire she asked about the true purpose of intercourse.) While a number of women in her study subscribed to the nineteenth-century view that sex was an act necessary to a man, tolerated by a woman, whose chief purpose was reproduction, other voices could be heard. One woman volunteered that "physical union possibly is necessary to complete harmony between two people." Another woman noted, "It seems to be a natural and physical sign of a spiritual union, a renewal of the marriage vows," while still a third said that sex was "a close bond making marriage more stable . . . [Sex] binds people together." Blending hygiene and theology, still another ventured, "I think to the man and woman married from love, it may be used *temperately*, as one of the highest manifestations of love, granted us by our Creator" (emphasis in the original).[62]

This is where my grandmother comes back into the story. The social hygienists, as these quotations attest, were articulating and popularizing new values about sex, gender, and marriage. By the early years of the twentieth century, earlier models of marriage were becoming outmoded. Women and men, especially in the middle and upper classes, were coming to expect to be friends and partners in companionable marriages, and marriage manuals began to focus on sexual pleasure and even mutual orgasm as a central part of the marital experience.[63] The stirrings of a feminist movement called for greater equality for women and, in the process, for debunking earlier views of women as passive sexless victims of male lust and permitting a new, equal, "comradely" partnership when it came to sex.

But as the researchers and moralists of the 1920s and 1930s belatedly discovered, the new model of sex also set the stage for experimentation with sexuality before marriage.[64] If sex and sexual pleasure were to be central to marriage, and if men and women were to use it as a bond to solidify their relationships to one another, it is not surprising that the young people Dr. Yarros observed during the early years of the twentieth century thought they had a right to make sure they were sexually compatible with each other before they committed to marriage.

I think my grandmother was caught between these two models of marriage. On the one hand, as a middle-class woman engaged to a man who would soon be a college professor, she was expected to be a friend, a companion, and an equal to her husband. For "new women," love, intimacy, and emotional compatibility were created, tested, proved during courtship, before they made the lifetime commitment of marriage. Yet as the heir to the Victorian tradition, such a woman, and not her husband-to-be, was expected to rein in that emotional intimacy when it threatened to spill into sexual intimacy. Thus she was caught between expectations for a certain equality in intimate life and the fact that when something went awry, the consequences were more dramatic for her than for him.

Maybe my grandmother was just unlucky. The technologies that men and women had available to prevent pregnancy in her day were not substantially better than those of a generation earlier, so risk was always part of the new intimacy. Premarital sex could and often enough did lead to premarital pregnancy. The question then was whether the man involved would do the right thing. Since my grandmother and grandfather were already engaged and were members in good standing of the Congregational church, and my grandfather was already an up-and-comer, probably nothing but moving up the wedding date occurred to either of them. Like many couples before and after, they found that getting married a bit earlier than planned solved the problem.

I will never know how and why my grandmother became pregnant before she got married. But I do know that she was fated to live at a time when men and women were questioning the verities of what it meant to be sexual.

Despite our assumptions about sex education, what little we know of its history over the succeeding years suggests that it was actually quite popular—not surprisingly, given its fundamentally pro-marriage cast.[65] The single standard of sex behavior was so persuasive that the federal government even enlisted it in World War I to help keep American troops free from venereal disease.[66] In promoting it to recruits, the government distributed over a million pamphlets; gave over 775,000 men approved lectures, complete with filmstrips and "stereomotographs" (automated slide shows); and commissioned a film, *Fit to Fight*, seen by 50,000 men. Even assuming that some men were exposed to more than one medium of persuasion, somewhere between one third and two thirds of approximately 2.8 million draftees received this revolutionary message of sexual equality.[67] From recruits, the federal government branched out, creating a slide show on sex education that it claimed to have shown to one million boys; a similar one was created for girls.[68]

The transformation of "sex education" into "family life education" was therefore built into the very bones of sex education and happened remarkably early in its history. Despite the fact that wary communities sometimes decided that family life education was really sex education in disguise and banned it, the sex education designed by the social hygienists to support marriage, and more broadly family life, was probably much more common and more accepted than we realize.[69]

As the goals of sex education expanded, so did the field. In 1915 the social hygienists largely had sex education to themselves, but as "social hygiene" came to include the broader realm of enhancing and supporting both marriages and families, new professions, organizations, and ideologies emerged to help with the task. Sociologists, marriage counselors, therapists of many hues, home economists, physical education specialists, social workers, nurses, "mental hygienists," and the newly invented "family life specialists" all claimed both expertise in and responsibility for families, and many of them produced their own versions of family life education.[70]

In the forty-five-year period between the end of World War I and the sexual revolution of the 1960s, this expansion of the role of sex education continued. Part preparation for marriage, part an attempt to discourage premarital sex, and part training for "responsible parenthood," sex education seems to have settled into a routine encouraged by the sex educators themselves. Rather than clearly focusing on the agenda that had brought it into being—the single standard of sexual behavior and the prevention of venereal disease—sex education became increasingly all-encompassing, expanding to cover almost everything under the rubric of "personal and family living."

To get a flavor of this expansion, consider the city school system of San Diego. In 1944, alarmed by how rapidly the city was changing owing to the rapid influx of military people in World War II, it revamped its existing sex education program to cover a wide array of topics, many not easily categorized as sex education. The program, successful enough to warrant an official social hygiene pamphlet describing it, presumed that its goals would be pursued in biology, English, home economics, science, social studies, and hygiene (health) classes. Topics proposed included the classic concerns of the social hygienists, but the "social" in social hygiene had already expanded dramatically, in ways that the first generation of sex educators would have found surprising. Included in the San Diego program were discussions of such issues as the

> disastrous results that interfere with happiness when an individual "bucks" social conventions. Difficulties commonly involved when marriage is made between differing races, religions and nationalities. Individual's responsibility to the next generation. Role of both sexes in family life. Family harmony. Value of family councils. Budgeting. Importance of the correct spending for the mental satisfaction of family members. What comprises the income. Family round-table discussion of expenditures and household management. Respect for the opposite sex . . . Aping opposite sex detracts from one's own heterosexualness . . . Social values of controlling the urge to fall in love. Petting. Selecting friends . . . Sharing the work at home . . . Differing problems of the sexes.[71]

As broad as this list was, the problems that family life education was thought to be capable of addressing were broader still. Picking up on Dr. Gruenberg's earlier dreams, a 1954 publication of the American Social Hygiene Association hailed family life education as the remedy for divorce, masturbation, lack of self-control in sexual and financial life, sexual maladjustment, delinquency, crime, and marriages of "differing races, religions and nationalities." In addition to preventing these ills, family life education, its advocates claimed, built character, prepared young men (and women) for service in the military, and helped young people present a good image of Americans abroad. In short, family life education had become the remedy for almost all the problems that plagued individuals or communities at midcentury.[72]

The expansion of family life education beyond the realm of the strictly sexual was possible because educators could draw on broad cultural agreements that sex outside marriage was wrong and dangerous, that intimate marriages needed healthy sexuality to bind them together, and that young people needed help in learning how to manage family life. If social hygiene had developed as a strategy to keep sexuality within marriage once it was no longer firmly tethered to procreation, then the social hygienists could consider themselves eminently successful. Outside of a few "sex radicals" whose opinions did not have much effect on mainstream American opinion, individuals, despite their own practices, agreed in principle that sex before marriage was wrong for both men and women.

By 1960, the evidence suggests, sex education in American public schools was often the expansive, diffuse, and usually uncontroversial family life education that social hygienists had thought they could accomplish by their careful incremental strategy of building consensus, and these programs were remarkable in their diversity. Events just over the horizon, however, would bring sex education abruptly back to its roots and to a new level of controversy.

CHAPTER THREE

Sex Education, the Sexual Revolution, and the Sixties

Sitting on her broad front porch with a warm afternoon breeze stirring the geraniums in their hanging pots, Mary Kay Malone pours me another chilly glass of sweet iced tea—the only thing ladies seem to drink in these parts, at least before the sun sets. In a drawl as soft and balmy as the breeze that has just come up, she reflects on the issues that led her to get involved in sex education in her small southern town.

"You know, I get shocked every year," she tells me. "I got shocked when we had a sixth-grader sitting there pregnant. I got shocked when my daughter had two pregnant girls in her class this year. I got even more shocked when we were at a basketball game and this little girl had this little girl and I made the assumption that it was her sister and I was saying, 'Honey, you have a cute little sister,' and she's going, 'This is my baby.' It scares you to death. Especially when you have a daughter. It really scares you. And, see, kids are not like they were when we were coming up, anyway . . . We came through—or I'll say *I* came through—the love-child and flower-power era, and your parents threatened your life because they wanted you not to be a part of that . . . But nowadays, it's like the kids know more than I knew when I was twenty years old."

Like Mary Kay, almost everyone I talked to about sex education takes it for granted that a watershed known as "the sixties" happened and that a—or as they call it, *the*—sexual revolution was a significant part of what made it a watershed rather than just another decade. Over and over again, people brought up the sixties as a time when the world changed forever, and almost without exception, "the sixties" was shorthand for the kinds of things that Mary Kay is shocked by.

If you look closely at Mary Kay's thoughts, you can see the revolution just below the surface. It's not as though fifteen-year-olds didn't get pregnant and have babies forty-odd years ago, although Mary Kay and I agree over our iced tea that fifteen's much too young to be having a baby. But still, it wasn't unheard of, especially in Mary Kay's part of the South. What's different now is that when Mary Kay and I were growing up, girls who got pregnant either got married in a hurry, just as my grandmother had, or were shipped out of town to relatives or to homes for unwed mothers. Either way, being sexual and being caught at it, which is what pregnancy meant in our day, meant that you were no longer fit to be seen in school. Well into the 1970s, even properly married schoolteachers in some communities had to step down when their pregnancies showed, lest their bulging bellies arouse speculation among innocent schoolchildren as to how those bellies got that way.[1]

Yet now in Mary Kay's small, rural southern town, girls get pregnant all the time, mostly when they're not married, and rather than hanging their heads in shame, they stay in class. They even go to basketball games taking their babies with them. In one conservative Texas town not that different from Mary Kay's, unmarried pregnant girls sued to be allowed to stay on the cheerleading squad, notwithstanding the view of the town fathers that pregnant cheerleaders didn't make very good role models.[2] (Showing the contradictions of sexual politics at this particular moment, the pregnant cheerleaders pointed out to their deeply religious fellow townspeople that they were worthier role models than the cheerleaders they knew of who had had abortions.)

The part of the story that is mostly unspoken, especially in the South, but that Mary Kay admits when I press her, is that these changes refer mostly to white girls. Between the late 1960s and the late 1980s, rates of premarital sex began to converge for African Americans and whites, and this was true all over the country, not just in the South.[3] In fact, premarital sex became more common for all young people. Not only did the rates for African American and white teenagers begin to look more similar (in part because of a drop in African American rates in the face of continuing increases among whites), but rates for boys and girls began to converge.[4]

And there's more. Although no national data are available to make the point, the data we do have support Mary Kay's example: the young woman with her baby at her side is now the rule rather than the exception. Where once white women who were pregnant out of wedlock were urged (and sometimes forced) to give up their babies for adoption, now, if they make the choice to continue the pregnancy, the odds are very good that they will go ahead and raise the babies as single mothers.[5]

In short, Mary Kay, like Jenny and Mclanie on the West Coast, is sure that something momentous happened in the sixties (which in fact included much of the 1970s), and that it affected how people thought about and experienced sex, gender, and the family. For the second time since Grace Hoadley Dodge and her friends invented sex education in the mansion on Fifth Avenue, sex changed, and not surprisingly, sex education changed along with it.

In the years following the 1960s, lively debates among academics have focused on whether or not a sexual revolution actually took place in this country; and if it did, when did it happen? As we have seen, some scholars still think that the "revolution in morals and manners" that got sex education going was the only real revolution, but others think not only was there a sexual revolution in the 1960s but it was a big part of what set in motion new and ferocious "culture wars." According to them, the sexual revolution and its aftermath eventually pitted religious fundamentalists and middle Americans against sophisticated urbanites across a whole range of issues—art, foreign affairs, and civil liberties—not just sex.[6]

Of course, some scholars think that *something* changed in the 1960s but aren't quite sure it was a revolution. They point out that public attitudes toward homosexuality and adultery did not change very much and that rates of premarital sex (to the extent we have data) were indeed on the rise but had been since Grace Dodge's day.[7]

Interviewing across the country, sitting on front porches, in crowded coffee shops, and in quiet living rooms, as well as in the offices of principals, sex educators, and clergy, I've become convinced that a sexual revolution really did take place, and that it's one of the great unacknowledged forces shaping much of contemporary social and political life. Just as the turn of the twentieth century saw profound changes in how Americans thought about sex and family, the 1960s were a time of remarkably unsettling change.[8] Just as people in the early years of the century watched hemlines rise, people in the sixties and seventies had much the same shock, watching dresses move from the mid-calf shirtwaists of the early 1960s (think Donna Reed or Beaver Cleaver's mother) to dresses so short that women had to learn a whole new way of bending over to pick something up. On the cultural front, not just dresses but other clothing and hairstyles, tastes in music, and the way people conducted themselves sexually and reproductively all changed.

At a deeper level, the sexual revolution held within it another kind of revolution, one in which men and women began to relate to each other in new ways, and parents and children fought about whether and how much youngsters would take part in this change. Sex, gender, marriage, and authority were all enmeshed in the sixties, and the sexual revolution represented them all.

People who were not alive in those years probably can't imagine it, and people who were alive may find it unsettling to be reminded, but there was a moment in the 1960s when it seemed as if all of American society might implode. The nonviolent civil rights movement of the late 1950s and early 1960s was followed by a riot-scarred period that forced white Americans to confront the fact that they lived, as the Kerner Commission Report told them, in "two societies, one black, one white—separate and unequal."[9] The war in Vietnam was so divisive that student protests roiled campuses large and small; attempts by the authorities to quell the protests at Kent State University in Ohio led to the killings of four students, and ten days later still more students died at Jackson State University in Mississippi.[10]

So the sexual revolution took place in an atmosphere in which many young people were both critical of established authority and suspicious of the motives of people who wanted to enforce traditional values. Young people were confident their values were authentic and noble ones while their elders were guilty of hypocrisy on a society-wide scale. And a remarkable number of their elders seemed to agree. Both the sexual revolution, and the gender revolution of which it was part, challenged everything that an older generation had taken for granted about men and women, gender and sex. (Older readers may even remember when a man's holding a door open for a woman, previously considered a courteous act, could earn him the epithet "sexist pig!")

Talking to people around the nation about the sex education of their children leads me to believe that for them, and maybe for a lot of other people as well, most of the culture wars these days are a response to the cataclysmic events of the 1960s. More to the point, most of the culture wars are really about sex, and all the other issues—clothing, teen pregnancy, family values, special rights for gay people—are different ways of talking about the same thing. And sex, as the social hygienists knew so well, is about how men and women relate to each other in all realms of their lives.

Going into the 1960s, the fruitful and multiplying married couple was the order of the day. Thanks to the social hygienists, of course, this couple had learned to treat sex as a source of marital intimacy and stability, but laws left over from before the first sexual revolution were still on the books. Contraception was nominally illegal, as was abortion. Contraceptive clinics existed, but a combination of local mores and federal and sometimes state laws meant that they were typically unadvertised and served only married couples, and at least two states had no contraceptive clinics at all.[11] Upper- and middle-class married women could and did visit doctors to obtain reasonably effective contraception, but it was under the legal fiction that they were protecting their health, not preventing pregnancy. Probably as a result, the most common contraceptive married couples used was the condom, followed by withdrawal and douching. Although a few upper-income women had diaphragms, most other Americans were relying on pretty much the same kinds of contraception people had used a century earlier.[12] Even more telling, although subsequent studies established that in 1971 32 percent of women were sexually active before marriage, no one knew at the time, because national studies asking unmarried women about their sexual practices were unthinkable.[13]

Other cultural norms also make it clear that the United States in those days was a country almost unrecognizably different from the one we now live in. The social hygienists' stance toward masturbation—that it did not cause either insanity or hair on the hands but was nonetheless a potentially harmful habit that could become addictive—was the conventional wisdom. Homosexuality was so distant from public acknowledgment that the idea that it was a "lifestyle" would have been unimaginable.[14] Even the founders of what were then called homophile organizations called only for an end to blatant discrimination, not affirmative acceptance of their orientation.[15]

Sexual activity during the engagement period had become increasingly widespread, but getting pregnant outside of marriage was still so shameful that women whose families did not arrange a shotgun marriage (or at least white women whose families did not) were sent out of sight, counseled to give up their babies for adoption, and told to resume "normal" life as quickly as possible.[16] As late as 1970, when an unwed mother in liberal Cambridge, Massachusetts, decided to keep her baby, she was fired from her job—for moral turpitude—and discovered that the local diaper service would not deliver diapers to such a patently immoral person. Even men could feel the pressure: a pharmacist I interviewed some years ago confided to me that before the 1960s, many of the pharmacists he knew would not sell condoms to men whom they knew or suspected were unmarried.[17]

By 1975, just a few years later, that world had disappeared almost completely. Contraception was legal for the unwed and for teenagers, and contraceptives were sold over the counter; ads for them competed for attention in the mass-circulation women's magazines you could buy at the checkout counter in any grocery store. Abortion was legal, and there was a new constitutional theory of privacy. Men and women lived openly together without being married, and out-of-wedlock birthrates began a steady rise.[18]

This brings us to why the sixties were so revolutionary. Scholars tell us that before the French Revolution of 1789, the word "revolution" simply meant a return to a previous state, as when we talk about the earth's revolutions around the sun. It was only with the French Revolution, with its radical new notions of the rights of man, that the word came to stand for the upending and redistribution of power, the total restructuring of everyday life.[19] In other words, it came to signal the idea that life had changed dramatically, because *the revolution had changed the fundamental power relations on which everyday life is built.* Thus, the way people addressed one another during the French Revolution, or the way that months came to be named or years counted, stood in for a set of *political* claims about the nature of society and how it should be organized.[20]

It is in this sense of the word that the 1960s were so revolutionary, because for the first time since the days of social hygiene, ideas about gender and sexuality were called into question, and thus power relations between men and women were questioned too. Whether or not the sexual revolution intended to challenge the power relations between the sexes and whether or not it actually did are still open questions.[21] For my own part, I think that much of this sexual revolution was accidental (which is probably true of the French Revolution as well), and it is hard to make the case that it created equality, no matter how that term is defined, between men and women. My colleague Arlie Hochschild calls it a "stalled revolution" and that sounds right to me.[22]

On the level of lived experience, however, the sixties and the sexual revolution broke down a set of hierarchies that most people took for granted. Kathy Lemoindre summed up what I heard in many different interviews when she said, "I challenged the way things were. I didn't always understand, I didn't always like the way things were . . . just the rebelliousness of the teenage years, plus the explosive sixties that I was living in at the time—you know, I did a lot of challenging." John Rockford also caught the temper of the times when he pointed out to me, "In college in the seventies, everybody was liberal, even if you were really conservative." So discussions were arguments, not discussions.

In that context, the claim that women and men were equal sexually as well as in every other way seemed of a piece with everything else that was going on—the challenging of authority in all its realms. For some, this was liberating. As Elaine Devoto said, "I was about nineteen years old when I had my first sexual experience. And that was great. That was right around the time of the sexual revolution, and I just went out and had a wonderful time. And traveled through Europe and had a great time, just really enjoying myself during those years. And of course nobody ever worried about anything. Of course I took precautions against pregnancy and venereal disease, because I was also very aware of venereal diseases, since I had educated myself. And I never did develop a venereal disease. I didn't develop any pregnancies that were unintended."

For others, it was traumatizing. Echoing the thoughts that several men shared with me, Jared Donnelly said, "I ran into a dichotomy in my life. On the one hand I had a value for my mother and for my sisters and for women, but on the other hand I kept getting bombarded, you know, in the sex revolution of the late sixties, of 'This is the way men are and this is the way women are, go for it, do it.'"

By 1975, the most cherished ideal of the first generation of sex educators had begun to come true—men and women had began to share a single standard of sexual behavior.[23] Unfortunately, it wasn't exactly the one they had in mind. In fact, the standard that Anna Garlin Spencer had so confidently predicted would never happen did: women began to conduct their sex lives in much the same way that men did. And both law and social policy seemed bent on helping them do so.

It's this part of the revolution that Mary Kay was referring to when she said that kids today know more than she did at twenty, and perhaps even do more as well. In another part of our conversation, she shared her grudging admiration for a very young man she watched buying condoms: "I saw a child buying a condom the other night. I could die. I was really embarrassed, you know, I was like *do-da-do*"—she mimed a person elaborately not paying attention to what is going on—"but for whatever reason, the child was taking responsibility for his actions. You know, whether I approved or not was not the question. Whether he was taking responsibility was the question."

Between 1964 and 1975, sex became possible for millions of women in the way it always had been possible for men, as something you did when you wanted to, because you wanted to, for its own sake. With legal, readily available, federally subsidized, and highly effective contraception, and with abortion available as a backup if pregnancy occurred anyway, sex for pure pleasure rather than sex necessarily tied to an ongoing and committed relationship became an option for women. And they didn't have to be ashamed of it.

This change took place in part because for the very first time, women had the *choice* of motherhood, and optional motherhood as a cultural and technological possibility occurred just as a new wave of feminism was burgeoning. Not only had the link between sex and reproduction been definitively broken, the women's movement made the political claim that this was just as it should be. After all, hadn't parenthood always been optional in some sense for men, and especially for unmarried men?

All the indicators we have suggest that in several different ways, men and women were becoming more alike in terms of their sexual practices. For example, in 1970, it was estimated that only one teenage woman in four was sexually active; by 1984, the proportion had risen to just under half. Teenage men in this same period showed similar trends.[24]

By the same token, in 1971 approximately six out of ten sexually active teenagers in metropolitan areas had had only a single sexual partner; eight years later, this figure had declined to only one in two. By the early 1990s, more than 70 percent of teenage women had had more than one partner and 20 percent had had six or more. (This is in part because recent cohorts of white teenagers face on average a decade between first intercourse and first marriage. Since marriage rates for African Americans are so low, the figures are twelve years for African American women and nineteen for men.)[25]

More surprisingly, sexual behaviors began to converge along racial and class lines as well. In 1988, the rate of premarital intercourse among young white women was only three percentage points lower than that of young African American women, who traditionally were more likely to be sexually active before marriage. Likewise, as teens within all groups become more sexually active, the traditional differences in premarital sex associated with class have declined.[26]

As men and women became reproductively and sexually more similarly situated, so to speak, women were able to become what liberalism had always claimed that they were—namely, free and equal individuals, different in no essential way from the men around them. Before, in different ways and in varying degrees, biology meant that women were always, in politics as in life, mothers or potential mothers.[27] With the spread of the pill and the ability to subordinate procreation to pleasure, women were freed to begin to think beyond motherhood and family. Like men, they valued intimate married life, and like men, they could now enter it on their own terms and view it as only a part of a complete life rather than the whole of it.

More relevantly, unmarried women who had access to the pill could now aspire to and invest in long-term professional education. Between 1960 and 1998, the number of "high-powered" professional women leapt from just under 5 percent to over 25 percent. Women applied in droves to medical school, law school, and schools of dentistry and business administration. While admitting that many other factors played a role, scholars who have analyzed the timing of these factors conclude that the pill alone accounts for much of the change.[28]

Thus the watershed of the sexual revolution and all it stood for: women, whose ties to motherhood were loosened, started to become *individuals*, and individuals who claimed they were different in no essential way from men.[29] Public opinion agreed; not only did American attitudes and behavior regarding both sex and gender change, and change rapidly, these changes diffused quickly among different sectors of society.[30]

In retrospect, it is astonishing how fast it all changed. As the pollster Daniel Yankelovitch put it in 1974, "So startling are the shifts in values and beliefs between the late 1960s, when our youth studies were first launched, and the present time that social historians of the future should have little difficulty in identifying the end of one era and the beginning of a new one. Rarely has a transition between one decade and the next seemed so abrupt and so full of discontinuities."[31]

I know how "abrupt and so full of discontinuities" that transition was from personal experience. In the spring of 1965, when I was a college freshman, I attended the senior prom with my fiancé, an "older man" of twenty. After the prom, a group of us, maybe a half dozen in number, ended up spending the night at the apartment of one young man who was lucky enough to live off-campus. We didn't do anything untoward—there were too many of us, and all of the women were encased in the standard prom wear of the time, which included such restrictive undergarments that even going to the bathroom was a challenge. Our modesty and chastity were safely protected that evening.

We were also protected by something subtler and less tangible than our clothing and numbers. The young man whose apartment it was woke us all up before dawn so he could rush us out of the building before any early risers caught glimpses of us. He knew that he would be evicted if anyone saw him with a woman in his apartment, and I am reasonably sure that not one person so rudely awakened that morning thought to question either his conviction or its legitimacy.

In the spring of 1965, almost everyone except a few Beatniks and bohemians lived out in daily life the assumption that society had a perfect right to try to make sure that most young women stayed virgins and did not become sluts. What individuals (especially unmarried individuals) did with their sex lives was accepted by everyone as a completely appropriate matter of public concern. Almost every detail of my prom night, from the unwieldy garments to the parietal rules (which meant that each girl had to sign out from her dormitory to an approved hotel) to our hasty departure, reflected the belief that the chastity of young women (and to a lesser extent of young men) was a public matter. Tellingly, young women, even in ultraliberal Berkeley, California, who sought contraceptive services in 1965 felt compelled to buy false wedding rings and use false names, playing out a drama not much changed since Mary McCarthy's heroine in *The Group* sought birth control in the 1930s.[32]

Yet that ritual, and the worldview it was based on, came undone in remarkably short order. In 1965 the sexual *ancien régime* was still substantially in place; ten years later it had vanished. Public opinion polls show quite convincingly that between 1967 and 1973, a set of rules about proper sexual conduct that would have seemed both comforting and familiar to the social hygienists was radically overturned. These polls show that whatever people might have done in their private lives, in the early 1960s they pretty much agreed about what people should do. Moral people, and specifically moral women, did not have sex before marriage, did not have sex with anyone other than their legal spouses, and did not have sex for the fun of it.

But things were very different just a few years later. In 1969, almost 70 percent of Americans told pollsters that they were opposed to premarital sex; four years later, that number had dropped twenty percentage points, to a little less than half of the population. The number who found nude photographs in magazines or nude actors in Broadway plays offensive (*Hair* and *Oh, Calcutta!* were playing on Broadway at the time) dropped a similar twenty points, from three quarters of those surveyed to just over half. The number of people who found topless waitresses (remember them?) offensive dropped seventeen points.[33] During these same years, people who thought birth control information should be available to anyone who wanted it, presumably including the unmarried and the young, increased ten percentage points.[34] Even attitudes toward abortion became substantially more liberal, with most of the change occurring *before* the Supreme Court decided *Roe v. Wade* in 1973.[35] Changes of this magnitude are extremely rare in the sixty or so years that public opinion has been polled. The sheer size of the shift in opinion and the very short time in which it took place make it clear that the sixties were indeed a watershed. When the sexual revolution was over, sex was in the public eye, motherhood was a voluntary choice for women, and marriage was no longer the only acceptable and legitimate place to have sex or babies.

The first sexual revolution, the one that brought sex education into being, changed the meaning of marriage by dethroning reproduction from its preeminent role and putting sexual pleasure on an equal footing with it. But as the social hygienists so presciently understood, valuing sexual pleasure raised troubling questions of whether or not such pleasure would be allowed to go its own way. If sex and reproduction could be severed from each other within marriage, what was to stop people from simply having sex without bothering to get married at all?

As it turned out, a variety of social forces kept sex within marriage—more or less—for much of the twentieth century. But for whatever reasons, sometime between the late 1960s and the early 1970s sex and marriage parted ways, just as sex and procreation within marriage had parted ways under the worried eyes of the social hygienists.

Already by 1969, for example, college students had come to accept what was earlier called "casual" sex; two out of three students surveyed found nothing morally troubling about it at all. Despite the fact that young people who are not college-bound tend to be more socially conservative than college-bound students, just four years later, disapproval among this group dropped from almost 60 percent of those polled to numbers much like those seen among college students. By 1973, substantial majorities of young people, whether in college or not, agreed that they wanted more sexual freedom, that abortions were morally acceptable, and that gay sex was acceptable too.[36]

Although less visible at the time, essentially the same thing began to happen to childbearing. The 1970s saw a national crisis over teenage pregnancy, but the behavior that was driving that crisis was not so much pregnancy as birth, and not births to young people but births to young unmarried people, like the girl who so unnerved Mary Kay Malone.[37] (It was characteristic of the whole debate that these very different things became amalgamated under the rubric "teenage pregnancy.") By 1992, when Vice President Dan Quayle made his famous "family values" speech denouncing the fictional (and adult) TV character Murphy Brown for having a child out of wedlock, the battle was essentially over. By the year after his speech, Americans' nonmarital birthrates had increased by almost 30 percent from 1960, and nonmarital births accounted for almost one out of every four births. These figures, as stark as they are, understate the change, just as the figures for premarital sex do. Where in an earlier era out-of-wedlock births represented miscalculations and accidents, in this a new era they increasingly represented conscious choices.[38]

What now seems to be happening is that Americans, including those who are having sex and children while unmarried, agree that marriage is a good place to have sex and give birth to children, and maybe even the best. But they differ from earlier generations in believing that marriage is not the only choice for either. Many women and men feel comfortable with the idea that they may well get married someday, when they meet Mr. or Ms. Right, but in the meantime they are willing to have sex, and in many cases children, while they wait for that day. In a term used by economists, they are "satisficing"—settling for good enough while they wait for something better.

Although the first public response to the "sexual revolution" and the "new morality" was largely one of alarm, Americans became accustomed to the new sexual lifestyles in remarkably quick order. In one 1974 survey, pollsters asked people to agree or disagree with the statement, "There is no reason why single women shouldn't have children and raise them if they want to." The fact that they even asked this question makes clear that something fundamental had changed in American society in the four years since the young woman in Cambridge had been fired from her job and refused diaper delivery simply because she was pregnant and unmarried.[39] What had once been the terrain of a small, sophisticated minority of Americans, the heirs of the Greenwich Village bohemians whose radical attitudes on sex were ignored by the social hygienists, became mainstream. Starting out among the young and the highly educated, more permissive values vis-à-vis sexual behavior spread within a remarkably short period of time to the less well-educated and to older people.⁴⁰

But this picture of unfettered choices had a dark edge, as interviews for this book have made clear. When marriage and parenthood became choices for women, they also became choices for men. What is different, and substantially so, from the world in which Mary Kay Malone and I and the young woman from Cambridge grew up, is that men who want to sleep with you no longer have to promise to take care of you "if something happens." That "something"—in our day, the euphemism for pregnancy—might be less likely to happen today than in our day, since more effective contraception is easily available, but if a woman does get pregnant, both parties confront a deeply transformed social reality.

When Mary Kay and I were coming of age, hopeful young men carried a condom around in their wallets, sometimes for so long that it wore a ring-shaped pattern into the leather. Because sex with "nice girls" was so rare and didn't usually happen unless the couple was committed to each other, the young man took all responsibility for preventing pregnancy, finally liberating that elderly condom from his wallet with fumbling fingers when and if the young woman said yes. But the advent of highly effective, non-intercourse-dependent (as the demographers term it) contraception, in the form of the birth-control pill, changed assumptions about how men and women related to each other when it came to preventing pregnancy.

Now, since effective contraception usually means contraceptive methods used by women, the decision to use contraception increasingly has become the woman's responsibility (offset to some extent by the growing use of condoms to prevent disease, which has a very different meaning in a relationship). More weightily, the task of not getting pregnant has become a woman's responsibility, and her responsibility alone. Furthermore, the existence of safe, legal abortion means that because women have the option of choosing to end a pregnancy if they want to, men increasingly feel that they do not have to support what is now seen as a personal choice.

The preceding paragraphs might read as if they were written by a card-carrying member of one of the groups that Jenny turned to when she found out about the sex education planned for Josh's classroom, such as Focus on the Family, perhaps, or Concerned Women for America. And that's the point. The risk of pregnancy in the 1950s brought women together. Contraception and abortion have divided them. On the one hand, there are women like me and Mary Kay, women for whom choices about sex, marriage, and motherhood opened doors. We were among those who took advantage of the pill and abortion to go on to higher education and from there to compete with men in the professions of law, medicine, and academia. Unlike the vast majority of women in earlier generations, we combined education and professional life with an active sex life, either as single women or as married women who had children when we and our husbands thought it would work best for us.

But on the other hand, there was another, less visible group of women, who did not particularly want to have and who were not eligible for the kind of payoffs that sexual autonomy brought to women more economically fortunate or ambitious. Women who had dropped out of high school, for example, or who had dropped out of college, or who just didn't like school and schooling, were not able to rush off to law school or medical school or a graduate program in sociology. As a result, while out-of-wedlock birthrates for highly educated women—the Murphy Browns—did not change, unwed motherhood for the least well-educated women tripled.

So for women as for men, the rich got richer. Women who were well-situated in terms of education or social background, or who just had high hopes for a future on a par with men, did very well as the sexual revolution unfolded. In fact, the sexual revolution (and state and federal responses to it) is an unheralded success story of the 1900s in public health. Quickly legalizing contraception and then abortion and committing federal and state funds to making contraception inexpensive and easily available, public policy enabled two generations of teenagers to become sexually active without becoming pregnant. (The available evidence suggests that the sexual activity started first and was not, as conservatives claim, a response to liberalized abortion and contraception.)[41]

But revolutions have winners and losers, and in this case the losers were women who looked forward to marriage and family as the most enticing and life-affirming future. Now they were confronted by men who could have sex with many different women and who did not have to commit themselves to a relationship in order to have it. When and if a pregnancy occurred, rather than doing "the right thing," as his father or grandfather might have done, today's young man did not necessarily feel that he had to endorse what was now seen as the woman's choice about pregnancy and parenthood.

My interviews indicate clearly the declining fortunes of women who would prefer to be married mothers but who have fewer resources than before to make that happen. A Nobel Prize–winning colleague, George Akerlof, along with Janet Yellin and Michael Katz, has independently concluded the same thing based on game theory analysis.[42] When a new technology comes along, they argue—in this case, contraception and abortion—those who do not adopt it are "emmiserated," in the same way that loom weavers were when factory weaving came into being. Not, of course, that intimate relationships can be reduced to weaving. But the point holds: when a new technology allows some women to reduce their dependency on (and their preferences for) marriage and intimate relationships, those who can't or don't want to are disadvantaged.

As it happens, sex education, which came into being as a way of managing the first sexual revolution, was now called on to manage the second sexual revolution, which separated sex from marriage. Sex education was increasingly remade, and increasingly it was remade into exactly what the founders had dismissed as "emergency" sex education—sex education taught alone, designed to warn young people about the dangers of sex outside marriage, or, in the new incarnation, to teach them how to manage those dangers more effectively.

Implicit in the sexual revolution, and especially in the changing standards of female behavior, was the threatening idea that people—particularly women, the traditional guardians of the home—were having sex for their own reasons. Sex was no longer part of a courtship process that would lead to a spiritualized eroticism designed to confine more entertaining, more satisfying sex neatly to the marital bedroom. Now sex was just another pleasure to be indulged in whenever two parties agreed. Worse yet, although sex educators largely recognized this only in the context of teenage pregnancy, people who were having sex just for fun were increasingly moving on to the next stage, building families without bothering to get married.

Alert to the threat, a new generation of sex educators moved to make sure that sex was safely tethered, if not in marriages, at least in committed heterosexual relationships (what Ira Reiss calls "permissiveness with affection").[43] More important, the language that sex educators increasingly began to use was one of risk reduction.

The sex educators of the 1960s, perhaps because they were surrounded by a youth revolution as well as a civil rights revolution and a general sentiment that young people couldn't trust anyone over thirty, fled from the monolithic self-confidence that had marked the sex educators of the first sexual revolution. While Grace Hoadley Dodge, Charles Eliot, Anna Garlin Spencer, and their colleagues may have disagreed among themselves about how to achieve their goals for young people, by and large they were in agreement about what those goals were. Sex outside or before marriage was wrong, and they took this for granted and easily moved on to the larger goal of making "wholesome" sexuality (married sexuality) happier and more fulfilling.

But the new generation of sex educators was living in a very different time. Rather than urging young people to avoid petting, masturbation, and premarital sex entirely, they decided since most young people would be having sex outside marriage, their task was to make that sex safer rather than denounce it. In other words, they took for granted the core assumption of the sexual revolution—that marriage was just one sexual lifestyle among many.

Mary Calderone, M.D., who founded the Sex Information and Education Council of the United States (SIECUS), the lodestar for the "new" sex education, wrote in 1968 that "one of the great issues of this era is the question of how to reframe our moral values in terms relevant to the needs and conditions of a world that grows more complex and demanding every day"; it was something she could well have written in 1915. But her next sentence reveals that she was speaking of the second rather than the first sexual revolution: "Many of the moral dilemmas relate in one way or another to sexual behavior *within, as well as outside*, marriage" (emphasis added).[44]

In 1967, the Illinois Sex Education Advisory Board, a committee created by the state legislature, made the point even more clearly:

> Illinois youth should be sex-educated, not merely sex-informed or indoctrinated. Illinois youth are growing up in a democratic pluralistic society wherein many traditional ways and standards are being challenged. In sexual matters they are being confronted—in news media, magazines, advertising, movies, plays, TV, radio, and books—with "situation ethics" and an emerging, but not yet widely accepted, standard of premarital sexual permissiveness with affection. They need to be sex-educated so they can meet and adjust to current conditions by making intelligent choices and sound decisions—based upon progressive acceptance of moral responsibility for their own sexual conduct as it affects themselves and others—when faced with alternative standards and patterns of sexual behavior. Sex education based upon a fear approach or moralistic preaching—instead of good teaching and sound guidance—is apt to prove self-defeating in the modern

world. Provision should be made for class discussion and communication among students, teachers, and counselors, which will guide and assist Illinois youth in critically and constructively analyzing current sexual problems and issues and in drawing sound conclusions, desirable from both a personal and a social standpoint. We must have faith that when young people in Illinois are given the facts and then guided in thinking things through, the vast majority will choose the right path instead of the wrong.[45]

In these few words are the marks of a revolution. No longer are sex educators confident that they know right from wrong in the array of choices facing young people. Rather, they see their job as providing information so that students, as the statement says, "can meet and adjust to current conditions by making intelligent choices and sound decisions."

The new sex educators gave less ground on unmarried childbearing, preferring to see it as one of the "risks" of sex to be managed rather than as a conscious (albeit often second-best) decision. Throughout this period, sex educators assumed that teenage pregnancy was the same thing as unwed pregnancy, and, true to an earlier era, they assumed that an unwed pregnancy must be unwanted.

The dangers of sexuality that students now needed to be educated about were no longer syphilis and the "commercialized vice" that so worried the social hygienists and family life educators of an earlier era. Their primary concerns were unwanted (although unwanted by whom was never clearly specified) pregnancy, abortion, and what were thought to be the relatively more benign diseases of the 1970s—gonorrhea, herpes, and the less well known sexually transmitted diseases.[46]

The task of sex education became one of reducing the risks of sexuality outside marriage among young people, and several things were thought to be critical for this, as the Illinois statement suggests. On the one hand, information was key: young people could not manage risks without being aware of both what the risks were and what means were available to reduce them. On the other hand, young people needed motivation to manage such risks, and this resulted in an emphasis on being in a "caring" relationship. This in turn gave rise to a new marker of when young people were "ready" to have sex. In an earlier era, of course, they were "ready" when they had married or, although few sex educators directly admitted it, when they were engaged. Now they were "ready" when they were prepared to manage risks actively on their own behalf and that of their partners. A young person who did not protect his or her partner from both pregnancy and disease was a person, by definition, "not ready" to have sex. Finally, sex education still tried to uphold the new ideal of caring relationships so that there would be no "slippage" into exactly what happened—the movement of sex and parenthood even further beyond the confines of imminent marriage.

In focusing on the management rather than the deterrence of risk, sex educators were in tune with a range of other cultural and social processes. Increasingly, in everything from crime to nuclear energy, the task of a more complex and heterogeneous society was not to preach a single moral vision but to provide information to morally diverse actors who would "clarify" their own values and act prudently.[47]

Like their forebears, who assumed that everyone could be taught to follow a single standard of sexual behavior, the new sex educators had a new ideal. It was still a single standard, but this time it was the standard of "intimacy," of "caring" and "nonexploitative" sex, that was the common goal. By the time that AIDS educators were preaching "safe sex," which was transmuted into "mutually monogamous sex" as the preferred ideal, this was simply a more clinical rendering of what sex educators had staked out as appropriate sexual behavior.

Although the new form of sex education was broadly congruent with larger social trends, it was not uncritically accepted by everyone. In fact, this new wave of sex education and the premises on which it rested struck many people as deeply troublesome. In the course of trying to convince young people that the best kind of sex was intimate, committed, and mutually caring, sex that took the other person into account, sex educators had effectively conceded that marriage was just one of several sexual options. In so doing, they planted the seeds of what would eventually become a harvest of controversy.

CHAPTER FOUR

Sexual Liberals and Sexual Conservatives

The sexual revolution of the 1960s and all that it stood for has divided the country into two groups, those who embrace the revolution and those who look back longingly to the old order it replaced. Having spent many hours talking to people around the country about sex education, I've become convinced that there is a chasm, wide and getting wider, between the *sexual* right and left—between people who hold liberal sexual values and those who hold conservative ones.[1]

The terms "liberal" and "conservative" came from those I interviewed.[2] As Emily Litton, a mother and a member of the school board, said, "Yeah, it got ugly. It did. Because people feel really passionate about it. But there were a lot of people—I hate to say on my side, but there were definite sides. And there was a split, and I guess the best way to label the split was maybe conservative and liberal. And I'm not saying that the conservative people were all exactly like-minded and came from the same backgrounds or anything like that, but they tended to believe one way and then the other people tended to believe another way."

Reverend Zebediah Miller, one of the very few African Americans I interviewed (I think I spoke with only three in over a hundred interviews), used much the same language when we talked on a sweltering spring afternoon, after we had fled the heat inside his century-old church to sit under a spreading oak tree that was already ancient when the Revolutionary War began. I asked Reverend Miller how it was that he and his colleague in that town, Dr. Kingston, both Southern Baptists in good standing, approached the sex education controversy.

Reverend Miller's courtly, old-time manner and soft voice belied the vehemence of his response, "Well, Dr. Kingston, for instance—

philosophically, he and I are on opposite sides of the fence. You know, he supports sex education. By supporting the sex education program, he's supporting abortion. Murdering babies. So he's a liberal and I'm a conservative."

Almost all the people I spoke with used some formulation of the conservative-liberal or right-left dichotomy to talk about where they and others stood when it came to sexuality and education about it. People clearly knew that common beliefs held them together with others on this same side of the issue, and they also understood that this was true of those on the other side. Moreover, they were unanimous in believing that people who supported comprehensive sex education were liberal or on the left and those who opposed such sex education and/or who preferred abstinence-only sex education were conservative or on the right.

The interesting thing about sexual liberals and conservatives, however, is that almost everyone I spoke with was raised as a sexual conservative, by which I mean someone who at least pays lip service to the sexual mores promulgated by the social hygienists in the early 1900s.[3] In other words, this is the view that men and women don't have sex unless they are married to each other, that gay sex is deviant, that sex is a healthy and normal part of marriage, but that a veil of seemly reticence should surround the entire matter. Sexuality was so hush-hush when most of the people I talked to were growing up that more than one of them confessed shamefacedly to a furtive trip to the public library to look up words that most third-graders today have long since committed to memory, such as "vagina," "vulva," and "testes."

So although these people are not necessarily representative of the country at large, in this respect I would guess that their experience is typical of a certain age group. Only the youngest of them had the experience that Mary Kay Malone described, where real alternatives to the model of marital sex existed and parents fought with their teenagers about what kinds of sexual values and lifestyles they would adopt.

The flowering of choices during the sexual revolution created a division about how to respond to these choices, a division that has only widened over the past thirty-odd years. On the one side were and are those who hold fast to the idea that sex is meant to be intimate and satisfying, but only within the context of marriage. On the other were and are those who believe that sex is about pleasure, and moral sex is sex that does not harm the person involved or his or her partner. True, this latter group of people tend to agree that intimate relationships, whether gay or straight, married or unmarried, between teenagers or between the elderly, enhance the likelihood of pleasurable sex, but for them committed relationships are no longer the sine qua non of moral sex, as long as those involved are both careful and conscientious.

While pundits debate about what "right" and "left" mean in a post–cold war era, the people I talked to had no doubts.[4] In particular, the rise of "social conservatism" has signaled a whole new dimension within conservatism. To be fair, conservatism since the 1950s has always included a turn toward religion, a fascination with natural law, and a deep respect for tradition and hierarchy.[5] But my hunch, based on the people I've talked to, is that for modern social conservatives, the term "social" has come to be exactly what it was in 1913—a euphemism for sex.

This kind of sexual left and right doesn't always line up with the other dimensions of conservatism and liberalism. After talking to people across the country about sex education, I can see that right and left in foreign policy, the fiscal domain, and sexual life, although often correlated, don't always track along the same lines. Being sexually conservative or liberal may well be a predictor of attitudes on other matters, but if so, it's a somewhat weak one. (Of course, I did not talk systematically about foreign affairs in my interviews, as it seemed a bit far afield for a study of sex education. Comments made in passing, however, made it clear to me that attitudes toward foreign affairs couldn't necessarily be foreseen from someone's stance on sex.) Some of the sexual conservatives I met were economic liberals, in part because the same values that led them to be sexual conservatives also led them to be deeply suspicious of the market and the economy as metaphors for human life. By the same token, a good many of the sexual liberals were moderates in economic matters.

There is a funny thing about this, though. When I tried to get people to describe what it meant to be on the right or left sexually, they had a remarkably hard time articulating either a theory or details that would permit sorting people unerringly into one camp or the other. In fact, they looked at me as if I were a little slow when I tried to get them to spell out exactly what it means to be sexually liberal or conservative. A few issues—abortion, homosexuality, feminism, premarital sex—were often listed as things that liberals and conservatives disagreed over, but no one could describe either a set of principles that would encompass positions on all of these issues or why it made sense to speak of them as markers on a conservative–liberal continuum rather than, say, a traditional–modern continuum or a feminist–nonfeminist continuum. In short, "conservative" and "liberal" were catchall terms that people used to separate something important, but they had only the vaguest idea about what the boundaries of those categories were. In fact, the people I spoke with just assumed that any socially competent person would know what fits into each category and looked askance at me when I asked them to fill in the blanks.[6] For example, one of the southerners said, "Yeah, well, I happen to be Southern Baptist, so we have kind of strict conservative views, I suppose it would be. So we think that as Southern Baptists, the parents are really supposed to give the kids all the sexual information that they need."

As this quotation makes clear, the terms "liberal" and "conservative" cover important differences in the realm of sexuality, gender, and the family, but the categories are blurred. People tend to assume that being conservative is the same as being traditional or "hard-core" or "strict," and they often also assume that attitudes about sex are congruent with attitudes about politics and theology. Often people speak of themselves or others as generally liberal or conservative, meaning both politically and sexually liberal or conservative. At other times "liberal" is a stand-in for certain life choices, especially for women, as in being a "single, liberal career woman" or a "flaming feminist liberal" when the speaker is unmarried and childless.

Obviously, these categories were deeply meaningful for the people I talked to, and they used them all the time to separate what divided the pro–sex ed forces from the anti–sex ed (or pro–abstinence education) ones. But there was an almost maddening circular quality about this part of the interviews. "What is liberal when it comes to sex?" I would ask, and the person being interviewed would respond brightly, "Oh, it's someone who supports comprehensive sex education." "And why do they support comprehensive sex education?" I would ask, and the answer would come back, "Because they're liberals."

As I pushed people, it became obvious that they made assumptions about which cluster of values would and should be held in the two camps. A person who was a feminist and a proud agnostic, who believed in abortion and contraception, and who also strongly supported an abstinence-only curriculum would be deeply unsettling, because such a person (who does not exist, as far as I know) would transgress the tacit values that separate one side from the other.

Despite what everyone seems to think, the easy answer is not that theologically conservative churches lead their parishioners to adopt sexually conservative views; the path between religion and sex is a complex one.[7] Given the high visibility of conservative religions, and in particular fundamentalist Christian groups, on issues relating to sex and family, some sexually conservative people I interviewed actively sought out such groups because they wanted a church whose sexual teachings supported their own values, especially when they felt that their values were increasingly under assault in the larger culture. In these cases, people's sexual values preceded membership in a conservative church.

For example, Sandy Ames opposes sex education, but she described herself as a person who started out with a very different set of values. I asked her if any particular event had set her on the path to rethinking what she believed in, and she said, "There was, actually. I was actually quite a liberal, single career woman, I was going to join NOW [National Organization for Women], blah, blah, blah. I was moving up, I was in middle management, and I had my own company car. All that kind of stuff, at twenty-five. Married and got pregnant, and he left me, and it just kind of opened my eyes. I thought, 'Okay, I've made wrong choices in my own life, and obviously I'm not basing my choices on anything. I'm not grounded.' And that's when I moved back in with my parents, I had my daughter, and I started attending church. And I just really came to the conclusion that it's one thing to mess up your own life, but now I have a baby, and I have a baby without a father, and it's not okay to mess up her life, and I'd better get grounded or centered in how I make decisions now that I'm responsible for this life. And that's actually when I started attending church and I became a Christian."

While some people seek out a church that is more congenial to their beliefs about sexuality, others stay where they are, standing by their own beliefs about sexuality despite what their church or pastor might teach. Particularly in Billingsley, where being Southern Baptist was as much a part of a person's heritage as a treasured recipe for fried chicken or light-as-air biscuits, some people had no problem disagreeing with either their church or their pastor. Mary Kay Malone, for one, made a point of telling me that her pastor was much more sexually conservative than she was.

"You have to understand," she said, "my pastor does not even believe in mixed swimming." The term "mixed swimming" being a new one to me, I ask Mary Kay to clarify. "Mixed swimming," she said. "He believes that the boys should swim in one area and the girls should swim in another area. So we've sat on the line a couple of times with our beliefs. He said, 'I believe this sex education program is horrible . . . it's teaching our children to be trash; it's advocating they run out and have sex.' And I said, 'I do not see the program like that . . . I hope you understand,' I said, 'As far as I'm concerned, we serve the same Master . . . What you believe and what your convictions are, that's yours. And what I believe and what mine are, that's mine. And if I'm wrong, I have to answer for it, and if you're wrong, you have to answer for it.' He knows I'm on the committee supporting sex education. He still does not like it, but there is no more controversy between us."

So if it's not religion, what does separate the sexual right from the sexual left? Which values do people on each side hold in common? I started out assuming that abortion would be the dividing line, perhaps because I had previously studied the abortion issue and because historically, abortion was central in mobilizing the pro-family movement. In my early interviews, I took for granted that being pro-life was a given for a sexual conservative who opposed sex education, and that was generally true. But it was not a clear-cut division. People who support abstinence education and/or believe that sex education is purely a parent's prerogative, and who consequently oppose comprehensive sex education, tend to have a pro-life view of abortion, but not always.

Richard Delany was opposed to sex education, he said, but he had some pretty complicated feelings about abortion. Rubbing his hands together nervously, as if he could rub off the rough edges between his conflicting views, he explained: "Well, first of all, I don't believe abortion's right. But there are cases where I think abortion is probably better . . . Say the mother's whacked out on drugs or something and there's a better-than-not chance the child's going to be deformed or something like that . . ." His voice drifted off as he contemplated abortion because of a physical anomaly. "Well, that's like having utopia, where you can pick and choose, weed out the bad and keep the good, you know. I don't know if that's right either. But I do believe that there are certain cases in a situation like that, where you know a child's going to be neglected, going to have withdrawals and stuff, I think maybe it is better aborted. I don't know. I really don't. In normal circumstances, no, I don't go for abortion." You can imagine how unpopular this kind of to-ing and fro-ing would be at a right-to-life meeting, but it did not disqualify Richard from being part of the opposition to sex education in his community.

Likewise, almost all of the liberals—those who supported comprehensive sex education—were in favor of at least the right to abortion, although some people made the point that they themselves could never have one. But even some of them had mixed feelings about the issue. Jerry Gorton, who supports comprehensive sex education, said to me, "I have become a little bit more conservative, especially on the abortion issue. Whereas I used to be pro-choice, I am still pro-choice, but not very much. I'm more anti-abortion, but I believe it should be legal. Making abortion illegal I don't believe will cut down significantly on the abortions. And I don't think it'll further the understanding of the issue. I think abortion should be illegal except in extreme cases where it's the doctor and the woman who are making a choice, but I think it's way overused as a birth control method, as opposed to using contraceptives or abstinence, or being more careful. So I've changed in that way."

Again, I don't need to tell you that such a stance would at minimum earn Jerry Gorton some hostile glances at his local NARAL meeting, but it did not seem relevant in his views toward sex education. In short, it's not reproduction that separates the liberals from the conservatives, it's *sex*. To be more precise, it's about whether any kind of sex besides heterosexual married sex should be morally and socially acceptable.

This probably seems painfully obvious. After all, what else would people fighting over sex education be fighting over? But it has taken me years of sitting in living rooms, cafés, and porches and of poring over transcripts in the quiet of my office to understand exactly what it is about sex that divides the two groups. Not one person I interviewed could put a finger on how and why she or he knew that people on the "other side" didn't share his or her values about sex, but somehow they all just knew that they didn't.

Here's what I've come to understand: for conservatives, sex is *sacred*, while for liberals, it's *natural*, and sacred sex demands formal structures, namely marriage, to protect it, while natural sex does not. As Sandy Ames said, "You know, we were created to be sexual beings, and that is God-created, and we actually think that that's a healthy thing within marriage. A lot of people think that 'Oh, Christians are prudes,' or whatever. It couldn't be further from the truth . . . We just believe it belongs in marriage, and within that, it's fine. But you just don't go around having that kind of time with just anybody."

Pastor Forrest Langley, one of the most articulate and poetic of the sexual conservatives, told me of the sexual legacy (his term) he hoped to leave his parishioners and community: "I would want to influence people in such a way to respect it so that sexuality is a thing that's not all tangled up like a ball of yarn and knots, a thing that is very damaged and very difficult to find out even how to begin to unravel it, but something to enter into and to enjoy lifelong, and to really experience a real depth of blessing in it." He believes this can happen only if a person comes to marriage as a virgin. In fact, Pastor Langley's belief that the sacred nature of sexuality in marriage can be derailed by casual sex extends so far that he hoped his young son wouldn't masturbate. He said, "I would encourage anyone not to masturbate, but the reality is, the great majority of boys will. I have no idea what the percentages are, but I would estimate it's well in the nineties. It's just from where I am spiritually, I would encourage Joseph not to."

His words echoed something that Jenny Letterman had said to me early on, when she bewailed both the desacralization and the openness of sex these days. Jenny told me, "I still feel that sex is a private thing. But the way it's been commercialized so, the way it's been presented so, there's nothing sacred about it anymore. It's just an open thing. If you feel good, do it."

Although liberals might endorse much of what these sexual conservatives describe as their beliefs about sex—after all, liberals too believe in healthy, committed sexuality, and they too worry a lot about the blatant and vulgar commercialization of sex—they ultimately see sex as natural rather than sacred. As long as people meet the two central conditions of being careful and caring (that is, not exploitative), they have no trouble with the "if it feels good, do it" philosophy that Jenny Letterman so easily dismissed. Sexual liberals, like liberals more generally, are pluralists: they see many, many different kinds of sexuality, and to make too big a deal over sex is to reduce the choices surrounding it. Again and again, liberals stressed to me the "healthy" dimension of sex and the need to be relaxed and playful about it. In fact, that's the point: they think that you can't make good choices about sex unless you are relaxed and playful. The kind of sacred sex that is central to Jenny Letterman's thinking is a sure recipe for making people feel worried and anxious, they think, and worried and anxious people do not make good choices.

So what sexual conservatives see as honoring the sacred nature of sex, liberals see as making a big and detrimental fuss over something as normal and natural as any other human drive. Where conservatives see the mystery of the sacred in sex, liberals see only mystification. As one liberal mother declared, "In terms of my personal interest and my own evolution sexually, I came from the heart of the Midwest—conservative, you know. I never learned about sex, certainly not from my parents. I carried a lot of myths with me and really wanted to do something different for my daughter in terms of her own treating sex as a more normal function of one's body, without so much of the mystique and forbiddenness. Because I think that was detrimental to me in terms of my own sexual development. So . . . I was interested in having her grow up with what I call a healthier view of sex, particularly for women, certainly women's role in sex."

In fact, many sexual liberals worried about what would happen to young people if the information coming from the sexual conservatives was the only source of sex education. One woman told me, "You will have young people who somehow, if they're dominated by the loud voices of extremists, like we've seen in Shady Grove—these fundamentalist Christians—will come up with the idea that sex is a very unnatural and unhealthy thing and that there is something wrong with them. And I think that would be a great tragedy indeed. That's the antithesis of what I would want taught all the way along."

Several themes stitched across the interviews with sexual conservatives, and all of them, in one way or another, address the sacred nature of sex and thus the need to protect it in marriage. For some sexual conservatives, sex must be restricted to marriage because the Bible calls on men and women (and only men and women) to cleave together and become as one. Accordingly, sex can transcend the merely physical only when it is based in holy matrimony. As Reverend Erik Thomassen said to me, in sentiment if not terms that would have been familiar to the social hygienists, "Sexuality in Judeo-Christian teaching is to be learned—and it's to be learned within the confines of matrimony and marriage. It's to be learned within the confines of the personal intimacy with the one you've devoted and committed your life to. Because this is big-time, this is major league ball. Sexuality isn't peanuts and popcorn, although there are those who made it be that. Thinking of sex that way, it's such a diminution of what is actual and real."

Similarly, when I asked Dorothy Sunn what she would do if her daughter had sex outside marriage, she responded, "I would probably do what I could to get her to question why she felt that she needed to do that. But I would be very, very explicit about what the Bible says, and I don't think it minces words at all—it says not until marriage. That commitment needs to be there, and that it should be honored and it should be done within a relationship that is a committed one. Where it's before God. And not something that is taken lightly and you just do because it feels good."

But other sexual conservatives argued that there was a secular as well as Biblical reason to reserve sex for marriage: the protection, commitment, and trust of marriage permits sex to reach its fullest potential. Dave Webber, an eloquent father and a national proselytizer for abstinence-only education, made the best secular case for abstinence, although he drew on Biblical imagery when he said, "Sex has this human dimension, a personal dimension. And as I read it in the scriptures, which gives me a kind of a point of view of God's intention, I see that the man and woman are supposed to relate to each other in terms of a bonding which is not just physical. The bonding is a personal bonding, and it has a lot to do with a total commitment to that other person . . . And I find what's happening in our culture is that that union between a man and a woman is approached and talked about just in terms of what's physical. When you say 'having sex,' what you're doing is speaking in physical terms. So the words I use—and it becomes awkward, because people want to be free to use other terms and I want to be Biblical—I want to say that there is a union. And I really sense a difference in the experience of two people having a union in that way: physical, emotional bonding." (To understand how much such sexual conservatives are echoing views from the first sexual revolution, compare Dave Webber's comments to something Edward L. Keyes said in the early years of the twentieth century. Social hygiene's goal, he claimed, was "to turn lust into love, into the enthralling love of equal mate for equal mate, into civic love for freedom, home, and state, into the eternal love of God.")[8]

Moreover, sexual conservatives believe that waiting until marriage to have sex means learning skills and values that will enhance marriage later on. As Dave said, "What abstinence is doing is, it's building that maturity and that responsibility over time. Trust. Allowing you to pursue your career plans without any of these serious interruptions. Be a teenager, have a good time, do it in a controlled atmosphere so you don't have to worry about the problems. Life is just as enjoyable. You're not missing out on anything, you have something wonderful to look forward to, within the context of a marriage. Imagine if someone's willing to make a lifelong commitment to you before the physical has entered the picture. That relationship's got to mean something. That's got to mean something."

Sexual liberals are all for sex within marriage, of course, but they view marriage as just one among many acceptable options. And here the reality of different life paths shapes how people think about sex. The conservatives are involved in strategies and worldviews that play up the value of sexuality, and by arguing that this mysterious, sacred force can be enjoyed only in marriage, they boost the stock of marriage as well. Liberals, in contrast, want to downplay the role of sexuality. (Sometimes when they talk about sex, their constant emphasis on "healthy" sex makes it sound just like volleyball, except more fun.) Because they expect young people to spend many years in schooling and getting established in life, they expect marriage to come later, in the late twenties or early thirties. Consequently, they see no sense in (and are deeply skeptical about) asking young people not to be sexual for a decade or two, if not more. For most sexual liberals, marriage not only does but should come relatively late in a full life, and not by accident but by plan.

Irene Thomas picked up the class and educational dimensions that make marriage such a freighted issue in this debate when she said, "The other thing I see as getting terribly conflictual for our society is this discussion about delaying sex until marriage, and this might go back to your class-based issue, kind of . . . I mean, I had my daughter when I was thirty-three. I got married when I was twenty-eight. If we're asking people seriously to be abstinent until they're married, and a whole segment of us is also asking people to get their economic life formed before they get married, I think there are some biological and social issues that just need to be faced squarely. I mean, I think the twenties are a healthy time for people, in their lives. So I'm not a believer in abstinence until marriage necessarily, for a variety of reasons."

Judy Samson made the same point: "I don't like early marriage. I met my husband when we were twenty-nine, and I'd never lived with anyone before. We married when I was thirty, thirty-one. And I think that those are good decisions, but I certainly would feel a sense of loss if my daughter had no sexuality until she was twenty-nine or thirty. Sexuality is an important part of our lives and a wonderful gift if used well and enjoyed."

Irene Thomas agreed, with a laugh. "I don't think that early marriage is the answer, because early marriage is usually done on a hormonal basis. 'He's so cute, I'll marry him.' If we all married the boys we were first attracted to, we would marry jerks!"

The sense that marriage is something you work yourself up to is based on assumptions of what kinds of lives lie ahead. Conservatives do not imagine long years of education and they think that marriage is the best life for most women, so abstinence until marriage is not much of a hardship, since it looms much nearer in the future for teenagers than liberals think it does.

Although sexual liberals agree with sexual conservatives that caring and committed sex is the best and highest form of sex, they're not sure that marriage is the only vehicle for that commitment, and they devoutly believe that people cannot hope to enter into that kind of committed, loving sex without a lot of emotional experience and self-knowledge beforehand—experience and self-knowledge that presumes sexual experience. "Know thyself"—sexually, emotionally, and psychologically—is the central moral tenet of sexual liberals. If you do not know yourself, you cannot know your motives, and to enter into a marriage before that hard-won self-knowledge is achieved is to fetter the possibilities that marriage can hold.

But sexual liberals also worry about something even more sub-tle, and it's something that took a great deal of digging to uncover. For sexual liberals, "marriage" is a verb, while for con-servatives it is a noun, and liberals at some level intuit this and are concerned about it. That is, sexual conservatives (at least in the ideal) marry once, and once married they are (again in the ideal) forever in the state of marriage. For sexual liberals, in contrast, being married is not only a verb but an active one. For them, a good marriage requires work and discipline, communication and honesty, and it's a process that's pretty much ongoing.

So for sexual liberals, all the talk about marriage runs the risk of confusing the wrapping with the package. In other words, if you teach young people that the only moral sex is married sex, then legally married people can just rest on their laurels and skip the hard work of creating and recreating the marriage on a daily basis, and that includes sex too. These people think that sexual happiness is something that must be worked on, not necessarily taken for granted. One person told me, "I think that the opposi-tion's mindset has to do with . . . 'There is only one place for sex and that's in the marriage bed. And don't tell me whether you're satisfied and happy and enjoy sex or not, it doesn't make a differ-ence.' I think you would be amazed at how much sexual ignorance is prevalent in the lives of married people. It's just, 'Wham bam, thank you ma'am, let's go to work now.' "

The talk about marriage flows over a difference between the two sides that is never forthrightly confronted, and that is the role of sexual pleasure in human life. Like the early social hygienists, the sexual conservatives are terribly worried about the dangers of letting pleasure loose. I must have heard such people tell me a hundred times the theme that sex education teaches "If it feels good, do it." They are convinced that sexual pleasure is all well and good, *but only in marriage.* Not only do they believe that mar-riage is the one place that sexual pleasure can become something beyond mere physical pleasure, they devoutly agree with Sandy

Ames that "you just don't go around having that kind of time with just anybody."

But sexual liberals find this baffling. Why not have "that kind of time with just anybody"? If both parties know how to protect themselves, and both parties are fully agreed that they want to make love, then what's the problem? The fact that such sexuality may just feel good troubles them not one whit.

This cuts to the essence of the difference. Sexual liberals, like sexual conservatives, look forward to a time when their children will be in a relationship where sex and love come together, but there's no reason for them to deny themselves sexual pleasure as they wait for Mr. or Ms. Right. Zach Rogers is somewhat wary of openly endorsing sexuality for the fun of it, perhaps because his children are young, but he explained: "A lot of people don't really want their kids to get married out of high school. They'd rather have them get married in their thirties, or do things first and experience life, and then decide on raising a family when they're older. So it's difficult. You're not going to say, 'Well, yeah, go out and experience what you can, and sex is part of it.' I think sex is wonderful, and I think some of my better experiences in college were sexual experiences, but I don't know whether I'd want to encourage kids to go out and do that sort of thing."

There's a second theme below the surface. To talk about marriage as *a* place to have sex versus *the only* place to have sex is to talk about individuals in relation to a collectivity and men and women in relation to the family. Traditional marriage, as an institution rather than a relationship, rested both in law and in everyday culture on deeply held assumptions about who men and women were and how they were to conduct themselves. In traditional Anglo-American common law, a woman as a separate legal entity disappeared the day she married. She could not hold property in her own name, she could not dispose of any property she took into the marriage without her husband's permission, and her labor (and any income she earned from it) belonged to her husband. Most important, she and her husband could not make any special agreements about any of these matters, because such an agreement presumed two legal actors, and marriage by its nature dissolved the wife as a legal actor into her husband.[9]

The last one hundred years have seen a gradual and mostly feminist-inspired attempt to change this traditional doctrine, but progress has been slow. Until the late 1960s, a married woman in most states was legally obliged to live where her husband chose; as late as 1974, a husband could take out a mortgage on a home wholly owned by his wife without her knowledge or consent. Times have not changed as much as we might hope: in the 1990s, a court invalidated the agreement of an ailing husband and his second wife that he would leave her his property if she would quit her job and care for him at home. Reasoning that the wife was simply doing her wifely duty, the court gave his property to his children from his first marriage, drawing on the ancient idea that wives have no independent legal or property interest and, more important, that to recognize such interests is contrary to public policy.[10]

The court in this case understood, I think, just as the people fighting over sex education do, that deep assumptions about husbands and wives and, deeper still, about the tension between women as individuals with needs and rights of their own and women as defined by their commitment to others are at stake. In traditional marriage, as represented not only in the law but in the assumptions we carry about in our heads, a married man is both an individual and a husband and must weigh his commitments between his own needs and those of his family; a wife is a person who consistently puts the needs of the family before her own.[11]

Over and over again, people told me that three things sparked the sex education conflict in their communities, and each of them, I've come to believe, stands in for a debate about the competing roles of pleasure and duty in American society. First, of course, is the role of marriage itself, or conversely, the belief that young people can have sex as long as it is both careful and caring. Then, as

Bruce Dean, the sex education teacher in Shady Grove, told me, "There's also the section on homosexuality, and a section on masturbation. And that always throws a red flag up too, especially for the parents."[12]

I asked Susan Shelly what alarmed her about the sex education curriculum in Shady Grove, and she mentioned the themes I heard from almost every sexual conservative. "My husband and I believe that intimacy belongs in a marital-type relationship, and that's for a good reason, because how can you be intimate with someone without having a commitment? And that's the first bit of morality that needs to be talked about, we feel. Which is not necessarily done in the curriculum as I've seen it."

I wondered if Susan really did mean a "marital-type relationship," so I asked her, somewhat apologetically, if that was in fact what she had in mind. She quickly interrupted me and leaned forward with an intensity at odds with the rest of the interview: "I mean a marriage, I don't mean a marital type . . . I don't mean a live-in situation, I mean a marriage, definitely." Then she went on smoothly to the theme Bruce Dean mentioned: "I don't think it's appropriate for children to be given a lesbian or any other gay person as a model for an alternate lifestyle, because my husband and I don't believe that that is a wholesome alternate lifestyle. It has nothing to do with any person who may be at this time homosexual. But we don't think that that's appropriate to give as an alternate."

In terms of the hidden parameters of the debate, Susan Shelley is an almost perfect example of what I call a sexual conservative. She believes that sexuality is rooted in both pleasure and procreation, but only within marriage. From this flows naturally her worry about comprehensive sex education, which is based on the notion that choices are available and that it is the task of each individual to gather the information in order to make the best choice for herself or himself. As far as she is concerned, there is only one choice, and she is clear that this is the only choice that should be taught. Such topics as homosexuality, contraception, and masturbation are all problematic for her, because they all, in one way or another, suggest that there can be sexual pleasure outside the bonds of heterosexual matrimony.[13] This explains, by the way, why people like Susan Shelly are equally opposed to plans in several jurisdictions to extend the legal protections of marriage to gay people or the unmarried in the form of "civil unions" or "domestic partnerships." To do so would be to acknowledge that a range of possible variations on the theme of heterosexual marriage exist and that the law should be agnostic about which of these people should choose.

That is precisely the heart of what sexual liberals believe. Because sexual liberals are pluralists when it comes to sex, marriage, and family, they believe that there are many possible ways to have a meaningful sexual relationship and many acceptable ways to bear and raise children. Sexual liberals may well have a preference for heterosexuality and marriage, especially when children are involved, but this is only a preference, not a line dividing the acceptable from the unacceptable, the moral from the immoral.

A few weeks after talking to Mrs. Shelly, I found myself sitting in a café in Shady Grove with Debbie DeGroot, a poised, well-dressed nineteen-year-old whose view of the world and of sex could not be more different from Susan Shelly's. As a veteran of the sex education wars that the parents in her community were fighting, Debbie was quite literally at the center of the debate. But she was also a committed sexual liberal, as I'm using the term. She showed up to speak before the Shady Grove school board to support the expansion of sex education into lower grades, arguing that the sex education she and her peers had had was provided too late and was just not comprehensive enough. In her words, it was "damn inadequate."

I asked Debbie for details about her experience, and she told me, "I had sex education in fourth, fifth, and sixth grade at my elementary school . . . And in eighth grade, you did some of that in science, and I had an excellent teacher, that was a good unit . . . And then I believe you're supposed to do some in tenth-grade biology; some classes did and some classes didn't, and mine didn't."

Since she seemed so adamant that her sex education was inadequate, despite having taken it in four separate grades in the Shady Grove schools, I asked what she thought had been missing. She said, "In fourth and fifth grade, it was segregated. All the girls were together, and all the boys were together, and it was mostly menstruation. And that was good—I mean, you need to know about it about that age. And the teachers were fairly good, honestly answering questions, and I'd say the same for sixth grade."

"And after that?" I prompted.

"It wasn't a whole lot of ethics and it wasn't teaching kids how to *think*, how to evaluate whether this is the right time to have sex. They didn't talk about emotions. They did talk about contraceptives; just which ones were better than other ones, which ones were more effective . . . How to make a decision wasn't emphasized at all, and I suspect that might have been because parents might have gotten upset and seen that as encouraging kids to go out and have sex. Sex education emphasized the physical changes and what was going to happen to you, not making decisions about sex."

When Debbie began talking about her 8th-grade sex ed class, the "good unit," her eyes lit up, and she was clearly remembering something quite fondly. I asked what that was.

"The teacher was very relaxed about it, very easy about discussing everything. The first thing he did, and I think this is an activity that a lot of teachers do, is just he went up to the board, and he had us tell him, and he would write down all the words you'd ever heard for all of the body parts, and that kind of got the giggles out for everybody. So you could discuss it like rational beings."

When it came to the kinds of topics that upset Mrs. Shelly, Debbie wanted more, not less. She had already mentioned that there needed to be more discussion of the ethics and decision-making surrounding contraception, but she also thought that the "hot topics" Mrs. Shelly wanted to avoid mentioning in fact were points for discussion. As she put it, "I think that they need to talk about everything, including abortion, including homosexuality, which is really hard in a little town like this. The homophobia is just incredible. And that's really sad."

What specifically did she think needed to be covered? Stressing that teachers needed to "keep their own values out of it," she wanted more factual and dispassionate discussion. In her words, "Abortion: this is what happens, this is what some people do, this is an option . . . and addressing the pros and cons of it honestly. Homosexuality: just presenting it as 'This is how some people feel, this is what exists.' I guess you'd have to give them the AIDS talk now—that wasn't really an option, something to learn about, when I was getting my sex education. It's something that they still totally ignore, like it doesn't even exist. And I think that's really sad, because I'm sure there are kids who are homosexuals in high school, but they're certainly not going to admit it at Shady Grove High, because they'd get beat up or something. Some of them would. And I know I had a sociology class from an otherwise excellent teacher, but I went up to him after class and asked him to stop using the word 'faggot' because it has really negative connotations. He said, 'Oh, okay, I didn't realize it bothered you.' "

Hidden within the ways that Debbie DeGroot and Susan Shelly look at the world are deeply embedded assumptions that serve to separate sexual conservatives from sexual liberals. On one level things are obvious. Susan wants sex education to teach only abstinence before marriage rather than how to have safer sex before marriage; she wants to clarify that while masturbation is not intrinsically bad, it's not morally acceptable either; and for her, homosexuality is most emphatically not an alternate lifestyle. Debbie not only supports the opposite position on each of these matters, she sees the goal of sex education as informing and educating people about the array of sexual options.

In this, both are paradigmatic. Sexual conservatives almost to a person oppose homosexuality, and sexual liberals almost uniformly support it. Typical conservative responses are like one mother's: "The sex education curriculum is saying two guys living together, that's fine, or two girls, whatever it happens to be. And that's cool. That's an alternative family and lifestyle. That doesn't do anything for bringing up children in what should be a family structure. I know too many boys and girls go through that problem [homosexual experimentation] in their teens, depending on the child, which age group that they hit it, some later than others, of wondering if perhaps they are. Because they're trying to establish and find their own sexual identity. And somebody's coming in and saying oh, well, go ahead. Feel free to run with it. They wouldn't normally try, if they just, you know, thought about it, wondered, and whatever the mental process would be, and maybe six months or a year down the road, oh, it was just a phase that they went through, and they could see that that was a part of their development rather than something that they were given a free license to go jump into."

Another mother agreed, saying, "I'm not going to get into whatever homosexuals want to do sexually, but don't teach it to my kids. I mean, my kids come from a two-parent family home, where I sacrifice my income to stay at home with them. That is what I want my kids to see. I don't want them being taught that if you have a few feelings for another woman you might be a lesbian. You know what? I've got close friends and I have a great many feelings for those women and I'm not a lesbian! You know? So, I mean, I'm not going to get into what's right and what's wrong for them, but there are some things that are right and there are some things that are wrong."

One father, who assured me that he was not a "homo basher," touched on an interesting stance about homosexuality that a number of people mentioned in the interviews, namely, that while they oppose the behavior of homosexuality, they do not oppose people who are homosexuals. In church this is sometimes known as "hate the sin, love the sinner," and I was struck by how many people told me that homosexuality was not an acceptable practice and should not be taught about in the public schools but went out of their way to say that they had gay friends, acquaintances, and coworkers. Steven Kingsley in Las Colinas was one of these: "So for example, even though I would be against homosexuality, I work with people who are homosexuals, and I've always liked them and I can respect them as individuals. In my job now, I've had many conversations with this woman who's a lesbian. I never confront her. She knows how I believe. I ask her a lot of questions, and I like hearing what she has to say."

But sexual liberals'—and presumably most homosexuals'—understanding is that in this day and age, sexual preference is at the heart of who you are and is therefore profoundly personal. The distinction that the sexual conservatives make between the person and the behavior is meaningless to most sexual liberals, because being gay is not what you do but what you are. For liberals, homosexuals are not people making an unacceptable moral choice. Rather, they are a persecuted political minority, persecuted because they are practicing a form of sexuality that others (conservatives) find unacceptable. The term "homophobia," which often came up in my interviews with sexual liberals, was not used in its technical sense as a fear of homosexuality (although many sexual liberals suspect that opposition to gay rights simply masks insecurity about one's own sexuality). What is being contested under the term "homophobia" is the conservative insistence that anything other than married heterosexuality is or ought to be morally stigmatized.[14]

In my conversation with Debbie DeGroot, she talked about how she would teach her own children about sex: "I'd teach them first of all, before they get into a sexual relationship, to be comfortable with their sexuality, to know whether or not they like men or women, depending on what their gender—you know, no matter what their gender actually is. If I have a kid who's gay, okay, fine, no big deal, as long as they're careful about that, as long as they know the risks involved, especially if I have a son who's gay. As long as he knows the risks involved in that kind of behavior, that he would exhibit in the bedroom or whatever, that's fine. I would let them know their risks, give them all the information, and let them make their decisions. You know, if I've set a good enough example of my life so they can say okay, this is good, this is right, and this is wrong . . . And I have a high tolerance for [homosexuality]. I have several friends who are gay, or, you know, had a boyfriend last week and have a girlfriend this week. And it doesn't bother me at all and I openly talk about it."[15]

Likewise, conservatives and liberals vary dramatically on their attitudes toward masturbation. I started the sometimes awkward conversations by saying, "Here's an example of asking something that we don't normally talk about at the dinner table very much, but how about things like masturbation? Is that something that you think should be taught in sex education?" Bonnie Blake, a sexual conservative, grappled long and hard with this one, and came out in almost the same place as Pastor Langley, the man who did not want his son to masturbate while reluctantly accepting that he probably would. "That's a real hard one," Mrs. Blake said with a sigh as we talked at her kitchen table. "Well, I would say that any normal teenager, healthy teenager, would masturbate at times. But to be taught that it's okay and it's a healthy thing to do is then going to give them an okay to do it whenever, and more often, and maybe a lot more than they normally would—it would draw their attention to it in a way that isn't really necessary. And as a part of a natural self-discovery it's okay, but to teach them to go ahead and use masturbation as a release or an escape is, I don't think, healthy. Yes, it is a physical release. But I could see a teenager using it as an escape. And there's always trouble whenever there's an escape involved. You know, you tend to just become out of reality, and then, and then the growing process stops. You know, they kind of get stuck in that area. Get locked in."

The belief that masturbation can be damaging was alluded to by many of the sexual conservatives I interviewed, in words that could have come straight from a social hygiene textbook of 1910. One father said, "In a sense, there is an addictive habitual nature to both masturbation and intercourse, and learning at an early age, as 'It's okay, don't worry about it, kid, you know, because here's a picture of what it looks like' . . ."[16]

Compare this to how the liberals think about masturbation. Several sexual liberals even suggested to me that sex education should teach masturbation as a substitute for intercourse. Calling it "outercourse," some suggested that either solitary or mutual masturbation would have all of the pleasure of sex with few of its dangers. Other liberals found this position disingenuous, however. Bethany Burt said to me, "I guess that there are other ways of sexual stimulation that adolescents can participate in. Myself, I don't see any difference in that and sexual intercourse, but I guess some people do. I feel that if you're stimulating one another sexually, to me it doesn't make any difference if it's a finger or a penis."

Apart from whether or not they thought masturbation should be offered as a substitute for intercourse, most of these people thought that it was good in and of itself, an essential part of getting to know oneself sexually. There is no mistaking that liberals want the idea of masturbation to be accepted as calmly as any other sexual option. One father told me how he and his wife view masturbation: "We're both really into letting the kids do it, trying not to let them do it in public and to keep it private, only because you don't do things like that in public, you don't scratch yourself in public, but in the same sense, wanting to make sure that they understood that it wasn't wrong to touch yourself. We're pretty liberal about that type of thing."

A mother who was distressed over how "conservative" her daughter's sex education class was pointed to the treatment of masturbation as an example: "The sex education teachers talk with the boys in sixth grade about wet dreams and masturbation. They don't talk to the girls about the clitoris and masturbation. That's not something that is talked about. We have somehow acknowledged that it's fine to talk with the boys about masturbation, but we're still, 'It's not okay for girls to touch yourself down there,' you know." (Her moue of distaste as she said "down there" made it clear that she was being ironic, mocking the view that girls—and not boys—could refer to their genitals only in an abstract and confusing way.)[17]

Another mother noted, in a discussion of how her values differed from those of her husband, "The only place where I'd say he and I disagree is that he felt that Emma should not be masturbating at all. I felt that she should be allowed to masturbate, but that we encourage her to do it in the privacy of her room. And after a while he began to see things my way more."

What knits these positions together? Perhaps it's obvious, but both homosexuality and masturbation stand in for larger issues about sex in these conversations. Conservatives, because of their conviction that heterosexual marriage is the only legitimate place for sex, find both masturbation and homosexuality threatening to marriage.

I must admit that these stances surprised me at first. The strongly felt opposition to homosexuality in particular seemed odd, along with the prominence of opposition to gay marriage. The insistence that people can be "recruited" to the gay "lifestyle," as sexual conservatives call it, or can find themselves dabbling in same-sex love if they merely hear it discussed in a nonjudgmental fashion, seemed to me to betray a certain defensiveness about the inherent attractions of heterosexuality. The conservative assumption that gay sex needs to be stigmatized struck me as implicitly suggesting that only the stigma on homosexuality—or lack of knowledge about how to do it—keeps people firmly rooted in heterosexuality.[18] What was it about homosexuality that made it seem so attractive and so dangerous that only moral horror would keep people from abandoning heterosexuality in droves?

Likewise, why was masturbation such a hot topic? Compared to the conservatives' stance on homosexuality, their stance here is more conflicted, as they want to transmit the complex message that masturbation is not necessarily a pathology while not going so far as to offer what amounts to an endorsement of it. In a day in which jokes about masturbation appear all over the popular media, such an attitude seems almost quaint. And how does it connect with ideas about homosexuality?

I think what separates the conservatives from the liberals on these two topics is the nature and meaning of sex. As we've seen, sex is sacred to conservatives, and its restriction to marriage makes it something more than the merely physical. Homosexuality, which cannot (at least at the moment) be expressed in marriage in most states, becomes the stand-in for sex that is just the opposite. Based in pleasure and fun rather than duty to a spouse and the next generation, based in the moment rather than in committed relationships, homosexuality becomes strictly about the physical. This view overlooks the fact that a substantial portion of gay America is actually eager to get married, as recent events reveal, and to engage in just the kind of committed sex that the conservatives value, but in fantasy, gay sex is about pleasure and pleasure alone.

Much the same attitude, I think, surrounds the vision of masturbation. Sexual conservatives, while not wanting to stoop to an older generation's threats about the dreaded outcomes of "self-abuse" (hair growing on the hands and all that), nonetheless feel that actively accepting masturbation, as many liberal parents do, is legitimating sex based on pleasure alone. Earlier sex educators were convinced that masturbation, while not dangerous in itself, could lead men to a taste for self-indulgence and thence to the brothel; modern sexual conservatives feel that there can be something addictive about sex and that masturbation can focus people on the pursuit of pleasure rather than the duties of marriage.

In both cases, the pleasure of sex is uncoupled from duty and hence is both morally and socially problematic. And part of its problematic nature is that pleasure-based sex is dangerously attractive. Who wouldn't want sex without obligation? Or as John Bunyan's Mr. Badman said, foreshadowing generations of mothers to come, why bother to buy a cow when milk is so cheap?[19]

Well, sexual liberals would do so. As far as they are concerned, we are talking about two entirely different realms of human life, one an intimate relationship built on trust and commitment and the other the momentary physical pleasure of sexual orgasm with yourself, another person of the same sex, or another person of the opposite sex. They are very clear that one cannot be reduced to the other. In fact, if sex and marriage are collapsed into each other, as they were in the 1950s, then both marriage and sex will suffer, since both run the risk of becoming taken for granted.

This raises an interesting question: how do people looking at the same institution, marriage, decide that it is *the* sexual lifestyle for human health and happiness as opposed to *a* sexual lifestyle?

CHAPTER FIVE

Becoming a Sexual Liberal or a Sexual Conservative

G iven that many of the people I spoke to came of sexual age before the sexual revolution had fully taken place, what kinds of forces sorted them into the two camps of sexual liberals and sexual conservatives? Why do some people turn out like Jenny Letterman, a devout Christian and equally devout Republican, whose values about sexuality would have been mainstream in 1952? And what about her counterpart Melanie Stevens, a Jewish environmentalist to the left of the Democratic Party whose values about sex and gender show the clear influences of the women's movement?

Almost all of us, whether we know it or not, have some kind of theory about how these two women ended up not only on two different sides of the sex education controversy in Shady Grove but in two very different places in life. With only the description I just provided and the knowledge that Jenny holds conservative sexual values, we wouldn't be entirely surprised to discover that she goes to church at least once a week, that she's a full-time mother and homemaker, that she has five children and is pro-life on the abortion issue. Likewise, our not-very-carefully-examined notions of how the world works lead us to predict that Melanie works full-time in a professional job, or perhaps in the not-for-profit world, that she has one or perhaps two children, and that she is pretty actively pro-choice. (For the record: at the time of this study, Melanie was getting ready to go back to work part-time as a social worker and had one child, Devora.)

If we think about it for a moment, our assumptions about the world usually have two dimensions. On the one hand, we expect certain kinds of values to cluster together. We generally expect people who call themselves Christian to be on the conservative side, both politically and sexually, just as we expect people who fit the profile of secular humanists to be liberals, in the bedroom and elsewhere. We expect people who support saving the dolphins, banning handguns, and protecting old-growth redwoods to be accepting of gay marriage, tolerant about pornography, and supporters of drug treatment programs rather than jail for addicts. No matter how many times people remind us that Hitler was a vegetarian and reputedly very kind to dogs, we still go on expecting vegetarians to be pacifists and ecologists who vote for Ralph Nader and steak-and-potatoes people to support motherhood (in its traditional form) and apple pie.[1]

On the other hand, we tend to assume that certain values are more common in some quarters than in others. We are surprised by the devout Christian on Wall Street and the rifle-toting Harvard professor, although we could probably find at least some people who fit these descriptions.

We care about our shorthand assumptions—our stereotypes, if you will—because we believe or at least hope they are predictive in nature. With reasonably small bits of information, we want to paint a larger canvas.[2] Of course, we also aspire to understand why some people end up endorsing some clusters of values and other people line up behind others, particularly these days, when moral issues around sex seem to take over the political sphere at regular intervals.

Activists in sex education circles ask themselves this question, if only implicitly. How is it that people who in many ways seem to be so much like themselves—living in the same communities, shopping at the same stores, and even worshipping in the same churches—end up feeling so profoundly, passionately different about sex and how it should be taught?

The sexual liberals and conservatives I spoke with had their own answers. For the conservatives, opponents were at best benighted victims (or "pawns") of larger forces, at worst active conspirators in those forces. The names varied, but when pressed to describe the opposition, sexual conservatives were inclined to think that their opponents were "secular humanists," "New Agers," or, more vaguely, the bureaucratic industrial welfare state.

I asked Reverend Thomassen what had gotten him involved in opposing the sex education curriculum in Shady Grove, and he told me that two strands had come together. "About eighteen years ago," he mused, "I was introduced to what we now call the New Age movement—it wasn't called that then—and so I began to do research in that area. The other strand is that several people, and by several I mean four or five—one or two whom I knew, and others I didn't know—began to call my attention to the curriculum, as it was in the process of being enacted here in Shady Grove and elsewhere in the county, and when they brought my attention to it, I identified it as the very thing that I had been doing research on!"

I have to admit I was rather flummoxed when I heard this. My confusion was heightened by the fact that Reverend Thomassen was a minister in one of the old-line churches of Shady Grove, a denomination that everyone expects to be on the front lines of support for sex education. I later learned, in what was becoming a familiar pattern in the course of my investigations, that the reverend was just one example of Robert Wuthnow's point that virtually all American denominations are breaking into conservative and liberal wings; his church was on the conservative side, reluctant to ordain women, aghast at the thought of ordaining gays, and worried, as Reverend Thomassen said, about how the "New Age" was taking over.[3]

Although my chat with Reverend Thomassen was the first time I ran into the concept, it wasn't the last. Even Jenny Letterman brought it up. Speaking in tones of dark conspiracy, she confided in me, "When I got ahold of the curriculum, which wasn't available to the general public—someone kind of slipped me a copy and said, 'Jenny, you gotta take a look at this'—I've been studying the New Age movement for about the last four years, and so when I read the document I realized that a lot of the principles and the tone were very similar to what I'd been reading about. And so when I read it, I was pretty much appalled by it."

Sexual liberals, in contrast, described their opponents almost without exception as "Christians," as that term has come to be understood these days.[4] In a conversation with Hannah Snowden in Las Colinas, I listened as she tried to mull over the various parts of the puzzle that "the Christians" represented. She said, "I saw a real kind of a radical Christian element. Very male-dominated. But yet it was the women who were all out there talking. You know, it's so hard to argue against family values. I mean, how can you argue against that? It's God and America and apple pie and family values. And you almost sound like a fool trying to go against them. But yet they're so narrow-minded and so conservative."

This categorization was made even by liberals who considered themselves Christian, but who thought that the opposition was being very un-Christian when it came to contesting sex education. Mary Kay Malone, for example, indignantly denounced her neighbor, who was heating up the conversation in ways she took exception to: "Margery is obviously very good at convincing people that what she's telling them is true. And getting them emotionally worked up. To the point that they will step out. And I mean, she makes it sound like it's a black-and-white issue. On one side you have Satan, on the other side you have the Lord, and the Lord is telling her what to do, and these are the things that the people that Satan has control of are doing over here, and they're the ones who are getting to your children. I mean, that's what I hear when I hear this message. And as I said, I feel that I am a Christian. I'm not aligned with Satan in any way, and I just kind of want to throw my hands up and say, 'I can't believe this.'"

In addition to seeing the opponents of sex education as responding only or primarily from their Christian faith, sexual liberals had another, darker line of explanation, one that drew on theories about the inner lives—the emotional and particularly the sexual lives—

of people on the other side. One of the teachers in Shady Grove confessed, "I question the motives sometimes, in my odd moments, of some of the Christian fundamentalists who would prevent their young children from learning how to protect themselves from touches they don't want. And I think that's a primary function, say, for sex education at the early ages—how do you tell somebody, who will you tell, would you know how to tell, when somebody touches you in a way that makes you feel really yucky or uncomfortable?" The speaker's clear implication here was that Christian fundamentalists did not want their children to differentiate between "good touch/bad touch," as Shady Grove's sex education curriculum had it, because they either were planning to sexually abuse their children or had done so.

My hunch is that most people subscribe to some version of the theories that these combatants hold. If pressed, most would guess that sexual liberals are secular folk, that they are politically liberal, and that they are middle- and upper-middle-class. Likewise, the common assumption, particularly in the media, is that opponents of sex education are all conservative Christians, a category that is often associated with having less education and being of a more modest social background.

In fact, reality is much more interesting. If we look at the backgrounds of the people I interviewed, there is just enough truth to some of these assumptions for us to see why they keep being used. But when we look closely, lots of troubling inconsistencies crop up. For example, while it's true that most of the sexual conservatives were deeply religious members of traditionally conservative Protestant denominations, not all were. By the same token, a good number of very religious people, including some from the same conservative denominations, turned out to be active supporters of comprehensive sex education, or sex education that presumes that at least some adolescents will be sexually active outside of marriage and need information to navigate that sexuality with as little lasting damage as possible. Even devout Southern Baptists,

when arguing in favor of the comprehensive sex education curriculum, enumerated values that were more consistent with those
of the often secular or "culturally Jewish" liberals than with those
of their fellow parishioners who opposed sex ed.

Not to put too fine a point on it, although such people are
probably in the minority, some sexual liberals are praying in the
pews of the most conservative Christian churches, and some sexual conservatives are attending ACLU meetings. And here's where
things get tricky.

Without really paying much attention, most popular thinking—and most social science thinking, for that matter—still follows the old assumption that material reality causes values in some
way. That is, something about being working-class or a Harvard
graduate, being on welfare or clipping coupons, shapes how we
come to believe the things we do. When we see that certain values are more common in certain social groups, we tend to assume
that something about membership in the group leads people to
hold the values common to that group. In some cases this is correct. There are clear correlations between being a certain age or having a certain ethnic background and holding certain values; for
instance, older people are on average more conservative than
younger ones; African Americans are much more supportive of
affirmative action policies than whites, and the nature of the relationship suggests that something about being old or being black
does in fact influence our values.

What is less evident but becomes of central importance when
we talk about issues of sex and gender is that *our values may well
influence what social group we end up in.* Two thirteen-year-old girls
who look virtually identical in terms of the things social scientists
study—social background, religion, education of parents—but
who hold different family values can easily end up in two very different places forty years later. The thirteen-year-old who holds a
traditional view of marriage and the family, who longs to get married and have children, will likely marry at a younger age, spend

less time on her education, have a larger family, and be less interested in working in the paid labor force than her counterpart, who is a budding feminist. In middle age, the cumulative effect of these value-driven decisions about when (and whom) to marry, about how much education to get (which in turn affects whom you marry), about whether or not to work in the paid labor force (which also affects whom you marry), and about how many children to have (which in turn affects labor market participation) becomes clear. Taken together, all of these decisions can mean that one of these thirteen-year-olds in middle age may look to a social scientist like a member of the working or lower-middle class, while the other one looks like a member of the upper or upper-middle class, despite the fact that it was hard to distinguish between them when they were entering adolescence. In social science, the relationship between background and values—in terms of some values, at least—is recursive, or mutually reciprocal.

What is particularly interesting about this notion is that virtually everyone I talked to grew up as a sexual conservative, because that was effectively the only option when we were growing up. Keep in mind the interviews were conducted over more than two decades, trying to figure out what makes the two sides of this debate so similar and yet so different. By the time I conducted the last interviews, in the early years of the new millennium, some of the people I interviewed hadn't lived through the sixties but were born in them. But even they, whether sexual conservatives and sexual liberals, told me pretty much the same story about their own sex education, what little there was of it.

The stories they told about their own sex education convince me there was a sexual revolution in the 1960s, albeit a revolution that took some time to become established.

Most people mentioned in this book can remember generic warnings about sex, about what not to do, usually without too much detail. Two sexual conservatives illuminated the point. One woman said, "We knew there were things—guidelines—set up. I don't remember talking about abortion at home, but it was always kind of understood as far as, you know, by our values, that abortion was never even an option. Homosexuality didn't really come up until after I was away from home. So we never really discussed that. Although, you know, because of my religious views, for the Christian, that was just not acceptable." Diana Smith agreed: "With my grandmother raising us, you didn't talk about sex. That was a no-no word. So in a way, they would always go around the bush with it, and you had to kind of reason it out yourself. Well, why do they say 'Don't do this' or 'Don't hang around these boys' or 'You better not get too close to that boy'?"

Most liberals reported remarkably similar stories. One father said about his upbringing, "There wasn't an awful lot of sex information given out in my family, although my dad had sort of a science background and my grandfather was a medical doctor. I still didn't feel like I got an awful lot of information about it through the family. Church didn't really do much for me, and of course the youth grapevine didn't really have a lot of accurate information."

Another sexual liberal laughed when I asked him if he had any sex education growing up. His parents had passed on to him the same mantra that the social hygienists had popularized, namely, that one should treat all girls as one would want one's sisters to be treated. He told me, "I had three older sisters, and my mother would say, 'Now, you have three older sisters, and you wouldn't want anything to happen to them, so I don't want you to get involved with any girl that would cause anything to happen to them.'"

Another father in another town explained how he had learned about sex from his parents' failure to talk about it: "I came from a very noncommunicative family. It was really judgmental, and we knew sex was bad. Very antisexuality, and it wasn't ever discussed. It was done with sighs and tense breathing and things like that, and as kids we learned to pick up on those cues."

Even people from backgrounds that were remarkably liberal in other respects recalled what in retrospect was a large void when it came to talking about sex. Karen Danton, a liberal in both the political and the sexual senses of the word, who was married to a liberal and had been raised by an old-fashioned civil rights liberal, said, "Certainly what was around me as I grew, in terms of other social issues, was, I think, pretty classic sixties liberalism. My father was arrested in the civil rights march in 1963. He counseled conscientious objectors for the Vietnam War . . . I never talked to my parents about sex." I looked at Karen somewhat incredulously. "Not at all?" She answered, "Not that I remember. It was not . . . I couldn't tell you what their view is or was."

One of the most delightful conversations I had about people's own sex education came with a man my age, a liberal, who told me somewhat wistfully, "I sometimes think that I learned about sexuality from the Sears catalogue." As I thought about his comment, I realized that I hadn't recognized how profoundly things had changed in our society until I heard from so many men and women, both liberals and conservatives, how little sex education they had received and how remarkably indirect and vague even that little bit had been. For many women, the only sex education they could remember was information about menstruation. A sexual conservative told me, "My mom was really very . . . conservative, I guess, is the word that I'm looking for. She told my older sister about menstruation, and then my sister had to tell me. Even after I was married, I asked my mom, 'What did you do for birth control?' and she was embarrassed! She turned her head and said, 'I slept on the other side of the bed.' "

In what probably seems astonishing to younger readers, some women reported that their mothers engaged in such a baffling amount of euphemism when it came to menstruation that they failed to understand for many years what they and their mothers had discussed—if you could even call what they had a discussion. I heard stories of young women being told that "something would happen," that they were "becoming young ladies," or that they would "get sick" one of these days. (One hapless woman told me that her cousin had come down with appendicitis about the same time she was told that she would be "getting sick" soon; she had spent the rest of her teens anxiously examining her abdomen, awaiting the same fate to befall her.)

Something else became clear as I listened to these stories: to the extent that the sexual revolution was based on the belief that men and women were sexually more similar than different, it served to bring them closer to one another, to lower the barricades between them.[5] I know that one of the main complaints conservatives lodge against feminists is that the women's movement pitted men against women, putting them at sword's point over a wide range of issues, from diapering babies to unloading dishwashers. But listening to the stories of a generation's sex education, I realized that almost everyone in those days took it for granted that there was a real war between the sexes, between male desire and female virtue. As parents before the sexual revolution made clear to their daughters, sex was about danger, not about pleasure.[6] Whatever else the sex education of the 1960s may have done, by conceding that both women and men were going to have and enjoy sex before they got married and by making virginity no big deal, it took the sharp edges off the struggle between men and women when it came to sex. While it surely didn't eliminate sexual exploitation between men and women, it does seem to have lessened parental worries about it—or so it seems when I contrast the sex education that mothers and fathers had with what they report that they tell their own children. Conservatives may tell children that sex before marriage is morally wrong, and liberals may tell children that they want them to wait until they are "ready" to have sex, but not a single parent told me that he or she had warned a daughter of the dangers of male perfidy, a constant theme in their own sex education.[7]

Even sexual conservatives who want to move sex back into the sole context of marriage would have to admit that in this respect things really have changed for the better. Woman after woman told me that a parent, usually but not always a mother, had warned them in the "olden days" that boys want just one thing, and as a result women were much more likely than men to tell me that they had had "the talk" with a parent. Alas, the main theme of the talk was that boys were the enemy.

Of course, many of these conversations were couched in coded and sometimes confusing words. Many women reported vaguely menacing but remarkably unspecific warnings about the opposite sex, like this one from a sexual conservative: "In school . . . we were taught that we should say no. I came from a Catholic school background, and that was definitely taught. And by the time I had graduated from high school in 1966, things were changing already, but they were still teaching that."

Sexual liberals told very similar stories. One said, "I can remember being told you don't let people touch you, but not very much more." Annie Ledbetter was eloquent about her background: "I did not hear the word 'sex' come from the lips of any member of my family until the age of twenty-one, when my mother nearly choked on it. She couldn't even say the word 'sex' when encountering it as a question on a form, but would translate it as 'male or female.' In my family, sex education consisted of 'Boys only want one thing . . . Don't ever let boys touch you . . . Don't ever let boys kiss you . . .' and the response 'That's nasty!' to all questions remotely associated with sexuality."

Other women told me how having a first boyfriend triggered "the talk" with a parent. I asked Marion Ross whether she had ever had sex education, and she responded, "Are you kidding? It was so totally taboo. I think the only time my dad ever talked to me was when the first boyfriend I had and I were sitting outside in the backyard and exchanged a kiss, and then my father, who normally was quite distant and preoccupied with television, actually invited me out for a hamburger. I thought, "Well, I wonder why he's inviting me out for a hamburger?' and we had our hamburgers, and then he drove to a park or something and we sat there and he proceeded to lecture me about . . . I mean, it was totally inappropriate. All I had done was exchange a kiss, and he was telling me about how sex was dirty, how sex was bad, how all men, that's all they want, you know, and just on and on. And I said, 'Well, Dad, are you like that?' " Marion laughed at her own boldness in confronting her father, but her face grew softer and sadder as she remembered. "It was just a terrible, terrible thing. And it was just—the way they handled it with so much shame, and . . . ugh."

You hear in these quotes the sense of pain and betrayal that sexual liberals in particular felt about having the older generation withhold information from them, information that they would later come to see as being about something that was, or should have been, "natural." I also think that when liberals told me that sex is natural rather than sacred, what they meant was that making sex sacred, something out of the ordinary, was associated for them with the idea that unmarried men and women were natural enemies when it came to sex. Downplaying the stakes made it possible for them to be friends with the opposite sex rather than continuing the guarded wariness their parents encouraged them to adopt.

In the course of my interviews, I talked to a few young people who had had sex education within the past few years, and their experiences bore out what their parents told me they were telling their children. These were youngsters who had attended high schools in the communities where fights over sex education were taking place and who had been active participants in support of or opposition to the sex education in their schools.[8]

Two daughters of liberal parents described a sex education that might well have come from a different planet from the kind that their mothers and fathers described to me. Debbie DeGroot had long and frank talks with both of her parents in addition to the sex education she got in school. As I kept plying her with coffee drinks during our afternoon-long conversation at the local café, she told me, "I talk more with my mother than with my dad about sex. My dad with general relationships and things like that, but for the nitty-gritty details, I talk to my mom. We talk about it at home—responsibilities, and about different types of contraception. Different issues, kind of deciding when it's right for you, not getting involved too fast." Lanie Eton said pretty much the same thing: "My mom basically—when I went through puberty, she . . . covered everything from A to Z. You know, men's and women's development, birth control, drug use, you know, sexuality, everything . . . So going in high school I probably knew a lot more about sexuality and moral values, birth control, than a lot of the kids did."

The conservative parents told a rather different story. They claimed proudly that they were very open with their children and that they made sure their children knew they were available to answer any questions. But many of these parents marveled about the fact that their children just didn't seem curious about sex and in fact did not want more information. As Noreen Redding said, "I've had an opportunity to talk to other people in classrooms, and I see the development of children—I don't have a degree in child development, but I'll tell you, experience can give you more than a degree could as far as raising three kids. So what I'm saying is, when my son had an interest in my—our—pregnancy, he would ask certain questions, but he didn't want the answers. And they tell you that in all sorts of books. When children say, 'Why is your tummy growing?' they don't want to know that an egg was implanted and blah blah blah, and the uterus. They want to know, 'There's a baby in there. There's a baby growing in Mommy's tummy.' That's what they're relating to. And I'd say to my son, 'Do you want to know more about babies?' 'No!' and then he'd run off and play."[9]

I think that so many sexually conservative parents described their children as uninterested in more information because these parents have very different attitudes from liberal parents about information in general, and they absolutely do not subscribe to the sexually liberal belief that more is better when it comes to information. At the same time, conservative parents are forthright about their belief that sex belongs only in marriage, so much of the information that the children of sexual liberals need to help them decide about when to get sexually involved with someone and why is simply not relevant to many children of sexual conservatives. To the extent that conservative parents view sex as sacred, then long discussions about sexuality probably seem a bit profane.

Finally, many conservative parents are not all that sure that a shortage of information about sexuality is a bad thing. One parent told me, "I was a late bloomer as a child, and my mother had told me all the facts of life, and I didn't know what she was talking about. And so, being sensitive that way . . . And then when my puberty came, I didn't know what was happening and had to find out. If I had been taught that in school and didn't know and everybody else knew, I can only imagine I would feel even more left out, and probably the children would pick up on it and I'd be ridiculed because of it." Another said, "Well, yeah. I don't think that I needed to—as a high school student, as a young girl who was trying to develop healthy relationships with men—have my mind filled with sodomy and beating and the other things that were presented later on, as I grew up and learned about terms like '69' and some of these other things that we learn about." A mother who experienced the limited sex education of her era still found it upsetting: "It was just horrifying. I think I was in sixth grade, and so you're kind of on the peak of falling over the abyss into the curious stage, and there it is, right in front of you, black and white, with, you know, all the boys right there with you, and oh, it was just very embarrassing."

Contrast this with what the liberals thought about the lack of information in their own upbringing. They found that the squirming and vagueness and indirectness of the adults around them when they asked about sex was nothing short of a betrayal of what had previously been a trusting relationship, and often enraging as well, a sign that the adults were holding out on them. Elaine Devoto remembered having an argument at age twelve, a "knock-down, drag-out fight" with a neighborhood girl who had five older brothers. The girl had told Elaine about the facts of life, and Elaine reminisced, "I remember having an argument with her that this was impossible, this couldn't be true, because if it were true, you'd see people doing it everywhere, you'd be reading about it, you'd be hearing about it on the news, if it were really as common as she said." When the girl insisted, Elaine confronted her mother, who flatly denied the whole story and continued to deny it until Elaine confirmed it with another playmate. "He also had the same story to tell. So I again confronted my mother, and I said, 'Ronnie says the same thing.' So in a darkened room, where I couldn't see her face, her voice was trembling, she gradually was just sort of able to clunk out the words about the sacred event that happens between men and women."

Elaine thought that her mother's reticence was part of why she herself chose to become a scientist and why she resolved to raise her own children differently. "It was such a tremendous shock to me that I was terribly shy and embarrassed about the whole subject, and there always seemed to be something very furtive about it, so when I had my own children, I made up my mind that the minute they started asking questions, they would get whatever answers they seemed to want at their age, and they would be told the truth as early as they wanted to know. So that's what I did with my kids, and they both are very comfortable and very conversant about these areas."

This is a theme that comes up over and over again—the role of information in human life, and why the lack of it is either a good and protective thing or a bad thing that confuses and blights young minds. And information, in turn, is the key to understanding why people are sexual liberals or sexual conservatives. Information plays such very different roles in the lives of people on the two sides of this conflict because they look at the world through very different lenses. For sexual conservatives, morality is a clear code of rules that is true across time and across distance; what was moral two millennia ago is still moral today. For liberals, in contrast, morality is based on a set of principles that must be adapted to the changing contours of modern life.

This distinction has been written about extensively—so much so, in fact, that these many observers must really be on to something, a division between those who favor a strict and clear-cut morality and those who favor a situationist morality.[10] Thinking about sex is part of this larger worldview as well as the place where issues of morality are starkest.

The sociologist Steven Tipton argues that systems of morality (which he calls "distinct styles of ethical evaluation") are "quite few in number, although each possesses great range and subtlety in their application," and reviews the theories of why these kinds of moral divides exist in American life.[11] To simplify the argument (and remember that there is "great range and subtlety" in the types), people I interviewed differ over whether something is wrong in and of itself or whether an act is wrong simply because of its consequences.[12]

These two views in turn implicate one of the great dilemmas of modern American society, which plays out in almost every conversation I have had with people fighting over sex education. At heart, the difference between them is based on an argument over authority, and, more to the point, how to convince those who do not share your views to think your way about a substantive issue such as sex.

For the conservatives, sex outside marriage is wrong because the Bible says it is. They are bewildered when others simply categorize them as "Christian." From their point of view, many, if not most, Christian denominations historically have frowned on premarital sex (and gay sex and sex outside marriage), and so have traditional Jews and Muslims (although Muslim beliefs were rarely invoked in my conversations with people). So their conviction that sex before marriage is inherently wrong is not a religious position, they say, but rather part of our common moral heritage, our "Judeo-Christian tradition," a phrase that was used with some regularity. (Often sexual conservatives add an essentially sociobio-logical argument, to the effect that if marriage has been around so long and in so many different societies, it must be good for people. This conveniently overlooks the fact that the kind of marriage they are claiming as universal is less than a century old and owes much of its seemingly timeless nature to the far-reaching work of the social hygienists.)

The liberals, however, think the question of sex before and outside marriage comes down to facts. And facts, in their view, can be agreed upon by all reasonable people, provided that these reasonable people have been given the relevant information. Divine authority as encoded in the Bible and the Torah, even if divinely inspired, as some liberals believe, is still always filtered through the eyes of humans and hence reveals human preferences. (Facts, in contrast to faith, can be tested and examined, they believe, so although they too are filtered through human eyes, they can be corrected, something in theory impossible with sacred texts.)

Two of the most influential scholarly writers on the culture-wars thesis, Robert Wuthnow and James Davidson Hunter, joined by their colleague William Bennett in the popular press, have seized on this aspect of how people look at morality as the core of what the culture wars are about.[13] In broad outlines, they agree about what happened to divide us, as Robert Wuthnow puts it, into a nation of people who, while claiming allegiance to the same God and even belonging to the same denominations, disagree profoundly about what He wants for us. (We are, after all, one of the most religious nations, right up there with the Irish.)[14] According to these theorists, a rising economy and the expansion of higher education led to a democratization of values that had once been the province of a relatively small elite. In the period right after World War I, for example, fewer than one American of college age in twenty undertook higher education. In contrast, at present almost 50 percent of high school graduates go on to some form of post–high school training. Even the period when the people I interviewed were growing up was one of continued educational expansion. Between 1960 and 1980, the number of people over twenty-five who had completed at least some college education almost doubled. Whether it is primarily a case of higher education leading to higher income, which in turn leads to more "postmaterial" and hence secular values, or whether education leads to secularization independent of income is something that sociologists still debate. But in either case, rising educational levels and rising income are thought to lead people away from "traditional values."[15]

This upward trend in what sociologists call "educational attainment" was paralleled by a liberalization of attitudes. Wuthnow identifies several cultural forces that contribute to the phenomenon, but the result is clear: education becomes the single strongest factor differentiating religious liberals from religious conservatives. For example, 47 percent of the college-educated people in Wuthnow's research supported ordination of gay people, contrasted to 17 percent of those with only a grade-school education. Likewise, only one college graduate in three thinks that the Bible is absolutely true, while twice as many people whose highest level of education was high school think so.[16]

Liberal and conservative academics, of course, like sexual liberals and conservatives, view this matter from the vantage point of their own situations. Liberal academics, for example, tend to see the liberalization of American attitudes about sex and family in a somewhat benign light, as the natural outcome of rising levels of education. More conservative academics, in contrast, tend to see the rise of the highly educated as the rise of a new class of knowledge workers, whose values derive not only from their education but from their generally sympathetic view of "the state." As early as 1980, conservative observers were bewailing the "therapeutic state," implicitly run by these knowledge workers, whose views were at odds with those of most Americans.[17] This new class, then—the secular humanists that sexual conservatives worry about—brought all kinds of alien ideas to impressionable young people.

With half the population going on to some form of higher education, and with sexual attitudes fairly uniform among educational levels (once age is controlled for), it's hard to argue that a tiny new class is running things. But clearly Americans differ, and differ passionately, about key aspects of marriage and family, and sex education mobilizes the two ends of the continuum, the very liberal and the very conservative.

For the record, let me remind you that the design of my study probably precluded contact with what we might think of as a "sexual middle," because people who are mildly in favor of abstinence for their teenagers and yet hope that the school will give their children some information about how to navigate the risks of sexuality if they do become sexually active are not likely to become crusaders on this issue. By the same token, while there may well be sexual radicals, as there were in early-twentieth-century Greenwich Village, either they don't show up in a study of this kind or they don't have teenage children.

Given that this study selected for the two ends of the continuum, is the difference between sexual liberals and sexual conservatives merely a product of education? Are all the supporters of comprehensive sex education just more highly educated than their neighbors who support abstinence-only sex education?

Yes and no. While it is true that sexual liberals tend to have a bit more education than sexual conservatives, the truth is that there is a tremendous amount of overlap between the two groups. In all of the communities studied, most of the activists on both sides of this issue were college graduates. Thus the idea that the conflict over sex education in the four communities is a conflict between members of a new class and a middle class doesn't hold.

The fact that conservatives and liberals were exposed to essentially the same experiences when it came to their own sex education but evaluate it so differently now is a clue to how people become sexual liberals and sexual conservatives when it comes to the education of children in their communities. Many of the liberals told stories that suggest they were liberals waiting to happen. They hated the sexual limitations and conformity of their childhoods and found them—at least as they tell the story now—demeaning and hypocritical.

For instance, as Francie Laycock said, "By the time I hit adolescence, which was around the late 1950s, I ran into this other whole dynamic and reality, which was adults' fear of sexuality . . . I remember by the time I was seventeen or eighteen considering becoming sexually active. And when I approached each of my parents individually about that, one of my parents, my mother, could not really get out of her very Catholic background, and she made reference to the fact that, well, yes, did I notice that my older sister got married? And it was almost like hinting that that probably had something to do with why she got married—she was probably ready to be sexually active, so she got married. And I said, 'Well, what if you aren't ready to get married?' Oh, well—my mom just couldn't handle that kind of specifics at that time . . . I remember approaching my father about it, almost in the same vein, hoping for something a little more helpful and guiding. And he said something along the lines of 'Well, honey, have you considered going to college somewhere like far away, a foreign exchange student program?' It's like, whoa! What is this message? I remember at that time feeling extremely furious at those responses."

In fact, like many men and women of their generation, many liberals did become sexually active before marriage. But for those who became active before the sexual revolution, the limits on what women could do or be in sexual terms were felt keenly. I asked one mother, "Was there much sexual activity in your high school?" and she replied, "In 1962 sex was pretty secret. There were some girls who had reputations for being very easy. I know I certainly was not sexually active until late in my senior year, and I was going with a college student at the time. But [there was] not a lot of sex [around], not that I was aware of."

Annie Ledbetter told me, "Because of my age and the time that I was born into, I was raised by a turn-of-the-century family. I mean, I'm more nineteenth century than twentieth century. I was raised that you had two choices: you were either a virgin or a slut."

Not surprisingly, sexual conservatives look back with a very different eye. One father who became sexually active during the sexual revolution regretted his premarital sexual experiences: "There's ramifications for what you do that are beyond the moment, that are beyond the here and the now. And yes, you may love this person with all your heart, but until you are standing before an altar and you've committed your life, your heart, everything you are from this point on until you die, to that one person, until you're willing to make that kind of commitment, don't have sex. And I was never taught that . . . I would like to think that if I had been given that information, I would have made different decisions. That if someone had sat me down and said, 'My gosh, you have no idea what you're about to do,' I would have made different choices. But all I was, was teased. I was told about the candy store and not told about what happens when you come out of it, the gut ache that you get when you come out of a candy store, and so when I finally got to that candy store, I tore into the candy like a guy who hadn't eaten in weeks."

This theme came out strikingly in my conversations with Steven Kingsley, for whom the 1960s proved a turning point, but not a happy one. Steven is a lanky, handsome man, seemingly unaware of his remarkable good looks, which remind you of suntanned men in cowboy hats gazing at far horizons while longhorn cattle mill in the foreground. His wife was making dinner in a pretty kitchen adjacent to the living room where Steven and I were talking, and he was blunt in telling me that the sixties led him to take a path toward what he now sees as a wasted youth. (I always interview people where they can have complete privacy, so they can tell me things that they may not have told spouses or children. But when I offered to take Steven to a nearby café, he tilted his head toward the sounds of dishes and pans being taken out of cupboards in the kitchen and said with a rueful smile, "She knows all about it.") Steven told me sadly as we discussed his past, "Well, growing up in the sixties and raised in that whole culture, I think what happens is you find that the things that you think are important to bring you happiness end up not bringing you happiness. And in the sixties that was basically sex, drugs, and rock and roll."

This interview opened up a theme that was surprisingly common among a subset of sexual conservatives. As Steven suggested, for some people the attractions and the freedom (Steven would say license) of the sexual revolution ran against deeply held values about life, or at least about sex, as they tried on new identities and ways of being in the world, including having sex outside of marriage.

In a way this is the great mystery that has intrigued and baffled me for most of my professional career. How is it that some people who came of age in and after the sixties, when confronted with the loss of certainties that those years brought, rejoiced, while others recoiled? How is that some people look back on the sexual revolution with the delight and fondness that Elaine Devoto experienced, while others, like Steven Kingsley, rue the day that they started that walk on the wild side?

I said earlier that the sexual conservatives and sexual liberals I spoke with had more in common than they had differences. But closer inspection of the interviews and the background data revealed some surprising findings. While it seemed that liberals and conservatives had a great deal in common, it turns out that in this study, at least, the sexual conservatives actually were made up of two different clusters of people.

On the one hand were the people who found the sixties troubling and very much at odds with the values with which they had been raised. Patty Dennison was one of those. "I really felt my parents' values were right," she told me. "I knew what my parents were telling me was right. But it was a time of rebellion, knowing what was right but not wanting to follow. I was a virgin when I was married, but it was almost 'How close can I get?' An example was, I slept with a boy, but it was kind of a thing where 'I slept with a boy, but we didn't do anything.' Now I go, whoa! All the things that could have happened! But it was that I had those values ingrained in me, and although I would go so far, that was it—no more. That this is the line, and I won't allow myself to go over it."

I've come to think of such people as "birthright" sexual conservatives. They tended to come from socially or religiously conservative families, they grew up with conservative values, and while they may have tested the limits, they didn't test them very far.

But I also spoke with a small but significant cluster of very different sexual conservatives. These were people who were not necessarily raised in a religious or a conservative home (although for people of this age, virtually everyone was raised in a *sexually* conservative home). While they mentioned the same kinds of experiences that other people, both liberal and conservative, did when it came to sex education, they reacted sexually to the 1960s in a different way. As the father just cited said, "I tore into the candy store like a guy who hadn't eaten in weeks."

It turns out that when we look at the backgrounds of the sexual conservatives, they more or less divide into two groups socially as well as in the ways that they describe their experience. The people who were raised in fairly strict religious homes and never strayed too far from their parents' values tended to have fathers who did not go to college and mothers who stayed home with them full-time. To stretch the point, this is the profile that other academics have drawn of traditional social conservatives. People in this group come from fairly modest class backgrounds, and while they themselves might be highly educated, their families were not. The other conservatives, however, were as likely to have had college-educated fathers as the sexual liberals, and were as likely to have mothers who worked in the paid labor force. In terms of other social criteria, they also resembled the sexual liberals.

Only two things distinguished this group of sexual conservatives from their counterparts who were sexual liberals: they belong to a conservative church and now have or are stay-at-home wives. I say this with all due caution, since this was a small and exploratory part of the study, but when I went back to the interviews, I found that these sexual conservatives had been far more likely than others to tell me stories of having done things in their youth that they had come to regret. As they put it, the loss of the boundaries that had been so taken for granted in an earlier era lured them into going astray, in much the same way that Mrs. Boland was convinced that sex education had led her husband to rape their daughter.

Talking to one of these sexual conservatives, I said, "You graduated high from school in 1966, so there was a lot of wild and crazy sexuality going on around you . . . The values that we were just talking about, you really had to sort of hang on to them with both hands in the early seventies." She interrupted me. "To be quite frank, I think I flushed [my values] all down the toilet, to use a very bad metaphor. And I had my very wild times and was very much a part of the sixties. I've come back to my beliefs because I can see that there's really a lot of value in them. There are things to be learned."

Another conservative said to me, "I had sex before I was married. I had a long-term boyfriend in high school. My parents obviously didn't know, because they would have really had a fit . . . This comes from my parents not really being able to talk about sex, except to say, 'No, don't do it.' There was no reason not to do it. I mean, there was never any reason."

Anita Star told me, "I had gone to church for few years when I was young—when I was ten, I think, I had gone for a couple years. And then when I got into high school I made a deal with God:

'Okay. It's too hard to serve You now, so I'm going to do whatever I want throughout high school and then when I'm eighteen and I can move out on my own, I'll come back.' What kind of stupid, warped thought is that? Yeah, like 'God, I'm going to tell you how things are.' It's kind of stupid . . . But I kept my end of the bargain. I did whatever I wanted, and then when I turned eighteen I started going back to church, and then I realized I don't have to live like this. I don't have to keep having sex, you know. You know, it hadn't been that long anyway. But I just realized that I could change and that was okay and that didn't mean that I was 'used goods' and that didn't mean that I was 'less than,' which was really challenging for me to accept."

When sexual conservatives speak of people who have been sexually active before marriage, they often speak of them as being "used" or "damaged" goods; when Anita speaks of being "less than," she is using the language of the recovery movement. In essence, she is saying that when she made her way back to Christ, her acceptance of herself as a Christian meant that she no longer had to think of herself as degraded or damaged from her forays into sexual experimentation.

At least four sexual conservatives I spoke with found their way back from a troubled life through twelve-step groups such as Alcoholics Anonymous and Narcotics Anonymous, and several more, like Anita, used twelve-step language to describe themselves or their feelings about themselves. I'm not at all sure that this is a statistically significant finding, and I'm not sure exactly what such a finding might be, given the methodology of the study. Since I know many members of twelve-step groups who are confirmed sexual liberals (although no liberals in this study volunteered that they were members of such a group), it's obvious that being a member of one of these groups is not in and of itself a direct route to being a sexual conservative.

Rather, I think that for this subset of sexual conservatives, membership in a twelve-step group is an indirect marker of how totally out of control they felt earlier in their lives and how being out of control with drugs or alcohol or food was intimately tied to being out of control sexually. The group was the route back, and in the course of traversing that path they came to believe that joining a church with traditional family values helped them stay in recovery.

Thus a small but significant group of people who by background look as if they should have reacted to the sixties by becoming sexual liberals experienced that period as a vortex from which they just barely escaped with their lives and their sanity intact. They then turned to a conservative church, whether or not they were raised in one, and found the structure of that institution and its fellowship to be just what they needed. As part of joining their church, they dedicated themselves to traditional gender and sexual roles—that is, they became sexual conservatives—and as part of that change in values they elected to have a traditional family, where the wife stays at home and the husband works. (Or, more realistically in some cases, the husband has a career and the wife works only when she has to.)

In turn, this employment pattern is based on a firm conviction that women cannot in fact have it all, that women who try to do so cheat themselves and their families. In short, these people become converts to "family values." A deep religious faith, backed by membership in a church that supports these family values, is no coincidence. These born-again sexual conservatives, like the birthright conservatives, felt that families are in dire straits and that their only hope of having a happy family life is to practice a clear commitment to the family *based on an understanding that this is God's will as exemplified by church teachings.* As Sandy Ames said, "I did not come from a religious home, but I came from a home where my parents were involved with us, and my dad worked out of the house, and we weren't allowed to go out on weekends. We had to have dinner at home. And so that kind of thing, that kind of value I've brought into my family now, but again, that's not faith-based. I realize these things are even more important, and maybe our conversations are a little deeper now that I'm a believer. Because we believe when it gets tough that it's your commitment to God that actually keeps you committed to the marriage. It's your obedience to God that is what's going to keep you committed to the relationship." She added with a smile, speaking of those who shared her views on sex education, "Just don't believe everything that you hear. These 'extremists' and 'religious right' and stuff. All I can say is, at first I was shocked, and all of a sudden it's like, 'Oh, my gosh, I'm it.' All because I really feel like I want to parent my kids."

Sandy was being a bit disingenuous, since she was very active across a wide range of conservative issues, but her views ring true in the stories of many others. For those sexual conservatives who found the values of the 1960s emotionally and spiritually dangerous and who felt that this period without structure almost sucked them under, the sometimes fanatic commitment to marriage and family, which translates into things that sexual liberals find anathema, such as opposition to teen and gay sex, is based on hard-won truths. Commitment *is* fragile. Relationships *do* fail. Individuals, as they know all too well, make bad choices. Only structure, the kinds of things that were so assaulted by the sexual and other revolutions of the sixties, can help people survive in an increasingly fractured world. And marriage, particularly traditional marriage, is one such structure.

All this puts flesh on the bones of the idea that the relationship between values and religion is much more complicated than social scientists (and probably most people) commonly believe. While it is true that many people were raised with what we now call family values and for many the source of those values was religious teachings, the stories I was told indicate that reasonably few people went through the sixties without questioning those values. Whether or not they went so far as to challenge the values in terms of their behavior, almost everyone did some deep, hard thinking about sex, gender, and family, not to mention authority and whom to trust, although they wouldn't have used those terms. When this group of people who are now sexual conservatives came to believe, via one route or another, that the traditional values were the ones they wanted in their lives, they turned to the church of their childhood or joined a new one that supported family values clearly and definitively.

Categorizing the opposition to comprehensive sex education as merely "religious" in nature suggests that the religion is encouraging individuals to oppose sex education and what modern sex education has come to stand for. But for many of the people I spoke with, the relationship ran the other way. It was opposition to sex education (and, more broadly, support of family values) that led them either to become active in the conservative church in which they were raised or to seek out a new conservative church whose support of family values reinforced their commitment to these values.

The pastors I spoke to often represented extreme versions of this pattern on the conservative side. Although a few had attended theological seminary and become ordained in traditional denominations, most were pastors in evangelical churches, where being called to the pulpit was a matter of conviction rather than of professional training. And while I would not insult these pastors by claiming that their conviction is simply a function of their commitment to traditional gender, sexual, and family values (and, as we will see, moral values as well), it is certainly a key part of the equation.

The same was true of sexual liberals within the clergy (who were much more likely to have had formal theological training): an attack on sex education was seen as an attack on a broad set of values that had brought them to the ministry in the first place.

And that brings us to a still deeper level.

CHAPTER SIX

Boundaries, Life, and the Whole Darn Thing

I've been calling people sexual conservatives and sexual liberals so far because of their relationship to significant social changes in sex, family, and gender over the past thirty years. The conservatives want the status quo ante, and the liberals accept the present and hope to make possible a better future. The fact that the conservatives look back to a sunny (and often idealized) past, one that conveniently airbrushes out of the picture many social problems (like racial segregation) and the liberals look forward to a sunny (and often idealized) future, conveniently skipping over how hard it is to change human behavior, suggests that the underlying differences between the two groups are deep. One group looks fondly back to a better past, imagining that the trajectory of history is a bleak one. The other looks forward expectantly, convinced that despite the evident problems we face, tomorrow will be different, and better.

I'm unsure whether these are psychological differences or sociological ones, or a mixture of both. (Like many parents, as I've watched my children grow, I've come to respect the role of inborn temperament in shaping the way people view the world, and some political scientists now agree about this.)[1] What I am sure of, however, is that whatever the reason, on a whole set of issues that go beyond sex, people on the two sides of this debate live in very different worlds within the same communities. My brother sometimes jokes that the three children in our family were raised in three totally different families who accidentally happened to have the same name and the same parents, and the same could be said of the two sides of the sex education controversy.

The sexual conservatives and sexual liberals I interviewed live in the same towns, practice the same professions, have similar educational and social backgrounds (partly because of those born-again conservatives described in the last chapter), and often belong to the same church, but these are only coincidences, as my brother would be the first to say. Despite all the superficial similarities, the two sides have very little in common in other ways. For example, the sexual conservatives are modern-day Calvinists. They think that humans are mostly the victims of unruly desires and that only firm structures can keep those often destructive desires under control. Mrs. Boland exemplifies this position. As she saw it—and most sexual conservatives would understand—her husband, who raped their daughter, was not inherently a monster but simply a weak person whose all-too-human impulses exploded when the restraining ties of social morality became frayed. You will recall that Mrs. Boland opposed sex education because she thought that the way it has come to be taught—in a morally neutral, "values clarification" way—permitted her husband to rationalize his actions to himself. If there were no absolute "thou shalt nots" (the term she and others used quite a bit), she was convinced that individuals would be able to decide for themselves what was morally right. Faced with the enormous temptation to gratify one's own desires at someone else's expense, individual human conscience could be very weak.

Remember that Mrs. Boland did not think her husband was directly affected by the sex education in her community. Rather, and significantly, she felt that the kinds of values that were being purveyed in the sex education course were precisely the kinds of values that had contributed to the fraying of the social ties that in an earlier era would have kept men like her husband in line. Sex education was simply the most approachable and salient example of values and processes she saw as destructive.

It's tempting to second-guess Mrs. Boland and her view of the world. One could easily think, as I did at first, that if I were in her shoes, it would be a lot easier to blame sex education for what her husband had done than to entertain the hypothesis that he was a monster. Considering that you may have married a moral monster forces you to confront your own culpability in choosing such a man, in having children with him, and in not noticing what was going on under your roof until it was too late.

But Mrs. Boland believed (and sexual liberals often do not understand this) that any one of us is capable of monstrous acts. In support of her position, I would argue that on the level of the commonplace, most of us find ourselves quite regularly doing things that we would not do if we were the rational beings that we like to think we are. We eat too much, smoke cigarettes, have an extra glass of wine, drink an extra cup of coffee when it means we will never get to sleep, or, conversely, hit the snooze button even when it makes us late to work.

Of course, there is a world of difference between raping your daughter and having a quick smoke or indulging in a nice bowl of fudge ripple when your weight and your cholesterol are higher than they should be. Or is there? I suspect that all of us experience the pull of deep, visceral desires that our better selves remind us are not in our own best interests or the interests of others. More important, I suspect that all of us find that indulging impulses like these are in some way alien, as if our actions are not entirely under our control. I know very few people with perfect willpower in the small things, so who is to say that Mrs. Boland is not on to something in the big things?

I don't mean to be a moral relativist here; I know perfectly well that there *is* a world of difference between committing rape and giving in to that extra cup of coffee. But the essential point is that this is one of degree. How far are we from Mr. Boland? What is it that keeps us on the side of morality when we know perfectly well that our desires can drive us to behaviors that we are abashed about, if not downright ashamed of? It is on these basic questions about human nature that the sexual conservatives and sexual liberals disagree.

Sexual conservatives, for example, believe that humans are fundamentally capable of the worst, and that it is only the combined power of an internal morality and external constraints that keeps most of us on the straight-and-narrow most of the time. They are firm believers in conscience, and think that teaching children about morality is one of the most important things parents can do ("As the twig is bent . . ."). But as Mrs. Boland made clear to me, conscience can be a weak reed in the face of temptation. Given overwhelming desire, individual conscience can be persuaded by the passions of the moment, and therefore conscience must always be aware of how it will square itself, not with its owner, who is capable of rationalization, but with the outside world. When I hear sexual conservatives talk about temptation (particularly in the case of teenagers, whose temptations are thought be hormonally driven), I often think of those old cartoons in which an individual has an tiny white angel whispering in one ear and a tiny red devil whispering in the other. If I remember correctly, the devil is never arguing that the person should just go ahead and do something even though it is wrong. Being a connoisseur of human weakness, he prefers to insist that the act being contemplated isn't really so bad after all; it's something that most people do all the time.[2]

Because those old cartoons were really modern morality tales, either the angel won out or dreadful consequences ensued. The cartoon can end only if the individual accepts the error of his or her ways, makes amends for having done something wrong, and swears never, ever to listen to that little creature with a pitchfork again. This is the essence of the sexual conservatives' position. It's not that they necessarily want to live in a police state or even in a theocracy, but like Edmund Burke, that first great conservative, they think a well-ordered society is a necessary precondition for the workings—and the maintenance in good stead—of individual conscience.

Part of the reason sexual conservatives romanticize the past is that they are more worried about a well-ordered society than ever before. They see society becoming more and more disorderly, although that is only part of it. Although I think they would be the last to admit it, their view is that a stern, all-seeing, and watchful civil society may have to stand in for the role that God once held, especially for the nonbelievers who, they feel, surround them.

All of us are in daily contact with an increasingly diverse world. Not only do we live in a society that officially supports the separation of church and state, but there are more and more churches (and quasi-churches) for the state to be separated from. Although many of the sexual conservatives spoke of a Judeo-Christian moral tradition, which they saw as the basis of American morality, the anthropologist and theologian Diana Eck has argued that the United States is the most religiously diverse nation in the world.[3] At last count, about three fourths of all Americans identified with a Christian religion, broadly defined, but about one in six identified with no religion, about 4 percent identified with a non-Christian religion, and just over 5 percent refused to answer the question. Since almost every denomination in the country is fissioning into a conservative and a liberal branch, sexual conservatives cannot even count on their coreligionists to share their views. So "society," and perhaps even that newly rediscovered avatar "civil society," has had to give a hand to the Almighty, since His adherents are in so little agreement among themselves about what constitutes good behavior, especially when it comes to sex.[4]

Sexual liberals acknowledge this dilemma, albeit with a different conclusion. They know full well that there is no agreement about sexual morality in American society; if they ever thought so, they were rapidly disabused of the idea in the face of the controversies over sex education in their communities. But their response to an increasingly morally diverse society is just the opposite of that of the sexual conservatives. If sexual conservatives are the heirs of Edmund Burke, then the sexual liberals are the heirs of the Enlightenment. They invert the equation that the sexual conservatives hold, that society needs to be protected from the individual and that only a strong, morally coherent society can inculcate the values that will prevent the Hobbesian war of the each against the all. Rather, sexual liberals believe that the individual needs to be protected from society. True to their heritage, they recall case after case when "society" has turned a blind eye to, and often actively supported, the diminution of individual rights in the service of social order. Thus, while conservatives often look back with fondness and regret to the 1950s, before all of the "rights revolutions"—the sexual, civil, and women's rights movements—took place, liberals see that era as the quintessence of the Bad Old Days. For them, the 1950s were a period in which individuals were mistreated, shunned, and sometimes even hurt or killed because their ideas were "wrong" in the eyes of a larger collectivity. Whether it was an African American who wanted to vote, a woman who wanted to be a doctor, or a homosexual who wanted to be open about his or her desires, individuals suffered enormously, they think, and suffered needlessly.

In this respect, sexual liberals are good liberals in the larger sense of the word. The ones I spoke with told me stories of experiencing discrimination themselves or seeing it directed at others, almost always in the context of talking about right and wrong. One man reminisced, "In the air force, I was in a line going into one of these fifteen-cent movies. There was a kid about three or four people in front of me, and one guy came in and pushed him out of the way. He said, 'Get behind me—back of the line, Jew-boy.' I was part Jewish, and this guy was a pretty big guy. I walked up and pushed him, and I said, 'You wanna pick on somebody, you pick on me.' There wasn't any second thought about it. You see, it was just the right thing to do at that time."

The most powerful comments often involved the punishment of an individual for transgressing sexual boundaries. Elaine Devoto said, for instance,

I was reared in the bosom of my mother's devoutly Christian and matriarchal extended family, in which everything from avarice to leaving one's bed unmade was a sin. There were hard-

and-fast rules imposed by my grandmother, a woman born in 1885, who went to her grave in 1969 believing that women in slacks and women exposing their ankles were equally sinful, as dictated by her interpretation of the Bible. As a young child, I witnessed a cousin who was decidedly 'different' regularly being beaten to a bloody pulp and called 'faggot' and other words I didn't understand, which caused him to do everything from drinking peroxide to hanging himself from a backyard clothesline while still in elementary school, in the hope of ending his torment. A few years later he became a sexual predator, pedophile, and drug addict—not because of his homosexuality, certainly, but because years of heinous emotional and physical abuse spawned a monster.

Mary Kay Malone holds this view too, based on hard experience. She explained, "My sister came up pregnant when she was fifteen. She was almost destroyed, because she didn't know what to do. A lot of people stopped coming around her. My mother was very upset with her, to say the least. And it touched home. It taught me that there is no right or wrong, there's humans. To say that my child's not going to become pregnant is a fool's eye-distant way of thinking."

This fundamental difference in viewpoint about who needs to be protected from whom leads to a whole host of different consequences, which put sexual conservatives and sexual liberals at odds over many things, some of them only distantly related to sex.

Because sexual conservatives think that humans are weak vessels, they are great believers in boundaries and hierarchies. I use the latter word with some trepidation, because part of what the rights revolutions of the sixties did—and part of what makes sexual conservatives so unhappy with those revolutions—is to taint the notion of hierarchy, making it synonymous with the naked use of power, and unjust power at that. (In fact, the original meaning of the word "hierarchy" was simply order, as in "the order of things"; it only later came to mean people who had power over others.)[5]

But sexual conservatives believe that society and individuals are best served by an orderly world, and orderly worlds have both boundaries and hierarchies within those boundaries. Thus, in a well-ordered world, people earn rights by taking on more responsibilities, and everyone is at one and the same time subordinate to some and superordinate to others.[6] For the sexual conservatives, hierarchy reflects natural rather than arbitrary differences. I hasten to say that despite the fact that "natural" has come to mean "unchanging" in the eyes of many people, many of the sexual conservatives draw on a more dynamic notion of what is natural, one based on a notion of capacities and the employment of those capacities. (I think here of the parable of the talents in the Bible. People are given different amounts and kinds of talents, but they may use, ignore, or invest those talents as they will.) Thus people in authority, such as teachers and ministers, are owed respect and deference because they have earned it by studying hard and employing their natural talents.

Three sets of boundaries and their associated hierarchies came up over and over again in my interviews with sexual conservatives. First, as just noted, people in positions of authority deserve respect from others by virtue of their station in life. Second, older people deserve respect, even from other adults, because they are assumed to have accrued wisdom and experience. Third, children owe respect and deference to adults, especially their parents, because of their station in life as dependents. (Note that these are not the rigid hierarchies of the Middle Ages but the dynamic ones of the modern era. Ideally, in the ordinary course of events, children will become adults, adults will become elderly, and if we work and study hard, we can earn the respect of our peers by moving into positions of authority.)

In addition to these three sets of boundaries, a fourth one was mentioned repeatedly: the boundary between men and women.

Although this boundary separates two categories, it is not entirely clear to me that it indicates a hierarchy, though it used to do exactly that. That is, in the service of "protecting" women, men often denied women, as Simone de Beauvoir pointed out, the dignity of being autonomous and full human beings.[7] In these days, when men and women have a wide range of choices in front of them, that may no longer be true. In any case, the sexual conservatives insisted when they talked to me that while there is indeed a boundary, there is absolutely not a hierarchy.

Of course, the sexual liberals don't believe this for one minute. When they see men and women separating themselves into different spheres, their first impulse is to assume that discrimination, albeit subtle, is to blame, and that discrimination is always based on some kind of a hierarchy. Not to put too fine a point on it, for most sexual liberals, difference equals discrimination. One of the red flags that alerted many of the sexual liberals to the fact that the people on the other side of the sex education debate were fundamentally different was their support of traditional gender roles.

Sam McKinnaugh, a student at Las Colinas High who was active in opposing the abstinence-only sex education curriculum at his school, despite the fact that he described himself as a "strong Christian" and agreed that abstinence is best for teenagers, put it this way: "There was a lot of stuff [in the abstinence-only curriculum] that had a certain 1950s connotation of the role of women. I mean, even things as subtle as showing women in the book doing house chores, unloading the dishwasher, doing the dishes—there's no reason why these things should have been sex-preferential with respect to the topic the book was discussing."

The sexual conservatives I talked to see men and women as having different but equally valuable sets of capacities, and each owes respect to the other for how they realize their capacities within their own domain. When I listened, I was reminded of a corporation's organizational chart. At the top is the CEO or president, under whom is a tidy set of separate divisions (production, finance, R&D,

marketing, etc.), beneath each of which are separate departments, and so on and so on. To be perfectly honest, thinking about that kind of a social structure inspires in me the same envy and admiration I have when I imagine Martha Stewart's well-ordered linen closets. The orderly closets and the orderly world—the hierarchies, in the original sense of the word, I heard about from sexual conservatives—serve as symbols of homes, families, lives, and a world in order and under our control. In a rapidly shifting global economy, the longing for order is something that many people experience.

Literary types these days speak of transgressing boundaries, of mixing categories and genres. Part of what gives sex education its special edge in disturbing sexual conservatives, in addition to the concrete substantive issues we've looked at, is that sex education, like these literary types, transgresses boundaries. Sex, and information about it, puts people on the same page, so to speak.

Diana Smith talked about why sex education offended her, "When I was in high school, you respected the teacher. You didn't go to the teacher asking him for contraception because you felt you wanted to be involved with a person. When I came along, you were put out of school if there was any such activities going on . . . [At the hearing on sex education] there was one of my teachers in school, and I told him, 'I respect you as an elder person, and I would feel ashamed to have to go to you and say, "Can I have a condom, because I feel like I can't keep myself" or "I want something safe to protect myself." ' And it loses the respect. It makes the child feel like 'Well, hey. I'm just as equal as this older person is, I don't have to respect him.' It breaks down that barrier. And I still feel that there still should be a level where the children have to respect older people. And that's being broken down. I drive the school bus, and I've seen such a tremendous change, and these were kindergarten students. Kindergarten to third grade is what rode on my bus. They talked about sex, they talked about their private areas. These are the things they talked about. They talked about some things that were just—I mean . . ."

In much the same way, sex education loosens the boundary between parents and children. Mrs. Smith had this to say about that: "And the thing, too, when I read the brochure about the sex education program they had, it was teaching the children how to be secretive to your parents. To rebel against your parents. Because in that teaching, it told them that you don't have to do what your parents say to do. I mean, not like that, but the way they did it, a child wouldn't know. It was so subtle to the child, that they wouldn't realize it was a form of rebellion. Because I ran into that with my teenage daughter when she was at that age, and I was wondering what was happening, and she made this statement, she said, 'I don't have to listen to you, because I can take you down to the court, and the court has a right to emancipate me over you.' So these are the little subtle things that they were teaching our kids. 'Hey, you don't have to do what your parents say to do.' You're your own boss, in other words."

Jim Highland couldn't agree more. "I think you've got to have some type of parental involvement," he said. "That means involved with the kid. That means, know what they're doing. That means teaching them moral principles and values. That means when they get—when they start having hormonal changes in their lives and they start noticing girls and boys, then you have to set up some really strict guidelines and rules. But you know, that doesn't start when they're thirteen. You grow up in a community and you see little tiny children who lack the respect for adults from the time they start toddling around the house, because there's no structure. You don't teach that kid that he shouldn't do something when he's fifteen if you don't have any control over him when he's two. So the question goes back to, there's got to be family involvement, there's got to be structure, there's got to be discipline, there's got to be moral values. And those things are taught from the time the child comes into life, and not—it doesn't start at seventeen. You never get it at seventeen. Then they're totally independent."

Thus for sexual conservatives, sex education by its very nature intrudes between parent and child and muddies the boundary between them. It puts in the hands of children information that the parents may not have—a point sexual liberals readily concede—thereby inverting the natural order of things, and it exposes children to values that the parents would rather they not hear about, particularly from authoritative sources such as the school.

And most important, sex education breaks down the boundaries between men and women. One father told me, "Back when I came along, there was a long time before I could take a girl out on a date, for instance, and talk about sex. And once I was able to talk about sex, the door was sort of open a little, you know, and I think you can advance toward sex more easily after you're able to talk about it than you could before. Now, I think it's real important that I as a man know about sex, and the girl, the woman, knows about sex. But when you sit in the classroom and talk about it, you know, all day long together, and then go out on a date that night, for instance, you know, you're already talking about sex. Boy and a girl."

I asked, "So it makes you more familiar with one another in a certain—in a bad sense?"

He heartily agreed. "Well, you know, you got some bridges that you've already crossed. And I suppose maybe the male is after a female, and it's easier for him to get where he's headed if he's already able to talk about these things. It seems to me, if a girl could tell him when the conversation might first come up about sex, 'Hey, you know, I don't want to talk about it, and I'd appreciate it if you just keep that out of our conversation,' but how you gonna tell—how would a girl tell a boy that when he's been sitting in the classroom with her all day talking about it?"

This sense of boundaries and how sex transgresses them was particularly visible in two realms. First, as these quotations suggest, is the realm of daily life with children. The word "innocence" came up often in the interviews, with sexual conservatives arguing that children have a natural innocence that must be protected as long as possible. (You may recall that Jenny Letterman in Shady Grove found a psychoanalyst to testify to the school board that exposure to information about sex within what the Freudians call the latency period would be developmentally harmful to young people.)

The other realm is that of male and female. I use that rather clinical term because for the people I interviewed, "male and female" covered both adult women and men and boys and girls. If innocence was the key word to the transgression of boundaries vis-à-vis childhood, then modesty was the key word to mark off the transgression of the boundary between the sexes. The frank and forthright discussions that the sexual liberals value so highly make conservatives cringe when they take place in mixed groups of boys and girls. While at least some sexual conservatives could live with (albeit grudgingly) a discussion of the biology of reproduction (what comprehensive sex ed proponents dismiss as "the plumbing"), any discussion of intimate matters or feelings in a mixed group is taboo.

In this context, one of the most interesting things was how upsetting some sexual conservatives found discussion of a topic that was the staple of 1950s sex education: menstruation. One of the sex education classes in this research passed around tampons during class and encouraged the students to unwrap them, examine them, and generally try to become comfortable with touching them. For many of the sexual conservatives, this class was only slightly less disturbing than the fabled act of putting a condom on a cucumber.

Drawing on the themes of innocence and modesty, sexually conservative parents said things like this: "I wasn't particularly happy with my children's sex education, because it's not presented in the manner that it should be, and things are discussed in front of boys and girls at an age when boys and girls can be a bit—when you are easily embarrassed—like how to insert a tampon, pads, and that kind of thing with girls. And then the boys come out and tease them, saying vulgar and rotten things. But that's not necessary, or I don't feel that it's necessary. People seem to think that it is, but I don't think it's necessary. I don't think that that kind of shame and embarrassment needs to occur. We should be trying to uphold the dignity of sex, the dignity of the sex act, which is a creation. You're creating children. It's also supposed to be an act of love, which is creative."

Sexual liberals can't begin to fathom why sexual conservatives find such benign things threatening. As far as they are concerned, the more men and women learn about each other—and especially the more men and women learn about each other in each other's presence—the better. So women menstruate? Big deal. Tampons? Also big deal. They can reluctantly understand why some parents might get tense about condoms in the classroom, since condoms are allied to more complex issues of reproduction. But tampons?

In fact, for sexual liberals, who view boundaries of this sort with suspicion, the task of education generally and sex education in particular is precisely to break down these boundaries. One physician told me about teaching in a medical school, where he saw his task as destroying these boundaries (or stereotypes, as he called them). "One of the things I do in the seminar is to bring out the idea of 'What's a male stereotype and what's a female stereotype?' They might say, well, they really didn't know it. Then I start asking questions: 'Well, what did you learn about sex? And what's expected of you, when you have intercourse with a female?' to the male. And to the female, 'What is expected of you?' And I'd say 90 percent of the time I got back just what I'd expected—the stereotypic answers. 'I'm going to do something to her,' and 'I'm supposed to be there for his pleasure, and if I get something out of it, that's all right.' And that was—these here— college graduates, in a professional school. Now, granted, they came, the majority of them . . . came from central, southern Illinois, small communities, mostly—the so-called Bible Belt."

Steve Kingsley talked about children in elementary school rather than doctors in training at a medical school—and age does make a difference, by the way—but this breaking down of boundaries was precisely why he took his daughter out of sex ed. "When I was in high school, I took a sex education class," he explained. "But what it was about this course is that when my wife went up and talked to the teacher after the presentation was over, and they showed her the materials and everything, her reservation was being in that mixed company, because kids at that age were naturally shy. And so the sex education teacher said their intention was to break down that shyness. And my wife's comment at the time was, 'That's not good, because we're naturally shy for a specific reason, because these are kind of embarrassing things for young people to talk about.' So in my mind that kind of shaped my perspective, going forward from there, knowing that there is a built-in shyness, I think, with kids, to talk about intimate things when they're in the younger grades and stuff. And so at that time we opted our daughter out of the program."

This theme proved a powerful one in the interviews, as much for the sexual liberals as for the sexual conservatives. Liberals talked about boundaries quite a bit with me, but with a very different flavor: where conservatives see boundaries, liberals see fences. If, as I noted earlier, the metaphor that captures the worldview of the sexual conservatives is the organizational chart of the traditional hierarchical corporation, then the equivalent metaphor for the sexual liberals would be a network, or perhaps the Japanese "quality circle," where people with a similar task get together to achieve a common goal. Managers and assembly-line workers, marketing people and financial people all work together to launch a new product. Boundaries, in the ideal, are porous, overlapping, and multithreaded, which suits sexual liberals just fine. The focus of attention is the individual, not the category. As liberals see it, boundaries and hierarchies serve only to separate people from one another and are just one more example of how "society" alienates people from genuine and meaningful connection.

Many of the sexual liberals I spoke with revealed considerable passion about the pain and confusion they felt as young people because no one would share information about sexuality with them honestly or forthrightly. Society, in its hypocritical way, they said, sacrificed their ability to come to know and appreciate themselves (including their sexual selves) in order to enforce a spurious morality that was already on its way out.

This in turn touches on the larger question of how liberals view human nature and the question of good and evil. If sexual conservatives see a world of sin and temptation, where people are kept in line only by the "collective conscience," as Emile Durkheim calls it, sexual liberals see a world in which the only way a diverse and heterogeneous group of people can be trusted to make good moral decisions is to ensure that all of them have the maximum amount of information possible. Because they are heirs to Descartes, not Calvin, they think that people will make good decisions if they are sufficiently informed.

As this view suggests, sex education brings into play, for liberals, two other deeply held sets of values. First, to be good decision-makers, people must be educated, and education implies information. Thus, while conservative parents resent information because it transcends the boundaries between the inside world of the family and the outside world, liberal parents value it because they believe that more information, especially the kind of accurate information that they imagine will be taught in a sex education class, enables the kinds of decision-making that will permit their children to become competent adults.

In fact, sexually liberal parents particularly value the information they imagine young people will get in a sex education class because they fear that accidents of their own history or circumstance have caused them to have blind spots that will get in the way of giving their children the information they need.[8] Traditional conservative parents may believe that parents are the people to educate their children about sex (although they may choose to delegate that responsiblity to a trusted source of moral authority, such as the church), but many liberal parents harbor the lurking suspicion that parents are the *last* people to teach their children about sex. From their point of view, parents are too old, too emotionally involved, and too vested in specific outcomes.

In this view, parents are not the guardians of what kinds of information about sex their children should get but barriers to that information. A consistent theme was the need for neutral, factual information passed on by a "professional," lest parents pass on their own misconceptions and hangups. Unlike the families of stereotype, who are uncomfortable talking to their children about the birds and the bees because they don't want to do it, these parents are uncomfortable because they are not confident that they will be able to give their children sufficiently up-to-date and emotionally untainted information to cope with a rapidly changing world.

In much the same way, sexual liberals expect that if their children are given education and information, they will grow up to be morally good adults. This is because they think of themselves as fundamentally good people (although not as good as they wish they could be, of course), and they assume other people are too. As far as they are concerned, people don't really need to be constrained by a watchful society but, on the contrary, need to be educated to be true to themselves, not true to the often arbitrary rules of society.

Again, this is a bit tricky. In general, sexual liberals think that many of the rules of society are in fact for the common good and that the common good is in general a good thing. Thus, in the interplay between individual conscience and the social order, most reasonable people will use the social norms of their society as a guide to good behavior. However, they also believe that because social norms are located in a given time and place (and although they don't directly articulate it this way, located in a given power structure), norms can generate all of the oppression and unfairness that they recount to me when they talk about morality: the oppression of African Americans by whites, of the poor by the rich, of women by men. (Children, as we will see, are an in-between category; sexual liberals take it for granted that children and young people need protection and guidance, but this does not mean that parental wishes always trump a child's wishes.)

As heirs to the Enlightenment, sexual liberals believe that individuals have been granted (by God, by evolution, or by their neural synapses) a unique capacity for reason and are thereby obligated to use that reason to question authority, not to follow it blindly. Moreover, reason needs information to function best, and boundaries impede the flow of information.

In a whole set of symbolic realms, this notion of boundaries (or fences) comes up with some regularity, especially in the context of education. In Shady Grove and Las Colinas, for example, some of the elementary schools were experimenting with open classrooms. "Open classrooms" can mean many things, but in Shady Grove it meant that classrooms lacked the traditional desks arranged in neat rows facing the blackboard. Instead, these classrooms had a number of tables in them, and students rotated from table to table depending on the task at hand. In contrast to the traditional classroom, where all the students would be doing the same thing in an orderly fashion while facing the teacher, in the open classroom small groups of children were doing different things and the teacher moved from group to group, encouraging them in their separate tasks. One table might be reading, another might be doing math problems, and a third might be doing a science experiment.[9]

Instead of the quiet and order of the elementary school classrooms I recall from my own childhood, these open classrooms always had a low hum of activity going on, always busy and sometimes boisterous. Rather than a distant and somewhat intimidating authority in the front of the room, the teacher reminded me of nothing so much as a consultant, appearing at each table and helping the group with its "process." Significantly, at least given my memories of classroom days, teachers were often in a fairly relaxed physical posture with the students, bending over, kneeling, and sometimes sitting beside them. Many of the open classrooms in Shady Grove had carpeted floors instead of linoleum ones, and it was clear that the carpets were there because sometimes students—even older ones—would be sitting in circles on the floor with the teacher. One classroom I visited even had a couch in it.

Not surprisingly, the sexual conservatives I spoke with detested open classrooms. From their vantage point, these rooms were invitations to anarchy and disorder. Listen to Steven Kingsley explain how he decided that his second son should go to another high school instead of Las Colinas High. As he suggested earlier, although sex education played a role, his decision was also based on his analysis of other values at play—what I am calling the question of boundaries. I asked him what factors shaped his decision to send his son to Brookview. He said, "Well, boy, that goes into a whole thing about a philosophy of education. It wasn't that I believed that Las Colinas would settle for anything less than a successful high school, but that their way of doing it was untried, untested. The saying that I held as true is that if anything shows in education to be unsuccessful, just wait, it'll reappear. And we talked about the open classrooms. Now, my sister is younger, six years younger than me, and she went to school here, and they had the open classrooms in those days, where all the kids were in one big classroom. So I guess everything kind of fits together, believing more in traditional education and those types of things kind of all fits in with your worldview and your morality. So Brookview had a good reputation, was a good school, was established, and Las Colinas was trying new things, and it's not so much being opposed to that, but it's a wait-and-see attitude."

In contrast, sexual liberals were generally passionate about the benefits of the open classroom and what it could bring to students.

In much the same way, some of the schools were experimenting with a new educational philosophy known as "outcome-based education," or OBE, which also offended sexual conservatives. I asked Chuck Finley, a sexual liberal and an advocate of OBE, to explain what it was, and he was kind enough to do so. "We patterned the curriculum on what's referred to as outcome-based education, which means the students have to take responsibility for their learning, and if they can't demonstrate what they've learned, then they don't move on. We elected to eliminate a failure scenario. If you get a D or an F at the Las Colinas High School, you get an incomplete and you must work to eliminate that incomplete. You can't get anything higher than a C [subsequently in that course], but once you've mastered the area that's been a problem, you get that C and you move on. To ensure that the graduate bore some resemblance to what our goals were for, there were sixteen outcomes established. You had to have such proficiency and do things like one hundred hours of community service during the course of four years. So it was a good, we thought, an assimilation of a lot of points from curriculums across the country as well as what we wanted. It was curious—at that time Littleton, Colorado, was in the forefront of outcome-based education. They came under severe attack. Their school board was transformed, and their entire system, after having been a model for the country, was suddenly jettisoned. It was a sad, sad happening. In any event, the outcome-based effects of what we were doing suddenly became hugely challenged."

"Hugely challenged" does not begin to describe it. From the point of view of the sexual conservatives, it was no accident at all that outcome-based education had flourished at Columbine High School in Colorado, a school now notorious because two teenage boys went on a bloody rampage there, killing twelve of their fellow students and wounding several more.[10] Rather than a curious coincidence, as Chuck Finley sees it, a direct, unimpeachable causal relationship is what the sexual conservatives see. If you take away the authority of the teacher, have no rules about passing a course ("no failure scenario"), and simply trust students to keep working until they get something right, they think, then what can you expect? Again, it's not as if sexual conservatives believe that the adoption of outcome-based education led in any *direct* way to the decision of two disturbed young men to pick up guns and kill their fellow students. Rather, they share with Mrs. Boland the conviction that murderous impulses may well lurk inside any of us and only a stern, morally coherent society helps individuals master those impulses. Outcome-based education then becomes a symbol of how the buttresses of morality—accountability in the classroom, responsibility for the consequences of your actions—are being dismantled moment by moment, stone by stone.

One last educational topic annoys and offends at least some sexual conservatives. Many American schoolchildren are now taught reading and writing with something called the whole-language approach. Whole-language teaches children, as the name implies, to get directly into the business of reading and writing, learning to guess at words and to approximate spellings as they go along.[11] In contrast to the spelling bees that adults remember, students are encouraged to express themselves, learning the finer details of how sounds combine to make words later.

Even this brief description should make it clear why some conservatives passionately reject the whole-language approach and strongly advocate returning to the traditional method of teaching reading, known as phonics, and to the old-fashioned spelling drill. Once again, the themes that come up when discussing the open classroom or outcome-based education resonate here in the most literal sense. Whole-language focuses on intent and self-expression, while phonics and spelling drills show students that there is a clear boundary between right and wrong. The daily action of teaching phonics and traditional spelling is seen as teaching children the larger lesson about boundaries, this time between right and wrong.

It is something of a play on words to say that this issue confronts sexual conservatives, who care about right and wrong in the sexual arena, with the idea of right and wrong in the classroom. But just as they believe that it is no coincidence that Littleton, Colorado, was the scene of the nation's worst school shooting (or that we even have such a noxious concept as school shootings), they think it is not a coincidence that right ("correct") and wrong ("incorrect") need to be taught in the literal as well as the moral sense. In other words, if children learn every day in school that there is a clear demarcation between the right way of doing things and the wrong way, this will instill the larger issue that in life there is also a right and a wrong, and that the boundaries between them are clear. In each of these issues, sexual conservatives support boundaries—what my legal colleagues call bright lines—between acceptable and unacceptable, between correct and incorrect, and by extension between right and wrong in the moral sense.

Just as the larger issue of boundaries offends sexual liberals, who see arbitrary divisions rather than neatly arrayed categories, all of the educational issues engage them on the other side, for much the same reasons that sexual conservatives reject them. It's not that they think that anything goes. In fact, they would be the first to tell you that kids need guidelines. But for sexual liberals, guidelines are principles, not rules. True to their Enlightenment heritage, they see budding citizens rather than budding truants when they contemplate schoolchildren. And children are best served, they think, by firm but fair guidelines, guidelines that children must eventually come to question as part of their intellectual, moral, and social maturation.

This attitude deeply offends sexual conservatives, not only in the sexual realm but elsewhere in the school as well. A mother in Shady Grove said to me, "I can share with you why I'm sending my daughter to Maplewood School and won't have her at the junior high school here in town. It's that there are three or four teachers specifically that I know of, two which I have even talked personally with . . . who have ideas about alternate lifestyles and basically authority. Just authority in general, and they have maintained in their classroom an attitude throughout the year to the students that you should always question authority, that you should always know that you are your own person and that you don't need to give yourself over to the authority of your parents, you don't come under their authority, you can stand up and refuse to obey them because it doesn't fit you. And this has happened on several occasions with friends of mine. And I'm real concerned—not because I want my children in a glass bubble, and I say, 'Gee, this is the way we think, and this is what you're going to think.' I'm not that unrealistic—I know we live in a changing world. But what I am afraid of is, in fact I've been very angry about, is teachers who use their influence, teachers that the kids really like, they've built up a trust and a bond throughout the year in a very casual way, they are saying, 'If your parents tell you no, that you can't do that, do you accept it? Do you feel that's okay?' Or can—you know—don't you say, 'Well, I have a right to do what I want, and I'm going to do it, whether you like it or not.' I mean, that's kind of what's been happening, what has happened. So the questioning of authority, and it's a breaking down of control, really. Of control."

A father and pastor in Billingsley agreed. "And then the sex education program expands their education in—they called it in helping people make decisions, but I saw it as a real humanistic kind of philosophy, to where there were no rights and wrongs, a big gray area. And authority was not—you don't really have to communicate to your parents about it, you're your own person, and you be your own person, and you do your own thing. And that's just calculated to destroy the family unit and level of authority."

There is one final boundary that differentiates the sexually conservative parents from the sexual liberals, and that is the boundary between the family and the school, both practically and philosophically. On the practical level, on average, liberal parents are more involved in their children's schools—they sit on site councils, serve in the PTA, write grants for enrichment programs, and, as Chuck Finley mentioned, help define the educational philosophy of the entire curriculum.

While many conservative parents are also actively involved in the school, and in some of the same ways, far fewer of them are as involved as the sexual liberals are. In part this is for practical reasons. Sexually conservative parents are typically much more involved in their church communities than liberals, and since many are stay-at-home moms, they spend a lot of time with their children and don't particularly feel the need to be involved with the school as still another social institution in their children's lives.

But there is a deeper reason as well, and it is a philosophical one. Parents, not villages, raise children, and the emphasis on the collectivity of the school, conservatives think, absolves parents from the serious obligation to raise their own children. In something of a reversal of the general trend, in which they worry about the collectivity as a container for unruly human impulses, here they feel that the enlarging role of the school in modern social life detracts from the role of the family. (Remember Jenny Letterman, who said that if schools were going to take over the moral and emotional raising of children, then what was the point of having a family?)

I suspect that this is because sexual conservatives, true to their conservative heritage, believe in what the Catholic Church calls "subsidiarity"—namely that smaller and more intimate social groups should shoulder more responsibility than larger ones. In this view, schools should educate children but should not take care of their moral upbringing, their health care, their stress reduction, or their self-esteem, as that is properly the role of the family.[12] (The principle of subsidiarity also showed up with reasonable frequency in the conversations of conservatives when we talked about poverty. Despite the liberal condemnation of their views as heartless, in fact many sexual conservatives supported help for the truly needy, and not a few practiced it in their daily lives. But what they wanted was a local, personal, responsive, face-to-face form of help rather than what they saw as a bureaucratized system of "welfare" administered from afar.)[13]

Sex education is the touchiest spot on the boundary between family and school, and before the AIDS crisis of the early 1980s, most sexually conservative parents thought that sex should be taught at home and that was the end of the conversation. For all the reasons we have explored, that position is no longer viable, but conservative parents still feel that how sex should be taught and to whom at what age is fundamentally a matter for parental decision. One mother told me, "I just don't believe this sex education should be taught in the ages of K through fourth grade. It should be left up to the families. The school can provide us, if they feel like the kids need to know certain things about it, then educate the parents, and let it be our responsibility. For heaven's sake, this country is over two hundred years old, and as children have grown up, sure, there's been different things going on in our society, but on the whole, I've been in the workforce for over fifteen years, and the majority of people there knew what was happening to their bodies."

Another agreed. "I don't like that the school assumes that they're going to do that for me, and that they're going to do it better, and many times contradicting my values. Again, you want me to be responsible and you want the buck to stop with me as a parent, but then you want to contradict me when it comes to something that I believe is an important issue, and reparent my kids."

Although sex education is the touchiest point of the boundary between parents and schools, it's not the only one. Parents are aware that teachers spend a great deal of time with children, that they can become larger-than-life figures for their students, especially in elementary school. Almost by definition, teachers disseminate their own values, whether they intend to or not. On the whole, the values of the school are not the values of sexually conservative parents, precisely along the lines of the boundaries and hierarchies we have noted. A father said to me gruffly, "Having read through the curriculum, I saw places in there where they found ways to challenge Mom and Dad. I told them, 'Hey, that's gonna be a cold day before I allow a teacher to challenge my family beliefs before my children, teachers who have my students longer in the day than I do, without my being able to defend myself and my position.'"

Not surprisingly, such parents often see their relationship to the school as an antagonistic one. Sandy Ames said, "I see when somebody speaks out, it becomes the school administration against the person, and then it becomes a big battle. And parents get worn out and tired and leave—maybe they'll hang in there for a few years, but then they leave. But our belief is that, I mean my belief in general, they—the administration of the school—don't want to hear it, and they don't want your input on curriculum, and really, they think they know best. They'll act like they're listening, but if you really demand too much, they'll do everything they can to stop you in the process and just hope that you either move on to another school or take the kid out, or whatever. But they're not interested in really adapting curriculum at any level to what parents want."

Another said, "We talked about some of the issues that led up to this, [getting involved in opposing sex education] and some of the things that caused us to oppose the direction the school district was going. And we sort of gradually took steps to try and bring about some change, which met with absolute failure, with no success at all, all the way up to the point where a group of people who were like-minded, we decided to try and start getting some people elected to the school board so that they could make some change. And so this all came to a head, probably unfortunately, in the election immediately following the controversy with the sex education curriculum. And our group ran a candidate. It was a single seat, it was like a mid-term election. Unfortunately, the whole thing got billed as 'the right wing opposed to the sex education curriculum,' which really was a very minor part of why we were involved, why all of us were involved. But we were defeated, and that really kind of was the jumping-off point for a lot of people. They realized that we didn't have the strength—and I don't think we were defeated because a majority of the people in Las Colinas were opposed to our views. We were defeated because there was no way we could match the immense resources that the NEA brought into that election . . . Oh, the teachers' union came in with big money and all kinds of political help. We were swamped, big-time."

In fact, to a surprising degree, sexual conservatives often saw teachers as part of a special interest group, one more committed to their own needs than to the needs of the children they taught. Speaking of a different but related issue—another mother's attempt to get a book off a required reading list—Sandy Ames echoed these themes: "Oh, it's the teachers, and then what happens is the union steps in immediately. And the union organizers, even though they're not supposed to put political activity in the mailboxes, they do. And they are behind the fliers, and they are the ones—it's the union. So when I say teachers, I mean mainly union. I think there are a lot of good teachers that just get caught up, and then they're forced in because it's the union . . . The union gets involved and uses this, 'They're trying to control your classroom and academic freedom,' and forgets the fact that with freedoms come responsibilities. They just want total academic freedom with our kids' minds, and we're paying for the public schools, there's compulsory attendance, and maybe that isn't what we want put in our kids' minds."

This sense that teachers are part of a special interest group coexisted with admiration and respect for particular teachers. Just as Jenny Letterman liked and admired Josh's teacher, Ms. Vasquez, but felt that allowing her to teach Josh sex education would be like signing a blank check, sexual conservatives often liked their child's own teachers but disliked teachers as a whole.

At the most abstract, although no one used this terminology, some sexually conservative parents described here too the layperson's view of "new class theory"—the idea that a group of educated professionals (and in this context, educational professionals) has come to be a class unto itself, as much at odds with ordinary middle-class people as those with inherited wealth once were.[14]

Thus the boundary between school and home is a clear one for sexual conservatives: teachers teach facts, families teach values. And when teachers move away from the simple teaching of facts, these parents get upset.

Sexual liberals, who view society as a web of relationships rather than a well-organized hierarchy, and who have a preference for porous boundaries, are deeply offended when conservatives say bad things about teachers. They too believe in a division of labor between school and home, but for them the differences are not so much about substance as about expertise. They mentioned over and over that teachers are trained professionals and parents must take their lead from teachers, who know what they are doing when it comes to children. A parent who tries to tell a teacher how to teach is misguided, if not foolish, said Olivia Henley: "I come from a background of believing that educators are trained professionals who deserve the respect and support of the community—that a partnership with parents is important, but that teachers are not slaves to do what parents tell them to do for their individual children."

Another mother said much the same thing. "I'm wondering who's judging the educational process. I've always felt when I sent my kids to school that I was trusting—there may not always be perfect teachers in every city, but that I was trusting my kids to go to that school. And what the teacher said, I was going to accept. If I didn't agree with it, I could talk to the kids about it at home, or they could talk to me. But I don't think that . . . I think a lot of people here feel they know more about education than they know. I know a lot about medicine, but I don't claim to be an educator. So I trust that to someone else."

As we've seen, on many grounds, not just sex, sexual conservatives and sexual liberals are deeply at odds when it comes to values. Perhaps not surprisingly, at the core of those values are two
very different views of morality, which reinforce their different
views of sex.

CHAPTER SEVEN

Morality and Sex

S ince the time of the ancient Greeks, and probably even earlier, humans have thought about what it means to be a
moral person. Across time and space, people have always
tried to outline for themselves (and each other) their desired standards of good behavior, even when these have been more in the
nature of wishful hopes than everyday realities.

In the modern era, morality, or at least the formal study of it,
is having something of a boom. Conservatives bewail the way
that "virtues" have been downgraded to "values," feminists urge
us to engage in an "ethic of care," communitarians call us to our
responsibilities to others, and liberals argue that the ground rules
of liberal democracy—tolerance, respect for others, respect for
differences—will create a space where morality can flourish.[1]

The odd thing about sex education is that whatever else you
might think about it, it is deeply grounding when it comes to
morality. Samuel Johnson admired the ability of an imminent
execution to concentrate the mind, and he would have been
impressed by how the combination of sex and children concen-
trates one's thoughts. Morality, given its history and its lofty aim
of helping us be better than we are in the ordinary course of
events, is abstract, grand, and general. The various scholarly disciplines that try to tackle morality in its many forms and ven-
ues—moral theology, moral philosophy, political philosophy,
bioethics—are often technical and sometimes impenetrable by
laypeople. But even the most sophisticated and most honored
scholar of morality has no edge on the parents I spoke with. A
scholar may be concise, elegant, logically rigorous, intellectually
subtle, and profoundly thoughtful; many of the parents are none

of these, but when it comes to how much they care, even the most passionately committed scholar has to take a back seat.

Just as these parents found themselves divided into the two large groups of sexual liberals and sexual conservatives, they found themselves hewing to two very different kinds of moral codes, and by and large these codes corresponded to (and are probably at the heart of) their sexual views as well.[2]

As a group, sexual conservatives tend to be Old Testament types. By this I mean that they believe in a moral code derived from God, not man. Since the code is divinely inspired, it is true across time and space. The Ten Commandments are not only as valid today as they were when Moses was handed the tablets, they are, if anything, more valid, given the perils of our modern world.

The sexual liberals—even those who were raised in and still attend conservative Protestant churches—have a more forgiving view of morality. God may well have given us rules to live by, but He also gave us human reason to adapt those rules to changing times and changing circumstances.

The relevant point is that whatever people's religious background and current religious practice (if any), their moral codes seem to come in two models. In the first, moral rules are clear, as are the boundaries separating right from wrong. There *are* moral absolutes. I asked one father what values he wanted his children to learn, and he replied, "Well, that's a tough question, because there's a lot of them. I guess if you wanted to categorize them, I think the values that are taught in the Ten Commandments, which most religious groups accept, whether it be Christian or non-Christian. The basic tenets of those things, about recognizing that there is a God and that there is a system of order where you don't lie or steal or cheat or rob or commit adultery or covet or murder, all those moral values we subscribe to and try to teach our children. Within those moral values, we believe and I believe that there is also responsibility to behavior and actions. And that responsibility not only lies with the individual, but also to some degree with the family. And that children need to be taught, perhaps more than anything, that there're consequences to their behavior."

Another father in another community echoed these words:

> We need a proper context. We need to say, "Yes, there are moral absolutes." Okay? "No means no." The kid gets busted for doing drugs and kicked out of school, and Mom and Dad go get a high-powered lawyer and get him back in. See, what are we teaching our kids? I suppose if we're going to teach sex education, we need to teach it with moral values. And I'm not saying religious values, I'm saying moral values. Yes, right and wrong, there is a right and wrong. And we live in such a wishy-washy society, where people don't want to take a stand . . . I just would say I hold to a strong belief in absolutes, and values, and let's stick with them . . . Yes, there are absolutes . . . we do not live in just a gray world. Tying in with that, you know, everybody says you can't legislate morality; I think you can. That little red stop sign out there is legislation of morality. The police say you don't pull a gun on a grocery store clerk and take all his money or you're going to go to jail. That's legislating morality.

Denouncing the liberal plea for tolerance, another conservative father said, "Because you go back to what's right and what's wrong. Tolerance for what's wrong, what's indecent, what's pornographic? That's tolerance? No, no, no, that's wrong. That's wrong, it's not tolerance."

The liberals' lack of absolutes signals to the conservatives that they are on a very different (and troubling) wavelength. I asked one pastor who the opposition was, and he told me, "Well, the liberal philosophy that almost anything goes." One father said simply, speaking of his moral values and how he hoped to pass them on to his children, "But I have to have a standard. If that standard is not absolute, then it's not a standard."

For the sexual liberals, however, life is—as usual—more complicated. They agree that general moral principles exist (summarized by a combination of the golden rule and perhaps the Boy Scout creed) and enjoin people not to hurt each other, to respect each other, to practice integrity, honesty, thrift, and courage, moral and otherwise. The trick is, of course, translating these general rules into actual daily practices. For them, making the right choice depends on context—and on information about the context. As one liberal father and pastor told me, "I make my choices, and then I have to live with the responsibility, or with the result of the choice. I don't think we have right or wrong choices, we just have choices."

Another father, a sex educator, told me, "Many times we've had people from clergy come in and talk on a subject—about abortion—you know, we had debates about it with the students. I think a very important underlying theme in this class is that we were not dictating how you should think about something, but we were trying to give them the tools to be able to discuss rationally and thoroughly any subject of human sexuality. So we never presented to them that we had the answer to any of the questions they were facing, but we were saying, 'Here are some different resources to use to be able to make some decisions, some evaluating that you're going to have to go through. Let's talk about this.'" This is exactly the approach that sexual conservatives worry about.

One way of thinking about these two models is that one puts a premium on obedience and one puts a premium on discernment. (I have deliberately chosen words that have long histories in the Judeo-Christian tradition, and I imply no value judgment between the two.) Despite all the fears of the conservative parents, liberal parents do in fact set boundaries for their children, and they set them regularly. Their boundaries, however, are not absolute boundaries between right and wrong but the boundaries of their authority over their children. In line with their views about hierarchy, they expect these boundaries to be negotiated regularly. As children mature, a key task for these more egalitarian families is to renegotiate parental authority to fit changing circumstances.

As one father explained to me, "Well, a lot of it was basically a trust boundary—this is what we expect. We were real clear. Every Sunday we would have a family meeting and we would talk about what was going on. The kids hated it, but we'd talk about issues that were in the family, issues that we had with them, gave them a real chance to lay out the issues they had with us. It was also during that time we did job cards, so that everybody had a job that lasted a month. Our kids were learning to cook when they were five and six years old, so [they had] a lot of responsibility there, but . . . the boundaries were the trust boundaries." He then elaborated: "The kids knew we were willing to negotiate. As it got to the point that 'Yeah, you can stay, your friends are staying out later than the curfew, then let's talk about that.' And so there was always that negotiation."

Because the parents I spoke with subscribed to one of these two moral codes, they (mostly unwittingly, as far as I can tell) expected their children to live according to the same code they did. None of them had the kind of "meta-conversation" about kinds of moral codes that we are looking at here. Rather, like Yankees fans or Dodgers fans, like passionate Republicans or Democrats, parents just assumed that their children would share their moral values.

As this brief overview may suggest, parents who subscribe to the Ten Commandments model mostly want their children to obey, and they want life, and social policy in particular, to back them up in their quest (or, at a minimum, not to undercut them). The "discernment" types, in contrast, want their children to make good decisions. And they too, usually without being fully aware of it, want social policy to affirm their view of the world.

Take, for example, the question of whether or not teenage children should have access to contraceptive advice, abortion services, and treatment for sexually transmitted diseases without their parents' knowledge and consent. Some years ago, it was easy to describe public policy in this field because most of it reflected a harm-reduction model of adolescent sexuality that most sexual liberals felt comfortable with. Holding that the benefits to adolescents outweighed the parental wish to have children stay chaste, courts at several levels permitted teenagers to have access to such services without informing their parents.[3] But because sexual conservatives experienced these decisions as an assault on their core values, they mobilized politically and persuaded first Congress and then the courts to put limits on what teenagers could do in this realm, by proposing parental consent and parental notification laws.

Today, teenagers across America face a policy world that reflects complex political struggles over moral codes in the arena of teenage sexuality. At one level, the conflict is a fairly straightforward one—conservatives oppose teenage sex, and consequently, like Susan Shelly, they oppose abortions and contraception and anything else that seems to make it easier for teenagers to have sex. Not surprisingly, they want to limit access to things that they think are morally wrong in and of themselves (in the case of abortion) as well as to things (such as contraception) that they see as paving the way to other moral wrongs, namely unmarried teenage sex. Liberals, in contrast, having few principled objections to teenage sex, favor increased access to contraception and abortion, precisely because these things make teenage (and other) sex less costly to the participants. So it is not surprising that while conservative parents would like to enlarge their area of control over a terrain they object to morally, liberals would not.

But this is only part of the story, and it misses a deeper dimension of values at play here. Sexual liberals generally do agree that parents are the people who are best positioned to help children and adolescents make complex and potentially risky medical decisions. But they differ from sexual conservatives in believing that the key part of raising a child successfully is teaching that child how to make decisions. They object to parental consent laws not (or not only) because they deprive other people's children of the right to make what they see as vital choices, but because these laws limit the capacity of their own children to make mature, responsible decisions and thus develop their character. At one level, the point is moot when it comes to the children of liberal parents; such parents support birth control and abortion, so when and if their children have to ask for permission, that permission is, in theory, promptly given.[4]

For liberal parents, parental consent laws enshrine in public policy the idea that teenagers are not allowed to make crucial decisions, and this undercuts very deep values. For such parents, the job of becoming a grownup is a tricky one, and the best way for children to do that is incrementally. Just as parents in these families encourage their children to start splashing in wading pools, then move on to swimming lessons in the shallow end of the pool, then into deeper water, and finally to the open water of the ocean or lakes, they believe that children need to learn to master a very complex moral world in gradual stages.

Mastering this world draws on two intertwined and cherished values for sexual liberals: decision-making and responsibility. These values are so basic that they cropped up in almost every interview I conducted. A good, moral child is one who takes responsibility for his or her actions. She or he thinks about the possible consequences of an action, prudently plans ahead so as to anticipate the entire range of those consequences, and then engages in a strategy of behavior that will minimize adverse outcomes.

If this sounds a little like the prospectus for a homeowner's policy or automobile insurance, it is because in some ways it is. A good liberal child, like the good middle-class family from which he or she comes, plans ahead. But the glitch, as liberal parents are all too aware, is that sex is a very hard arena in which to be so deliberate. Liberal parents, like conservative ones, see that children can easily be led astray. But while conservatives worry about temptation and sin, liberals worry about hormones.

The key difference is that for conservatives, the way to deal with temptation and sin is to avoid them, and the further one can keep away from them, the better. For liberals, however, the best way of dealing with hormones (and impulsive behavior generally) is to get children into the habit of making thoughtful decisions.

Liberal parents think that children learn to make good decisions by making a long array of decisions over the course of growing up, analyzing each decision in the light of its consequences. Each decision entails a little more reach, as children show that they can handle increasing amounts of responsibility. One father explained, "We have sheltered our children, in a sense. Kids have to be given the opportunity to make choices on their own, and if we shelter them completely and then send them to college or then send them out into life, they won't be ready to make those choices. They've got to be given increasing responsibility along the way. We're possibly a little bit oversheltering on our kids. They don't get into trouble. We do have exceptions, but I'll refrain from mentioning those, because I don't feel like talking about my kids' falls when they fall down."

If decision-making describes the process of how these children are to make moral decisions, then responsibility is the benchmark against which decisions are evaluated. A good decision is one in which a person anticipates problems and plans ahead for them. One sex educator told me that this was what was new in the sex education in her school. "Values begin in the family, and you learn about the family, and the role of the mother and the father, and some of those ideas that are associated with gender and communication and relationships. But, we have added more to it, and because our society's changed, we now have to teach responsibility for yourself and how to take care of yourself and how to learn about yourself. And so those are the kinds of major things that we have probably put into it that weren't there traditionally."

Many sexually liberal parents, when I asked how they would define moral conduct in the realm of sexuality, told me that their offspring would practice "responsible sex." And responsible sex, in turn, is sex that harms neither self nor others, something one does by anticipating possible harmful consequences and reducing the risk.

Mary Kay Malone somewhat ambivalently laid out for me what her priorities were, and in so doing illustrated the connection of responsibility with protection. Speaking of the sex education program in her community, she said, "At that time, abstinence was not the first thing that they were emphasizing. And I don't care what anybody says, because I talked to too many kids that sat there in class. They were stressing more 'protect yourself, protect yourself, protect yourself.' Well, my way of looking at that is, you preach abstinence first. But then you turn around—and maybe it's contradictory—and you say, okay, these events are what can happen to you if you do not practice abstinence, but if you're so bound and determined that the only way you can make it through life is to go ahead and have sex at this point, you take the responsibility of knowing that you have to protect yourself. And those are three steps: abstinence first, the consequences of having sex, and then the protection."

Sam McKinnaugh, who described himself as a "strong Christian" and who was upset about sexist material in the abstinence-only curriculum, said firmly, "There's a lot of guys out there that just want to get laid. And you know, in college I've found there's a lot of girls like that too. As high and mighty as it sounds, I don't think people should basically be sleeping together unless they've said either a) we're both pro-choice about abortion, and we're on the same page about that, or b) if they're not going to have an abortion, then the guy's going to stay around and he's going to be a father and take it like a man and do what he has to do to do right by that child."

Sex, then, is so important because it is like the Grand Prix of decision-making, where liberal parents and their children demonstrate to each other that the young person has successfully

advanced to a level where he or she can be trusted with the weighty
responsibilities of these decisions. It is the area in which the consequences are most serious, when what is at stake is an array of emotional, physical, and moral outcomes.

For sexual conservatives, of course, all this is confusing at best
and downright dubious and misbegotten at worst. Because they
have a value system in which right and wrong are clear and unambiguous, they really don't see the point of decision-making at all.
Conservative parents, like the medieval Catholic Church, are concerned that free will means only the capacity to move away from
God's will, not toward it. The more information that children
have and the more they are expected to make decisions, the more
tempted they are.

A public official on record as opposing the sex education
program in Billingsley was blunt when he talked to me about his
evaluation of decision-making: "Certainly we all have to make
decisions. But I don't think if adolescents were involved in church
and related activities that they would be placed in situations where
they would have to make as many of these decisions as frequently.
So the temptation. You take away some of the temptation there."

This analysis just doesn't make much sense to sexual liberals.
How can spending time in church keep children from making "as
many of these decisions as frequently"? They don't see how spending time in church can take temptation away, unless the church in
question is a maximum-security convent or monastery. If anything, they see the opposite—because churches teach absolutes,
children are poorly prepared for the complexity of choices they
will be facing. To the extent that children face a complex world,
what parents on both sides call the "thou shalt nots" are a thin
reed upon which to rest.

But from the conservative point of view, to teach without a clear
line that separates good from bad is to rear a generation of students
who have no ground on which to make decisions at all. One conservative father said, "I was a school bus driver as well as involved

in the school as a wrestling coach. And so it was very exciting, and good hands-on with the kids. I really enjoy it. But one of the things that bothered me was to watch the kids grow up, I guess you'd say, without any supervision. They were going through the educational system, but they were coming out unable to make any decisions, unable to say this is right or this is wrong. We were putting out a whole system of what I call wishy-washy kids."

Sexually conservative parents value responsibility too, by the way, and mentioned it often. But they did not have the same thing in mind as the sexual liberals when they used this word. For liberals, responsibility is planning ahead, but for conservatives, it is accountability, not preventing the consequences but living with them.

Dave Webber, the abstinence educator, put it this way: "For humans, the big word that I write on the board, because this is what it pretty much boils down to—and I write this one in capital letters—on the human side, humans are responsible for their actions. Whether so-and-so talked you into doing whatever, if you did it and something occurs, you're going to be held responsible. I said, 'At this point, you might think, "Oh, gosh, if we as humans are going to be held responsible, then we're doomed as humans." No, we're not. Why? Because one of the greatest traits that every single one of you in this classroom possesses right now, and many of you don't even know you have it, is the ability to control yourself. Humans have the ability to control themselves. So that if they're not ready for these consequences, you could make a decision to be totally free of those consequences. An incredible amount of power that you have that many of you are not using.' "

Knitting together the themes of moral absolutes and taking responsibility, one father told me, "I suppose that would be another absolute—that you are responsible for your actions. That we cannot develop social agencies to take care of pregnancies, that we do not develop agencies to take care of this and take care of that. That we are responsible for our actions. And I think we as parents need to teach that to our children. You get a car and you wreck it, you still have to pay for that car. But too often Mom and Dad will say, 'Well, it's easier to get the kid out of the house. I'm going to go buy him another car, and I'll pay for it.' I think we do our children a disservice when we do that. Even if it's fifty cents, it comes out of my daughter's piggybank."

A public official from Billingsley epitomized the conservative point of view that churches reduce temptations because they teach values, and values are shorthand algorithms, if you will, about how to make decisions. "The bottom line there I guess is the Ten Commandments," he said, "The basic laws that were set forth in the Bible, they give all of us a guide to live by. They're the basis for a lot of the things that are in our Constitution. Judeo-Christian influences are very much a part of our day-to-day life. And those values and all that were taught through the Ten Commandments, and hopefully a lifetime relationship with God through Jesus Christ. Or a faith—for a lot of these young people, they have nothing to believe in, and I believe that contributes to their feeling of helplessness. It certainly contributes to the lack of self-respect. I think that's what I meant, instilling those values. Literally the Ten Commandments, that will lead them to a faith in Jesus Christ."

Coded within these very different notions of how to exercise morality are profoundly different attitudes toward information. If sexually liberal parents expect children to make increasingly complex decisions over time, it stands to reason that they want their children—and all children—to have access to as much good information as possible. As far as they are concerned, the more, the better. After all, information surrounds decision-making on every side: the existence of a great many sometimes competing pieces of information leads to the need for decision-making, and still more data are needed to evaluate how a particular decision worked out.

Sexual conservatives could not disagree more. As far as they are concerned, the more children are exposed to information, the more confused those children become. For them, children are tainted, not informed, by all the information floating around them. Since they view children as having a certain natural innocence, which can only be corrupted by talking to them about sex, especially before high school, they want a minimum of information. Information just makes young people jaded, they think, and gives them ideas that they would not otherwise have had. As one conservative said, "Well, I think sex education is harmful at a young age. It's like giving a kid a loaded gun. They're inquisitive, you know. Children are very inquisitive, and who knows, they could start trying."

In part, these views of information grow out of two different family styles. Since liberal parents are not authoritarian, since they expect their children to make decisions on a regular basis, and since children need guidance in evaluating their decisions, liberal parents talk to and with their kids a lot. A cherished self-image of liberal parents is one in which family give-and-take occurs at the dinner table, in the carpool, on walks, and pretty much all the time. New information simply expands the array of things that parents and children can talk about, and one of the cardinal virtues of sex education that liberal parents single out over and over again is that it starts conversations. The real problem, as they see it, is that parents and children just don't talk enough. Not only does the information purveyed by sex education prompt discussions in families that are not doing a very good job of talking, it can enhance the conversations in their own homes by prompting children to talk about things that came up in class.

Sexually conservative parents, with a focus on obedience and values, find such attitudes disturbing. Since the key thing about values as defined in these families is that they are true across time and cultures, children are distressed to discover that other values exist. Not only does this call into question which values are the true ones, it creates distance between parents and children. From the liberal point of view, the good thing about sex ed in the public schools is that it highlights differences between parents and children and leads to more, and more interesting, conversations. Conservative parents agree that sex ed highlights differences, but these differences are upsetting, not interesting. The key arena for their concern is of course in the boundaries between parents and children. One of the most common expressions that I heard as I interviewed people who opposed sex education was the phrase "too much, too soon." While sexual liberals are careful to note that information about sex should be "developmentally appropriate," and because information about sex has traditionally been so secret, sharing information with youngsters will empower them and make them more confident, capable young people.

The metaphor that comes to mind is the computer, that quintessential emblem of the information age. Conservative parents want to be gatekeepers for the information that their children are exposed to. They want to preview the information, sort it, and let their children have access only to the information that passes parental screening. Logically, the conservative parents I talked to supported the V-chip (a computer chip that can screen out materials that parents deem offensive) and what they called "family friendly" libraries, where parents can either forbid their children to use computers or the computers have screening programs to prevent children's exposure to inappropriate materials.

Sandy Ames, for example, made a point of telling me that she keeps a careful eye on what her children are exposed to. "We pay attention to what they watch [on TV], and our kids are not allowed to watch MTV . . . Our daughters now have the password to the Internet, but they had to earn that kind of freedom, and the computer is in a common room . . . so it's not like hidden away so that they can read about how to make bombs and get some attention. I go in and I will every so often go back and into the history [on the computer] and see where the kids have gone on the Internet."

Such concerns about what children will see if parents don't protect them are nagging ones, and they are not easy to calm. On the

West Coast, parents by law have the right to preview materials that will be taught in any sex education class. But parents understand that examining the formal materials that will be used is only a very small part of the process. One mother made this point explicitly: "Yesterday I went and talked to Mr. Sarnon, because they're having sex education at the junior high, and I just said, 'Mr. Sarnon, I understand you're having sex education. May I have a copy of the curriculum which you're teaching, so that as you're teaching it I can say to my daughter, Emily, "Today you went over this, how did you feel about it?" ' And he said, 'We don't have a curriculum. I just kind of go along with what I use, and I can show you.' I said, 'But I'd like a hard copy of that.' As a parent, I feel like I have that right. He said, 'Well, we don't really have that.' 'Well, do you have a class for parents, do you have something to show?' Now, see, I think that's important. As much as the kid will bring home a textbook and I can see what they're doing in math and social studies, I think I need to see that too. But that's not really available in the sex education class. In fact, a lot of even the things that are proposed in the curriculum are sort of not tangible things. They don't have books to go with it, you see. So that's another reason why I feel like it's a sort of a separation of parent and teacher and child. Now, I want to be able to support the teacher. I don't want the teacher to think that I'm against that, what that teacher's presented. I want to be all for her. I want to back her up—her or him—as much as she will back me up. You see? So that is lacking, I think. It's the curriculum itself."

Such parents know full well that teachers may improvise, joke, and generally purvey information that they would have preferred to see first. When Jenny Letterman said that she was not prepared to sign a blank check, this was what she was worried about.

Sexually liberal parents find this attitude confusing. They argue that for better or worse, we live in an information economy, and no one can possibly preview all the information that children will be exposed to. Not only is it not possible, it isn't desirable either.

If conservative parents want to be gatekeepers, liberal parents
want to be programmers. They want to instill a few key principles
in their children, so the children can define for themselves what
they will look at and be able to evaluate what they see. Which is
not to say that liberal parents aren't sometimes aghast at what
even young children come home with these days. Like parents on
every side of this issue, they find themselves amused, bemused,
and sometimes downright horrified at what their kids say and
think about, and what television, and more recently the Internet,
bring into the home. But they are separated from the sexual conservatives by underlying assumptions about the world. While the
conservatives see their children as being immersed in a precarious
innocence, one that is too easily shattered and impossible to
replace, liberal parents see their children as relatively immune to
the assaults of the information age.

These beliefs are reflected in the way that the two sides appropriate developmental psychology. The conservatives, as noted,
think there is a latency period during which it is unwholesome
and possibly dangerous to permit information about sex to
intrude. Liberal parents argue that children just don't notice
things unless they are developmentally ready to see them, and if
they are capable of seeing them, they are capable of understanding
them, with appropriate adult input and guidance.

Though information plays a key role in the differences in how
these parents think about their children, it is only one small part
of the picture. Parents care about the information their children
will see and have because attitudes toward information reflect
attitudes about power and how to regulate it.

An old saw has it that information is power. One of the
strongest engines driving the fight over sex education is exactly
this: in some odd way, liberals and conservatives agree that information is an arena of power and a power source as well. They also
seem to agree (although they do not know that they agree) that
information breaks down barriers between categories of people,

that information is equalizing, that it levels the playing field. Where they differ, as you might imagine, is over whether that leveling is a good thing.

What parents articulate in very personal and concrete ways when they talk about their children becomes more global when they talk about the world at large. Although they are hard put to say exactly why, both liberals and conservatives make it clear that information, and especially information about sex, traditionally the most secret and closely held information of all, breaks down barriers—not only between parents and children but between people generally.

On the one hand, it breaks down barriers between people of different ages. To the extent that almost any society has a hierarchy based on age, to talk about sex across age categories is to lessen the social distance between those categories.[5] As might be expected, sexual liberals welcome this. Talking about sex is the gold standard of getting young people to talk to older people, and from their point of view, if older people withhold information from younger ones, the outcomes can be dire. The people who teach sex education state this very clearly. One sex ed teacher explained, "I intended to have some pretty good communication with my students, and I realized that they needed a lot more information. They also needed a place to discuss their feelings, and to talk about what other people were feeling, and to break down some of the stereotypical barriers that existed between those kids at that age group."

More important, information about sex breaks down barriers between men and women. As with parents and children, the two kinds of families have very different values about how men and women should relate to each other. Generally speaking, most sexual liberals are liberals in this part of their lives as well and subscribe to some version of feminism, defined as meaning that men and women are fundamentally equal and are more similar than dissimilar.

By the same token, sexual conservatives are generally conservative in their family values as well. While men and women may be equally valuable, they would never say that men and women are equal, because to them equality means sameness. As far as they are concerned, the genders are fundamentally different, not similar, and consequently they have very different roles to play. If conservative families can afford it, they prefer for women to stay home and take care of children, since in their view having a husband who works in the paid labor force and a wife who is a homemaker reflects the natural differences and capabilities between men and women.

Sexual liberals, in contrast, believe in equality and think that men and women should choose the role that most fits their talents and inclinations. They find no natural correlation between anatomy and a desire to work in the paid labor force, or between hormones and a desire to stay home and nurture young children. To the extent that liberals acknowledge differences in the everyday world as we know it, they think those differences are made, not innate.

Of course, these different viewpoints play out in the realm of talking—and not talking—about sex. When sexual conservatives talk about sex, I find myself thinking about the Woody Allen quip to the effect that sex is dirty, but only if you do it right. Based on our discussions, the bedrooms of conservatives appear to be dimly lit places, metaphorically speaking, in that no one seems to want either too much or too explicit information. Euphemism, indirection, and a certain glancing away from some of the basic aspects of sex are the order of the day. But sexual conservatives would argue—and I can see their point—that their bedrooms are not so much dimly lit as romantic.

To continue with the metaphor, liberal bedrooms resemble sunny places indeed. The windows are open; the shades provide privacy but permit sunlight; the talk is frank, and information is freely exchanged. The less romantic parts of sex—the smells, the sounds, the technology of birth control—are all forthrightly accepted, and a willingness to accept these dimensions is proof of mental health. As one sexual liberal said to me brightly, "Sunshine is the best disinfectant!"

I have never been in the actual bedrooms of either the sexual liberals or the sexual conservatives who participated in this study. (I even went through my notes to see if I had ever accidentally traipsed through one on my way to the bathroom after a long interview, and the answer seems to be no.) Moreover, for the record, I did not ask a single person what his or her bedroom looked like, felt like, or symbolized. My metaphors about the bedrooms grew out of my understanding of the bundle of values that the two sides hold. Since a key point of this book is that we often don't know our own deepest values, I've drawn on the values that came up when we talked about how children should think about sex.

What I heard time after time was the quintessentially Foucaultian point that information about sex profoundly changes the experience of sex. How these parents assessed that change revealed their deeply held but different values. Despite what every single person in this study took as an article of faith, there is no inherent moral hierarchy between the dim romantic bedroom and the sunny open one. A room, and by extension an attitude toward sexuality, can be dimly lit by the lamp of information and be either murky or romantic. A room or a sexual attitude that is brightly lit by information can be either sunny or shamelessly brazen.

These dichotomies come up clearly in attitudes toward what children should be taught. From the point of view of the conservatives, too much of the wrong kind of information takes all the mystery out of sex. From the point of view of the liberals, access to good information and plenty of it is necessary to demystify sex. But what is the mystery that needs to be protected, or unveiled?

The key mystery, I suspect, is that men and women in the bedroom, as elsewhere, share one humanity but two genders. What the conservatives want to do is protect the differences between men and women by keeping certain kinds of information at arm's length. Put another way, using the concepts of the brilliant sociologist Erving Goffman, they want to keep the backstage of the everyday life of the two genders dimly lit so as not to detract from the action going on at center stage.[6]

This means that sexual conservatives have a strong preference for giving information about sex to girls and boys separately, in order to maintain the mystery. A mixed group of adolescents (or preadolescents) learning about menstruation, wet dreams, and the mechanics of reproduction is a group for whom barriers have been broken down. Each side, so to speak, knows the other side's secrets.

One sex education teacher told the story of a sexually conservative mother who did not object to having her daughter learn about sex but did object to having her learn about it in a classroom of boys and girls together: "She said to me, 'My daughter came from a Christian school, and we've already, she's already learned some of this information. I don't mind if she knows some more about it, but she should not learn about it in the presence of a boy, because it is degrading.' And I went, 'Wow! Okay. Whatever you say, ma'am.'"

Liberals often forget that the conservative worldview was the predominant one until very recently. In fact, although most people I talked to described very limited exposure to sex education in their own lives, a substantial number on both sides recalled that their sex education took place in single-sex groups. For some, this was because sex education happened outside the schools. For middle-aged women in particular, groups such as the Girls Scouts were a major source of what little sex education they received—when they saw a film made by the makers of sanitary napkins. Those who had sex education in their public school recall a short lecture of the kind that was prevalent in much of the country until the late 1960s, in which a school nurse explained menstruation to a class of girls (and/or showed the sanitary-napkin movie) and a coach explained nocturnal emissions to a class of boys. On the cultural plane, grown men and women recalled in detail the excruciating humiliation they felt when they had to buy tampons or sanitary napkins in front of males (if they were young women) or condoms in front of females (if they were young men). So the kind of embargo on information that the conservatives want was, in an earlier era, simply tact and discretion.

The interesting thing, then, is not where the conservatives' values come from, since most of us grew up with them, but what changed. The short answer is the women's movement. In the course of arguing that men and women were substantially equal, feminists attacked the double standard on a multitude of fronts.

Blackstone, the famous seventeenth-century legal theorist, stated clearly that women were the property of their fathers until wed and then became the property of their husbands. "Unchastity," which meant that a woman made her own decisions about whom to have sex with, was a crime against property, namely the property that men held in women. Thus, when feminists agitated on a range of issues, including birth control, abortion, and rape, they were challenging the belief that women, unlike men, held no property in themselves.[7]

If men and women were (or were to become) really equal, then the double standard had to go. Of course, like their predecessors in the early part of the twentieth century, late-twentieth-century feminists could have argued that men should be more like women.[8] But that didn't happen: Men and women became more similar, but this time male behavior was the model.

Once men and women become more similar, especially and most visibly sexually, all of the old dilemmas about how to parse "I-ness" and "we-ness" rear their ugly heads. Since our society has believed for at least the past one hundred and fifty years that there is a fundamental division of emotional and social labor between men and women, in which men are stoic, ruthless, and constantly girded for the battle for survival and women are passive, self-sacrificing, loving, and moral, how are we to reconcile these differences?

My guess is that these anxieties are especially acute in a globalizing and volatile economy, where the survival of the fittest seems both the order of the day and unrelenting. I suspect that almost everyone in American society these days longs for a haven in a heartless world, where someone else will take care of us, putting his or her own needs on hold for at least a moment while our needs come first. I suspect that all of us, men and women alike, want someone to put our needs first and a place where we are loved for who we are, not what we do.[9]

But whose needs get put on the back burner? Who nurtures and cares? If men and women are both gainfully employed full-time (which is increasingly the case) and we still expect women single-handedly to fill what my colleague Arlie Hochschild calls the care deficit, then women indeed have a double day.[10] And on what grounds of fairness does this fall to women? After all, weren't men and women supposed to be equal? For many of the women I spoke with, sexual conservatives and sexual liberals alike, "equality" isn't what it was supposed to be. Many women feel guilty both at work and at home and do not fully accomplish what they need and want at both places.

This raises the final paradox of sex and morality. As must be clear, a concatenation of values and life experiences and choices means that sexually conservative men and women are likely also to be conservative about gender; that is, they believe that men and women are fundamentally different rather than similar. As a result, conservative families are much more likely to have a stay-at-home mother; sexually liberal mothers more often than not work outside the home.

So the fight about sex education is not only about sex but about education, about the value and place of information, about how men and women are to comport themselves, about the role of sexuality in human life, and about whether the world is or should be a place of firm lines and boundaries, or of interconnections and informed decisions.

To make things worse, most of these values are implicit, tacit, and only barely visible to the people fighting over them. With all of these compelling differences—differences that people care passionately about—it's not surprising that the conflict over sex education shows no signs of being resolved anytime soon.

CHAPTER EIGHT

The Politics of Sex

I t's a surprisingly sunny June day in Stockholm (spring comes late to these northern climes), and the classroom I am sitting in is bright and cheery. A middle-aged woman—the school nurse—is discussing sex with a room full of interested, alert fourteen-year-olds. Other Americans are here with me, wanting to see at first hand the vaunted Swedish sex education miracle, and when the teacher tells the students that they have visitors from America, they shift effortlessly into almost unaccented English. (I find myself wondering where, if at all, such a scene could be played out in the United States.)

Sweden is the gold standard of what most American sex educators imagine an ideal comprehensive sex education program looks like. It begins in kindergarten and continues cumulatively throughout a student's entire school career.[1] It is detailed, open, and by American standards remarkably frank (I am about to discover just how frank it is.)

Under the pressure of abstinence advocates, many American sex educators have slowly come to believe that a more directive sex education, one in which educators tell students exactly what is expected of them, may serve young people better than the values-clarification model that was so central a part of most comprehensive sex education until recently.[2] In this, Swedish sex education is exemplary, and far ahead of most American schools.

On this day, the school nurse conducts a ritual that I have observed several times in American sex education courses: she passes out index cards to the students and asks them to write down any questions they may have about sexuality, in all of its various forms and confusions. She then passes around a large manila envelope, and students drop their cards into it. Then she pulls out the cards and reads the anonymous questions aloud.

The first question could have come from any of the sex education classes I studied in the United States: "What is an orgasm, and why do people talk about it so much?" In the American school where I last heard this question posed, the teacher answered by discussing the different phases of sexual excitement, drawing from the sexologists Masters and Johnson. As the instructor covered the excitement phase, the plateau phase, and the resolution phase, pretty much in those terms, I realized that this particular sex educator had done the remarkable: he had made sex boring. I found that discussion remarkably uninformative in terms of what I thought the students really wanted to know, and judging from their body language, so did they. In contrast, the Swedish teacher said that "orgasm is the moment of highest pleasure during sex, and that's why people talk about it." I realized at that moment that I had never heard any American participants in the sex ed debates, whether teachers, students, or parents, mention either sexual desire or sexual pleasure, except in the most circumspect of terms.[3] But this was just the beginning of the surprises in store.

Another question concerned homosexuality: how did a person know whether he or she was genuinely attracted to the same sex? The nurse teaching the class answered this by drawing on her own experience, but not in the way I would have expected. When she was younger, she said, she had thought that perhaps she would like to be a Mormon. So she went to services with Mormons, had a lot of social activities with Mormon students her own age, and read a great deal about the religion, including *The Book of Mormon*. After some months, however, she realized that her interest in this religion (a novel one in Sweden, where the vast majority of the population is nominally Lutheran) was not a real spiritual calling. She pointed out to the students that she had nonetheless come out of the experience with a deeper appreciation for her own religion and a better understanding of how Mormons view the world, and she had made lifelong Mormon friends in the process.

Just as I was beginning to wonder what the link between Mor-monism and homosexuality could be, she made the connection: if a student wondered about homosexuality and about whether he or she was gay, then that student should get to know gay students and gay life. She recommended contacting the RSFU, the Swedish sex education association, which would help the student find gay organizations and clubs. Anyone who was questioning his or her sexual orientation should make gay friends, socialize with gays, and generally become familiar with what American conservatives would call the "gay lifestyle."

In the end, the nurse concluded cheerfully, the student would dis-cover whether or not he or she was genuinely gay, and if the stu-dent turned out to be heterosexual, then, as had been the case with the Mormons, he or she would have a deeper appreciation of who homosexuals were, a more broad-minded attitude toward those who were different, and, if all went well, lifelong and interesting friends. (As her comments indicate, Swedes tend to believe that homosex-uality is an inborn trait that cannot be "learned" in any meaning-ful way. The specter such recommendations raise among American sexual conservatives, that the student could be "recruited" to homosexuality, is incomprehensible in terms of official Swedish sex education. In this view, one could no more be recruited to homo-sexuality than one could be recruited to being six feet tall.)

More frankness was still to come. At the end of the session, the nurse handed around a bowl full of condoms, much as a hostess might pass a bowl of mints at the end of a successful dinner party. Mixed in the bowl, in a variety of colors and flavors, was the astonishing array of condoms available in Sweden. The nurse urged the students to help themselves and to take several different kinds home. To the boys, she said, "Take these home and mastur-bate with them on, so you can see which kinds feel good and what kind you like." And to the girls she said, "And girls, you too take some home and open them up and handle them and make sure that you feel comfortable with them, so you won't feel shy when the time comes to put them on your boyfriends."

As she handed around the bowl of condoms, the nurse added, "We don't want you to have sex. Fourteen is too young for sex. Swedish young people don't have sex until they are sixteen. But we want you to be ready when the time comes." She was being a bit disingenuous, in that sixteen is on average when Swedish teens become sexually active, so some will start earlier and some will start later. But generalizing about the statistic helped the teacher give the students a clear message: wait for a while to begin sex, and take precautions when you do.

Perhaps the most interesting thing for a visiting American was how relaxed the students were. I was struck first of all by how young they seemed—much, much younger than fourteen-year-olds I had observed in the United States. This sense of youth was directly connected to sexuality, albeit in a roundabout way. The American teens that I saw walking in the school corridors when I interviewed sex education teachers, or drifting in twos and threes down the sidewalk when I met a parent at a local café for an interview, or sitting in a sex education class, were typically dressed in a much more mature and sexually provocative way. Even the boys, and even in the early years of this study, seemed to draw their sense of style from the MTV videos that Sandy Ames adamantly refuses to let her kids watch. The children of the sexual conservatives, particularly when those conservatives were also Christians, were the only exception to this general observation.[4] As in Sweden, children of sexual conservatives in America, boys and girls alike, were dressed in modest, clean outfits, with none of the bare midriffs, pierced bellybuttons, and acres of visible underwear that seem to be the style in much of suburban America.[5]

So the Swedish kids seemed young—ten or eleven years old, perhaps, not fourteen. And they were surprisingly calm about the whole matter of sex education. Remember when Debbie DeGroot, the young woman who had taken sex education in Shady Grove, said that the teacher had written all kinds of words on the board so the class could "get the giggles out"? The American sex education classes I observed did seem to have their share of squirmy and embarrassed teenagers. So why do Swedish and American teens approach adolescence so differently? (As noted earlier, the available evidence suggests that Swedish and American adolescents are more alike than different when it comes to how old they are when they first have sex and how many of them become sexually active while they are still teenagers.)

Partly to find the answer to that question, I traveled from Stockholm to Paris to conduct interviews with French specialists in sex education. As I crisscrossed Parisian boulevards, going from one ministry to another, I was struck by another set of surprises. Official sex education in France is much closer to what American sexual conservatives would favor, almost 180 degrees away from the comprehensive, frank, and open Swedish sex education. Although a conservative government passed legislation authorizing school sex education in the 1980s, sex education in the public schools is remarkably limited, found mostly in the context of after-school programs. School-based programs are typically short, and, in the words of various functionaries in the ministries, limited to "the facts" (*les données*).

As I chatted with people in the several bureaucracies that deal with sex education, the reiteration of "the facts" was oddly jarring. After all, this is the country that gave the world Foucault, Derrida, and most of the other luminaries of deconstruction. How could the French insist all they were teaching was the facts when left-wing academics and conservative Christians in the United States agree there can be no such thing as "simple facts" when it comes to sex?

My sense of being on an entirely different wavelength continued as I probed the origins and social meaning of sex education in France. I asked several people, for example (before their astonished stares began to make me falter), what the Catholic Church thought about the creation of sex education courses in the public schools. Eyebrows were raised in that particularly Gallic fashion. Why, my informants wanted to know, would the Catholic Church have any-thing whatsoever to say about sex education in French public schools? Perhaps I was unaware of *la loi de Jules Ferry*, which these French bureaucrats invoked as Americans might invoke mother hood and apple pie. *La loi de Jules Ferry*, it turns out, is the legis-lation that mandates that publicly supported schools be secular, and hence to the French, the idea that the Catholic Church might have any say at all on sex education was quite literally unimaginable.

Feeling properly chastened but also still curious, I followed up my question about the Catholic Church with one about the grand imam of Paris, since Islam has been France's second largest reli-gion for some years now. Even more astonished stares and elevated eyebrows greeted my question. It's hard to convey the sense I had that these bureaucrats felt they were talking to someone who had just arrived from an oddly theocratic country—Afghanistan under the Taliban, perhaps, one in which religious figures could be pre-sumed even to *have* opinions on what happens in public schools. (This has changed in recent years, as conflict over headscarves, yarmulkes, and "large crosses" has prompted the prime minister himself to ban all of these religious items from school grounds, pre-sumably in the spirit of upholding *la loi de Jules Ferry*.)[6]

Finally, and somewhat desperately, I asked several people in the ministries what the gay community had said about sex education. The astonishment that had greeted my first two questions was now replaced by a blank stare of incomprehension. When they thought about the question carefully, they realized that they in fact knew homosexual people and knew what a community was, but the idea of "homosexual" and "community" occurring in the same sentence was something they could not begin to fathom.

Here is the paradox at the heart of my Swedish and French inter-views. Although France has relatively little sex education by American standards and offers virtually nothing to young people by Swedish standards, the results of adolescent sexual activity in France are far more like those in Sweden than those in the United

States. All the things Americans worry about—unintended pregnancies, sexually transmitted diseases, out-of-wedlock births—are
comparatively rare in both Sweden and France compared to the
United States, despite the very different levels of sex education
offered in those countries. And sex education in both countries is
by and large uncontroversial, an accepted fact of educational life.
(I asked so many pointed questions about the French program
because it was relatively new. My Swedish informants told me that
their sex education programs, established in 1921 for secondary
schools and 1942 for all grades, had long been accepted by virtually all Swedes.)[7]

So what's the deal here? Why do two European countries with
such totally different sex education programs have such similar
outcomes? And how is it that the United States, which has now
brought fights over the future of sex education to the very heart of
partisan party politics, has such dismal ones? And are the two
questions related?

As I've said, American sex educators of the comprehensive variety look longingly toward Sweden (and to a lesser extent to
France) as something of a promised land. Many of these educators
have taken as an article of faith that if Americans could only put
in place the kinds of programs Swedes take for granted, teenage
sex in this country would begin to resemble the accepted, relatively unproblematic sexuality of European teens. (As an example
of accepted and unproblematic adolescent sexuality, the sociologist Amy Schalet notes that Dutch parents whose teens are
becoming closely involved with a girlfriend or boyfriend start
teasing them about when they are going to bring that nice young
person home to spend the night.)[8]

But American sex educators are sadly confused. It's not the programs that enable French and Swedish teenagers to get through
their adolescence without much in the way of serious trouble, it's
the people. When American sex educators and sexually liberal
parents hear that I've conducted interviews about sex education in

Sweden, they often ask me if the sex educators there are doing anything that Americans are not, and my answer is "Yes, they're being Swedish."

Although that's a flippant answer, this may well be the most important finding in this book. As I noted earlier, Americans as a group, teenagers and adults alike, have a great deal of trouble dealing with sex. It's not their age so much as their nationality that puts American teenagers at risk.

What is it about American society that makes teenage sex so risky? Whenever I posed this question to American or European sex educators, they almost always came up with some version of the Puritan hypothesis—that we are troubled about sex because of our puritanical heritage. There are two things wrong with this theory. First, the new historiography on American Puritans reveals that our stereotypes about them have very little basis in truth. In fact, they were lusty, sex-loving people who took for granted that women had strong sexual desires and believed that female orgasm was necessary for conception. Courts granted divorces to couples when the man was impotent, and failure to pleasure a woman was considered a serious problem. All this sex was firmly rooted in marriage, of course, and Puritans did worry about becoming so fixated on erotic and marital love that it would crowd out the love of God. But sexual pleasure was a central part of Puritan marriage, so much so that they had their share of babies who arrived, like my grandmother's, a bit too soon after marriage.[9]

The other problem with this theory is no one has been able to show convincingly just how any kind of sexual ethic, Puritan or otherwise, can be faithfully recreated generation after generation, especially in the wake of the two sexual revolutions examined in this book.

Americans have trouble with sex not because of the Puritans in our past but because we are an incredibly diverse nation, and our diversity is reflected in our attitudes toward sex. Although things are changing rapidly, most European countries are (or at least were) remarkably homogeneous. People in those countries have historically tended to be of the same race, largely of the same ethnic group, and often of the same religion (many European countries have "established" or state religions that enjoy special privileges), and class and educational differences are much, much smaller than in the United States.

These countries also have centralized governments and centralized political parties. This means that the bureaucrats I talked to in France and Sweden were insulated from the kinds of political pressures regarding sexuality that Americans have come to take for granted. Technical expertise, rather than politics, tends to shape what goes into European sex education.

In addition, European multiparty systems, combined with the higher level of centralized control, make it harder to establish single-issue movements in the political process, while American political parties take on many of the tasks of the centralized bureaucracies of Europe.[10] Policies concerning alcohol, sexuality, gambling, and many of the other moral issues that confront societies have typically been fought out in the political arena in the United States, rather than in the technical one. To take an example from recent times, an American who actively opposed abortion could easily run for political office, as a Democrat or a Republican, if he or she could rally like-minded supporters. If that person was someone like Ellen McCormack, a self-described New York housewife who ran for president in 1976, entering twenty primaries on a right-to-life platform and winning enough votes to qualify for federal matching funds, she could be assured her issue would gain attention from the national parties. Such actions are much more difficult in the multiparty European countries.

So the United States is a country with many different religions, many different races, many different ethnic groups; income disparities are much sharper than in Europe (although almost every patriotic American denies this), and we have a political system that welcomes single-issue movements, provided they can generate a certain level of popular support. Sex, which is usually tightly controlled by cultural norms, often provides the ideal arena where contesting groups can fight out their differences in what social scientists call "symbolic politics."[11]

Even the social hygienists who were so active in the first sexual revolution saw themselves as managing, by education, the different kinds of sexual behavior that they saw among young people, members of the working class, and immigrants. For example, social hygiene made special attempts to take sex education to those in the ghetto, which in those days meant Jewish immigrants, not African Americans. (The social hygienists, like most of the Progressives, were not particularly concerned with African American sexual behavior, probably because at the time most African Americans still lived in the South, and social hygiene, although it had southern outposts, was more prevalent elsewhere in the country.)[12]

When the great sexual and gender revolutions swept the United States in the 1960s, sexuality became a way in which different kinds of people sorted themselves out, since sexuality is so central to our images of who we are. The young and the old were the most visible groups to come into conflict, as Mary Kay Malone reminded us, but other groups joined the fray. Abortion in particular became a turning point for many people. Surprisingly, at first religious denomination did not seem to matter very much in terms of predicting opposition to or support for abortion or the other sexual issues emerging at the time. American Catholics, for example, were not particularly distinct from those of other religions when it came to opinions about abortion, although their church was at the forefront of organizing the institutional response to *Roe v. Wade*.[13] Jews were far more liberal on abortion than was the average American, but when their generally higher levels of education were taken into account, much of that difference disappeared. Finally, Protestants as a group were spread across the spectrum on this issue. One sector of Protestantism, the fundamentalists who had emerged as a distinctive group in the early twentieth century in reaction to the Progressive movement, were not at first a particularly visible part of the opposition. Because of their pietistic tradition, they preferred to remain detached from the profane world of politics, rather than to become actively involved in something so potentially disturbing to religious faith.[14]

I bring this up because I have so far focused here on individuals, people like Melanie and Jenny and Steven and others whose voices make real the passions that animate people about sex education. Unless you are a particularly careful reader, you could well think that individuals like these tell the story of conflicts over sex education today. In some measure you would be right—there really are a great many people at the grassroots level who are worried that their values about sex are not being taught in the public schools and who are working almost the equivalent of a full-time job to see that their values will be the dominant ones in public sex education. Like any other social movement, though, the grassroots effort both shapes and is shaped by larger political organizations, and in the case of sex education, those organizations stretch all the way up to national politics.

Although other people have told the story of how "social conservatives" have changed the political landscape much better than I can and with much more detailed evidence, I think that with some notable exceptions, those accounts tend to overlook the central role of sexuality in the transformation of American politics. True, abortion is often given the credit (or the blame) for mobilizing a great many people into what is now being called the New Right, a name meant to signal that this group is distinctly different from the old right, much as the New Left broke with the traditions of the old left. But accounts of the rise of the New Right often end there, overlooking the extent to which the same broad values of this group shape everything from international AIDS policy to policies on contraception, stem cell research, and the like. Yet understanding how sex has moved from the periphery to

the center of American politics is absolutely central to understanding the larger world in which we find ourselves. (Recall that
sex education is such an evocative symbol that both the national
Republican Party and several state-level Republican organizations
make a point of either denouncing it or advocating abstinence-
only education in their platforms.)

Drawing on accounts that detail the rise of the New Right as
well as on my interviews with high-level movers and shakers in
these movements, I think I know how sex moved, as the historian
James Reed has so memorably said about contraception, from a
question of "private vice" to one of "public virtue."

Most commentators point to key social changes that took place
in the past thirty or forty years, changes that were intertwined with
but not reducible to the sexual and gender revolutions of the 1960s
and 1970s. Much like the Progressive era, the last half-century has
been one of increasingly national rather than regional consciousness, of increased immigration, and of new forms of corporate
organization. All these forces meant that a somewhat alien culture
intruded into small towns like Billingsley, Las Colinas, and Shady
Grove. (Remember the café in Shady Grove where Hell's Angels,
farmers, and dot-commers found themselves sitting side by side,
where only a decade or so earlier, only farmers and people who made
their living from agriculture could be found?) Despite the lack of
a Starbucks and the plentiful presence of hard-shelled Southern
Baptists in Billingsley, these days satellite TV brings *The Simpsons*
and MTV even into this pocket of innocence, and on the outskirts
of town a garish adult bookstore has recently set up shop.[15]

In response to that reality, conservative Christians in Billingsley and elsewhere began to set up separate schools that embodied
their religious and cultural values, including, of course, those having to do with sex and gender. Between 1970 and 1980, for example, the number of Christian schools almost doubled.[16] To their
critics, these schools represented not so much a commitment to
common religious or cultural values as an attempt to flee recently

desegregated schools. In 1970, the IRS began to deny tax-exempt status to these Christian academies on the grounds that they were racially discriminatory. (The two eventual defendants in the resulting court case, Bob Jones University and Goldsboro Christian Academy, did in fact have policies that treated African Americans and Caucasians differently; at Bob Jones University, no interracial dating or marriage was permitted, and such activities were grounds for expulsion.)[17]

Mobilizing to protect the tax-exempt status of Christian academies is seen by many scholars as the key factor that brought conservative Christians into organized politics. Fearing the loss of this tax exemption would make these schools financially out of reach for most Christians, supporters began to protest the IRS's activities. Once mobilized, however, Christians became active across a range of political issues. The proposed Equal Rights Amendment of 1972 and the legalization of abortion in 1973 enraged those with traditional views about sex and gender, and they organized what soon became known as the pro-family movement, which was able to piggyback on existing structures (organizations, mailing lists, and the like) that had grown up to protest the withdrawal of tax exempt status for Christian schools.

Historically, sex education has always engendered some degree of opposition. When Ella Flagg Young first introduced sex hygiene to the Chicago schools in 1913, scandalized Chicagoans protested that sex was not at all something to be discussed in public.[18] Scattered protest marked sex education in the period between its institutionalization in the early years of the twentieth century and the sexual revolution of the 1960s, but such opposition was rather muted—not surprisingly, given the fundamentally conservative cast of much of the sex education of the era.

It was only when sex education moved to respond to the sexual revolution and to acknowledge that sex and marriage were two different things that opposition began to take on a national rather than local cast. In 1964, for example, a chapter of the John Birch

Society in Anaheim, California, a group of ardent anti-Communist conservatives who looked on Republican presidential candidate Barry Goldwater as far too liberal for their taste, found themselves in the national spotlight thanks to their passionate attack on sex education in the local public schools.[19] Sex education courses, they fulminated, served merely to "make sexual promiscuousness fashionable, marriage a temporary convenience, divorce commonplace, chastity a joke, and fidelity a symbol of backwardness. [They] encourage premarital sexual experiments and relations, the unlimited use of contraceptives, and a widespread resort to abortion . . . [They] *convert the sexual act from its natural reproductive function to solely a source of pleasure, without corresponding responsibility"* (emphasis mine).[20]

In the years afterward, the John Birch Society went on to found MOTOREDE, the Movement to Restore Decency, the first national group to oppose sex education.[21] In short order, the John Birch Society was joined by the militantly anti-Communist Christian Crusade and the prolific Gordon Drake, who published such books as *Is the Schoolhouse the Proper Place to Teach Raw Sex?* and the less titillatingly titled *Sex Education in the Schools*. Both groups followed staunch anti-Communist opinion in believing that sexual liberalism was a Communist plot meant to undermine the moral fiber of American society.[22]

Although historical data are lacking, it seems to me that this opposition to sex education, although national, never really gained many allies outside its own extremely conservative adherents, and it sputtered into occasional cranky letters to the editor for the better part of a decade. In fact, the period between the early 1970s and early 1980s was, as I've mentioned, a moment in which opinion leaders of almost every stripe believed that sex education was the best response to the twin problems of teenage pregnancy and HIV/AIDS.

That consensus was both brief and fragile; starting in the early 1980s, a new opposition to sex education emerged, and this one was far more formidable than that of the John Birch Society and the Christian Crusade. In the late 1960s, the latter groups, whatever their relationship to sex education, were decidedly on the fringe (some would argue the lunatic fringe) of American political debate. Yet opposition to sex education, once the purview of what was called the "radical right," moved in just a little over a decade to the center of the Republican Party.

As the gender revolution began to challenge traditional sexual as well as gender arrangements, it spawned its own opposition. Opponents of abortion, the ERA, pornography, and, increasingly, sex education began to build coalitions and to resemble a real social movement, one that its members called the "traditional values" or "social issues" coalition, when they were not calling themselves simply the pro-family movement.[23]

Central to this movement were not only newly mobilized groups of conservative Christians but groups and individuals with ties to traditional conservatism (that is, the "old" right), such as Phyllis Schlafly's Stop ERA (Schlafly had been an ardent supporter of Barry Goldwater), which subsequently became the Eagle Forum; JoAnne Gasper, the editor of *The Right Woman*; and Connaught (Connie) Marshner of the Free Congress Foundation.[24] Conservative Christians turned to these organizations to express their dismay with changes they saw around them and began to build their own organizational framework to represent Christian views as well. Dr. James Dobson, for example, founded Focus on the Family in 1977; Beverly LaHaye, the wife of the conservative Protestant activist and best-selling author Tim LaHaye, founded Concerned Women for America in 1979; and the Reverend Pat Robertson founded the Christian Coalition a decade later. (*Time* reports that Dr. Dobson's organization in Colorado Springs, Colorado, is so large that it has its own zip code.)[25]

With the rise of the pro-family movement, sex education moved onto the horizon of social conservatives. In response to Senator Edward Kennedy's landmark legislation in 1978, expanding comprehensive sex education and contraceptive services to young people in the wake of growing concern about the "epidemic" of teenage pregnancy, two conservative Republican senators, Orrin Hatch and Jeremiah Denton, sponsored the Adolescent Family Life Act (AFLA) in 1981, designed to transfer federal monies away from proponents of comprehensive sex education and toward more pro-family organizations. AFLA is where the idea of "abstinence education" made its debut on the national scene, at least as far as I can tell.

Although the amount of money spent on AFLA was tiny in comparison to the money spent over the previous decade to fund contraceptive services and education for young people, it was a strategic boost for the pro-family activists, who wanted to create alternatives to comprehensive sex education. As Connaught Marshner said in a 1988 *Conservative Digest* article, "The Adolescent Family Life Act was written expressly for the purpose of diverting [federal] money that would otherwise go to Planned Parenthood into groups with traditional values. That noble purpose has certainly been fulfilled here."[26]

AFLA money permitted networking among the like-minded and led to the development and testing of prototype programs. Themes and concepts in these prototypes became the basis of many of the abstinence-only programs that spread across the country in the 1990s and subsequently. The value of these programs cannot be overestimated. In the wake of the increasing prevalence of HIV/AIDS, when people like Jenny Letterman found themselves in the untenable position of arguing that sex education should occur only in the home, the existence of already developed sex education curricula that supported their values— "programs in a box," as they are sometimes called—was a godsend. Now Jenny could, and in fact did, argue that she was entirely in favor of sex education and understood the need for it. All she wanted was for such programs to be abstinence-only, like the popular *Sex Respect* or *True Love Waits*.

that men as well as women are encouraged to be abstinent, to take care of their children, and to eschew divorce, my interviews made it clear that when people talk about "traditional values," what they have in mind is traditional gender roles. Republicans could and did change their stance on sexual and reproductive issues— the social issues Gary Bauer mentions—because the sexual revolution created a new kind of conservative, this time a *sexual* conservative, and gender, sexuality, and marriage had become partisan issues.[38]

The existence of a well-mobilized and politically sophisticated opposition to the sexual and gender revolution in turn reenergized older organizations that had traditionally supported gender equity as embodied in birth control, abortion, the ERA, and comprehensive sex education.[39] Planned Parenthood, the Sex Information and Education Council of the United States, and the [N]ational Education Association all began to respond to the con[serv]ative grassroots activities they saw around them. New organ[izati]ons brought into being by the ERA and *Roe v. Wade*, such as [N]AL and the National Organization for Women, began to [organi]ze on issues related to sexuality as well as reproduction. [The e]xistence of these national groups made a big difference, as [I was] while listening to parents (and others) fight about sex ... Over and over again, people complained to me that the [other side] was "sneaky." Liberals thought that conservatives had [o]utsiders to help with the fight and/or had recruited [new] members of local evangelical churches, to swell the [ranks of edu]cation opponents. Conservatives thought that lib[erals were in lea]gue with school administrators and teachers and [that th]e teachers' union were secretly backing the [liberals and] tacitly undermining the message of chastity ... [Both] sides were right, of course.

[These group]s typically called on conservative organiza[tions like Focus o]n the Family and Concerned Women for [America and cons]ervative legal groups to help them with

The development of what became widely circulated (and widely implemented) abstinence-only curricula turned out to be both cause and effect, politically speaking. Federal money was available for producing abstinence-only curricula because traditional sex education programs offended sexual conservatives, who were now getting mobilized under the banner of the pro-family movement. And bringing together like-minded sexual conservatives meant that networking and coalition building among various groups could take place. The result of the process was the furthering of a new kind of conservatism, one that bridged the gap between the traditional old right and the emerging New Right. Rosalind Petchesky, one of the most astute observers of the role of sexuality in modern American politics, argued as early as 1983 that issues over sexuality could well serve as the glue to bind a new generation of conservatives together, with opposition to changes in sexual and gender roles taking on the role that anticommunism had once played in binding diverse conservative constituencies together.[27]

Although nowadays everyone assumes that the Republican Party is the natural home of those who support traditional family values, the marriage between social conservatives and the Republican Party is of relatively recent vintage. Before the sexual revolution, not many sexual (or gender) issues came to the attention of either state or federal legislators, but the few that did were more likely to find support among liberal Republicans than among Democrats. The Democratic Party, with its historically strong constituency among immigrants and workers, had reasonably close ties with the Catholic Church and generally seconded the Church's traditional family and gender attitudes. Although both parties tended to give the Church what Gene Burns has called a "moral veto," the Republicans endorsed the ERA before the Democrats did, and Republicans were traditionally much more supportive of both divorce reform and attempts to overturn the 1873 Comstock Act, which made contraception illegal.[28]

In terms of who Democrats and Republicans were before the 1960s, this made perfect sense. The Republicans were typically the party of the affluent, the well-educated, and the professional, and a certain measure of gender and sexual equality flowed from their financial and educational status. Democrats, whose working-class status inclined them to economic liberalism, were also on the whole less well educated and less affluent and more likely to expect men and women to be different rather than equal.[29]

As I discovered in an earlier research project, the legalization of abortion in 1973 was a bolt from the blue for many people who supported traditional values. Almost all of those who later went on to be antiabortion activists can remember exactly where they were when they read that *Roe v. Wade* had effectively legalized abortion.

Abortion opponents saw this Supreme Court decision as a frontal assault not only on innocent human life as they had always understood it, but also on family and gender arrangements that they had long taken for granted. And slowly, like battleships at sea, the two parties began to respond. Before 1980, Republicans were almost as likely as Democrats to cast votes in favor of abortion rights, and conservative Democrats, still connected to working-class and Catholic voters, were as likely as Republicans to oppose abortion.[30] After 1980, however, "issue evolution" began to occur, as a pro-choice position became almost a requirement to run for office as a Democrat and a pro-life position became almost the sine qua non of being a Republican. Increasingly, moderate Republicans began to vote Democratic and conservative Democrats became the much-discussed "Reagan Democrats."[31]

Over time, conservative Catholics and evangelical Protestants began to move into the Republican camp, a process predicted by the conservative strategist Kevin Phillips as early as 1969.[32] A fundamental realignment of the two parties was taking place, and both race and sex were at the heart of it.[33] By the end of the 1970s, Republicans and Democrats, who began the decade almost evenly

split among themselves on abortion, had started to vote along party lines 80 percent of the time, with Republicans consistently opposing abortion and Democrats supporting it.[34]

As the parties began to polarize on abortion and subsequently on other gender and sexuality issues, including contraception, homosexuality, and sex education, there was a corresponding shift in the makeup of the typical Republican and Democratic voter and of the constituencies the parties spoke to.[35] Greg Adams, who has traced the issue evolution of abortion, argues that his data (bas on all congressional votes on abortion between 1973 and show that the changes began first at the level of Congress, w lic opinion following rather than leading congressional

As Gary Bauer, another astute political observer, ar

Clearly the landscape has changed. In the lifet ple here today, American conservatism h philosophy embraced only by a hand intellectuals and Western-style pol that put a president into office . . . cal eminence in the late sevent together a political coalitior "economic," "foreign po as I prefer to phrase and traditional valu brought us to deserves to b may unrav as less e the s P suc

But these
discussion of the

In terms of who Democrats and Republicans were before the 1960s, this made perfect sense. The Republicans were typically the party of the affluent, the well-educated, and the professional, and a certain measure of gender and sexual equality flowed from their financial and educational status. Democrats, whose working-class status inclined them to economic liberalism, were also on the whole less well educated and less affluent and more likely to expect men and women to be different rather than equal.[29]

As I discovered in an earlier research project, the legalization of abortion in 1973 was a bolt from the blue for many people who supported traditional values. Almost all of those who later went on to be antiabortion activists can remember exactly where they were when they read that *Roe v. Wade* had effectively legalized abortion.

Abortion opponents saw this Supreme Court decision as a frontal assault not only on innocent human life as they had always understood it, but also on family and gender arrangements that they had long taken for granted. And slowly, like battleships at sea, the two parties began to respond. Before 1980, Republicans were almost as likely as Democrats to cast votes in favor of abortion rights, and conservative Democrats, still connected to working-class and Catholic voters, were as likely as Republicans to oppose abortion.[30] After 1980, however, "issue evolution" began to occur, as a pro-choice position became almost a requirement to run for office as a Democrat and a pro-life position became almost the sine qua non of being a Republican. Increasingly, moderate Republicans began to vote Democratic and conservative Democrats became the much-discussed "Reagan Democrats."[31]

Over time, conservative Catholics and evangelical Protestants began to move into the Republican camp, a process predicted by the conservative strategist Kevin Phillips as early as 1969.[32] A fundamental realignment of the two parties was taking place, and both race and sex were at the heart of it.[33] By the end of the 1970s, Republicans and Democrats, who began the decade almost evenly

The development of what became widely circulated (and widely implemented) abstinence-only curricula turned out to be both cause and effect, politically speaking. Federal money was available for producing abstinence-only curricula because traditional sex education programs offended sexual conservatives, who were now getting mobilized under the banner of the pro-family movement. And bringing together like-minded sexual conservatives meant that networking and coalition building among various groups could take place. The result of the process was the furthering of a new kind of conservatism, one that bridged the gap between the traditional old right and the emerging New Right. Rosalind Petchesky, one of the most astute observers of the role of sexuality in modern American politics, argued as early as 1983 that issues over sexuality could well serve as the glue to bind a new generation of conservatives together, with opposition to changes in sexual and gender roles taking on the role that anticommunism had once played in binding diverse conservative constituencies together.[27]

Although nowadays everyone assumes that the Republican Party is the natural home of those who support traditional family values, the marriage between social conservatives and the Republican Party is of relatively recent vintage. Before the sexual revolution, not many sexual (or gender) issues came to the attention of either state or federal legislators, but the few that did were more likely to find support among liberal Republicans than among Democrats. The Democratic Party, with its historically strong constituency among immigrants and workers, had reasonably close ties with the Catholic Church and generally seconded the Church's traditional family and gender attitudes. Although both parties tended to give the Church what Gene Burns has called a "moral veto," the Republicans endorsed the ERA before the Democrats did, and Republicans were traditionally much more supportive of both divorce reform and attempts to overturn the 1873 Comstock Act, which made contraception illegal.[28]

split among themselves on abortion, had started to vote along party lines 80 percent of the time, with Republicans consistently opposing abortion and Democrats supporting it.[34]

As the parties began to polarize on abortion and subsequently on other gender and sexuality issues, including contraception, homosexuality, and sex education, there was a corresponding shift in the makeup of the typical Republican and Democratic voter and of the constituencies the parties spoke to.[35] Greg Adams, who has traced the issue evolution of abortion, argues that his data (based on all congressional votes on abortion between 1973 and 1994) show that the changes began first at the level of Congress, with public opinion following rather than leading congressional votes.[36]

As Gary Bauer, another astute political observer, argued in 1989:

> Clearly the landscape has changed. In the lifetimes of most people here today, American conservatism has developed from a philosophy embraced only by a handful of *National Review* intellectuals and Western-style politicians into a movement that put a president into office . . . Conservatism rose to political eminence in the late seventies because we were able to put together a political coalition built around a strategic cluster of "economic," "foreign policy/defense," and "social" issues—or, as I prefer to phrase them: free enterprise, anti-communism, and traditional values . . . This issue-mix is basically sound. It brought us to the great watershed election of 1980, and it deserves to be kept more or less intact . . . However, I fear it may unravel because some members of the coalition are treated as less equal than others. In a word, it is time to stop assigning the social and family issues to the back of the policy bus . . . Politically, the conservative movement was nowhere before it successfully reached out to social-issue voters.[37]

But these "social issues" have a special edge. While much of the discussion of the traditional family is formally gender-neutral, in that men as well as women are encouraged to be abstinent, to take care of their children, and to eschew divorce, my interviews made it clear that when people talk about "traditional values," what they have in mind is traditional gender roles. Republicans could and did change their stance on sexual and reproductive issues— the social issues Gary Bauer mentions—because the sexual revolution created a new kind of conservative, this time a *sexual* conservative, and gender, sexuality, and marriage had become partisan issues.[38]

The existence of a well-mobilized and politically sophisticated opposition to the sexual and gender revolution in turn reenergized older organizations that had traditionally supported gender equity as embodied in birth control, abortion, the ERA, and comprehensive sex education.[39] Planned Parenthood, the Sex Information and Education Council of the United States, and the National Education Association all began to respond to the conservative grassroots activities they saw around them. New organizations brought into being by the ERA and *Roe v. Wade*, such as NARAL and the National Organization for Women, began to mobilize on issues related to sexuality as well as reproduction.

The existence of these national groups made a big difference, as I found while listening to parents (and others) fight about sex education. Over and over again, people complained to me that the other side was "sneaky." Liberals thought that conservatives had brought in outsiders to help with the fight and/or had recruited people, such as members of local evangelical churches, to swell the ranks of sex education opponents. Conservatives thought that liberals were in league with school administrators and teachers and that evil forces like the teachers' union were secretly backing the liberal parents and tacitly undermining the message of chastity until marriage. Both sides were right, of course.

Sexual conservatives typically called on conservative organizations such as Focus on the Family and Concerned Women for America as well as conservative legal groups to help them with what philanthropic foundations call "technical support." Having a keen awareness that it makes no sense to reinvent the wheel, conservative parents in all four of the communities I studied quickly found national resources to help them with talking points, speaker education, and curricula that they could propose to replace a curriculum that did not represent their values.

The liberals did the same thing. They didn't have to do it quite as much, because in fact the conservatives were right in perceiving a certain attitudinal symmetry between liberal parents and the school system. In terms of the issues discussed earlier in this book, teachers and school administrators are generally in favor of more information, not less. The canonical virtues of the sex education curriculum as it emerged before World War I and was transmuted in the 1960s were and still are broadly consonant with the overarching values of most schools—the ideas of citizenship, critical thinking, and what the hygienists called "worthy home membership." Conservative parents understood this intuitively, as indicated by their frequent denunciations of John Dewey when we spoke. Although Dewey is coming back into vogue among academics, I suspect that most sexually liberal people and those involved in the school system recognized the name—if at all—only as a historical figure, a philosopher, and a friend of the social activist Jane Addams. Certain broad cultural values associated with Dewey's name, however—the commitment to the worth of value neutrality, if not value neutrality itself; the idea that if young people are given all the facts, they will make the right decisions; the idea that young people are innately good and valuable citizens in the making and need only the proper environment in which to flourish—are deeply embedded in most American public schools.

So sexual liberals probably felt they needed less outside support and advice than the conservatives did, because they and the school held many values in common. Probably because of these shared values, liberal parents were more likely to have been actively involved with the schools, as volunteers, mentors, and active PTA members, than the conservatives, and so they had closer social ties to the school and its administration. But that didn't mean that sexual liberals hesitated to call on Planned Parenthood, People for the American Way, or other such groups, and they did so for the same reason that the sexual conservatives did—they wanted to know what had and had not worked in other communities facing this same fight. All this is by way of saying that people soon gave up the hope of having a meeting of the minds with the opposition.

This brings us back to the main point: whatever organizations people turn to, different groups in our society have emotionally powerful reasons for supporting either a "traditional" or an "equal rights" view of gender and marriage. In part this is because of where and how they grew up, and in part it's because more and more people find the pace of rapid change in the world at large, as well as in the relations between men and women and between parents and children, unsettling.

For reasons explored earlier, the latter group may well be growing. The decline of stable working-class jobs makes marriage more and more of a luxury among poor people, and the affluent are waiting longer and longer to marry, as they get more education, travel, and enjoy themselves before settling down. So marriage is being cramped at both the top and the bottom—poor people can't afford it, and affluent people have all the benefits of it without any of the obligations for years of their adult lives. No wonder people whose values and life experiences have convinced them that traditional marriage is the best and most satisfying option for women (and men) want social policies that promote what they see as a profoundly threatened institution. Whether it's President Bush's plan to teach poor people the benefits of marriage or policies to stigmatize sex outside marriage, people like Jenny Letterman think marriage needs all the help it can get, and I think she's right.

Let me make this point in a different way. We are living in a globalizing culture, in which people's cherished beliefs are challenged as they never were before. My colleague Fred Block suggests that as nations join global communities and economies, local political figures are far less able to protect their citizens from the financial (and I would say cultural) buffeting that becoming part of a whole new system incurs.[40] When people feel less protected by the powers that be, they tend to polarize, to have less faith in a common middle ground.

Sexual conservatives want to turn the clock back to a period when there were sharp boundaries between entities, when there was an organizational chart of life and you knew where you fit. Family structure of that era both symbolized that world and embodied it on a daily basis. At least as a cherished cultural norm (I'm less sure about the lived reality of that era), men worked, women stayed home and took care of their families, and children obeyed their parents. But in our new world, as the epigraph of this book suggests, we are all immigrants to the future, and the children are learning the language much faster than the rest of us.

This is happening on a worldwide basis, not just here in the United States. Whatever it is about women as individuals in themselves and women within families, about authority versus consultation, about bright lines and hierarchies versus egalitarian networks, these issues are dividing the whole world, not just our country.

The political scientists Ronald Inglehart and Pippa Norris have undertaken an analysis of the World Values Survey, a large multinational public opinion poll, and have come to the conclusion that attitudes toward women, family, and sexuality are more strongly associated with a commitment to democracy than any other values they tracked. On the international plane, the people whose values most resemble those of the people in this book I have called sexual liberals. They are likely to be supporters of democracy on the international scene, while sexual conservatives are not. Samuel Huntington's much-vaunted "clash of civilizations," which posited that the struggle for the future would be between Islam and the West, was half right. There is a clash, but it's about equality versus hierarchy, something that is most visible when people think about women's roles and the family. The struggle between the sexual conservatives and sexual liberals with whom I spoke is being played out on a global scale, and every major religion has spawned a fundamentalist branch that defines itself by traditional values, and those values, along with religion, are almost exclusively about women, sex, and the family.[41]

It's clear from my interviews that boundaries and hierarchies are in the end one of the main fault lines along which liberals and conservatives divide, so I suspect it makes sense that as countries slowly merge into supranational entities such as the European Union; the "little commonwealths" of the family bring the issue of boundaries home with particular sharpness, separating those who want a bounded, protected family from those who want a flexible one. Even in the early 1980s, the people I spoke with were worried about globalization and the merging of boundaries at home (in the most literal sense of the word) and abroad.

The sexual right and left are therefore driving political conflicts across the world as well as in American political life. Thomas Edsall, for example, has pointed out that five questions about sexuality predicted votes in the Bush vs. Clinton election of 1992 better than any other factor except party affiliation and race—quite an accomplishment, given that African Americans are committed to the Democratic Party at very high rates.[42] I suspect that this is just an American example of what is being played out on the global scene.

So sex and politics are finding themselves entwined in a globalizing culture. The people who participated in this study have reasons upon reasons to feel the way they do. For a small but significant group of sexual conservatives, the blurring of boundaries that has occurred over the past thirty years has been enormously destructive. They feel as if they have emerged more or less intact by the skin of their teeth, so the formation and protection of boundaries in an increasingly boundaryless world has special importance for them.

For other conservatives, including those who strayed and came back, religious faith provides both boundaries and a community that supports those boundaries. And life within those boundaries is more comfortable than it is outside them.

If what is at stake is both a real and a metaphorical attempt to manage one of the largest and most pervasive cultural, social, political, and economic shifts of our times within the intimate realm of the family—a shift that in the end might well rival "the great transformation" that turned the agricultural world into the industrial world—you can imagine that it might be difficult to get opposing sides to sit down and come up with a working plan that meets all their needs.[43] The long history of sex as a divisive issue in American society, where attitudes toward sexuality are shaped by race, class, religion, and religiosity, means that coming up with the kind of consensual sex education programs that more homogeneous European countries take for granted is probably not in the cards.

In both France and Sweden, I interviewed members of the tiny antiabortion movement (movements that are inspired by and often financially aided by their American colleagues), and all of them were resigned to being what they thought of as a voice of conscience rather than a force for change. One well-dressed Parisienne, a member of Laissez-les Vivre (Let Them Live, a French right-to-life group), told me of her efforts to counsel women who were seeking abortions. She would tell them of the very generous options the French government offers to women who want to continue their pregnancies and then watch helplessly as they opted for abortion anyway. Shrugging her Chanel-clad shoulders, she said, "What can you do? They're adults"—a position of world-weary resignation that I have never encountered when interviewing American right-to-life "crisis pregnancy" counselors.

So here I am, having spent the better part of twenty years talking to people about sex education, and here's what I've learned. I think that both sides have something important to tell us about how to live in ways that do the least possible damage to ourselves and others. If this is a case of "going native," so be it. I think that the sexual conservatives, like my sociological predecessor Emile Durkheim, understand that morality is not only personal but deeply social as well. And I think the liberals are on to something when they insist on having faith in our fellow human beings. Their belief that more information will solve major problems means that in their hearts they cherish the belief that we can decide to do good. I find their faith inspiring, as is the more obvious faith of those on the other side. If you put me in a corner and asked whether I wanted to go through life treating my fellow citizens as potential evildoers or as basically good but misguided human beings, I think I would opt to think of my fellow men and women as basically good, not evil, even given the evil that I have seen in my own heart and my own lifetime.

But I would do so cautiously. That's the rub, isn't it? The world is filled with good and bad people, as I tell my children, and although I haven't gotten around to it yet, I will also tell them that the world is filled with people who are a mixture of good and bad. The great sociologist of morality Zygmunt Bauman wrote of people who had the misfortune to be on planes that were hijacked. After their release, a surprising number of couples divorced, presumably because under the extreme stress of the hijacking, they saw cowardice and perfidy in their partners they could not accept. Bauman makes the point that these people were not inherently cowardly or evil. If the hijacking had not happened, they might well have gone to their graves as happy, successful, moral citizens with blameless records of no harm to themselves or others.[44] Another friend tells me that the correct translation of the Lord's Prayer asks not that we not be led into temptation but that we not be *tested*. Both the conservatives and the liberals have a point: there is much to admire in human beings, and a good society is arranged so that as few of its citizens as possible are tested in the way that the original version of the Lord's Prayer (or Bauman's story of hijackers) implies.

For obvious reasons, people are more moral and committed to the welfare of others when they live where there are ample social and cultural supports for altruism. I myself long for some of the boundaries (and even hierarchies) that the conservatives miss so painfully.

It's not at all surprising that as the world becomes more and more a market, people long to protect and preserve places that the market does not penetrate. I teach in a university where law and economics have become one of the most energized intellectual fields, and the whole point of the enterprise, as far as I can tell, is to reduce complex social and moral transactions to just that— transactions. (A tipoff is that economists have just begun to worry about "norms"—about why people keep their promises and do things that are not in their immediate self-interest. Sociologists have been worrying about norms for over a century.)

But one of the hierarchies is the one that makes women responsible for morality and caring while men are (relatively) self-centered in the larger world of the market. I find it hard to imagine and would vigorously resist a stratified society like the one that existed in this country until the 1950s, where women knew just what they would do when they grew up, which was be wives and mothers, and where ruthless ambition, self-centeredness, and take-no-prisoners action were strictly limited to men; where people of color knew their place and whites never thought of themselves as especially privileged; and where children were seen and not heard. In that world, women, people of color, and children were simultaneously valued and devalued for their unworldliness, but the value was of a second-class kind.

As a sociologist, I know that projects to turn back the clock are always doomed to failure. One can never rerun the past as it was, and it is not even clear that we can remember the past as it was in a totally accurate way. As my postmodernist graduate students tell me, the best that we can have is a representation of the past.

So the wish to bring back the sexual and moral certainties of the fifties is almost certainly guaranteed to remain a wish. This is not to deny that in terms of a sexual spectrum, things have moved a great deal to the right in the past twenty years, as sexual conservatives have mobilized over abortion, contraception, and sex education. Sex education teachers no longer assume that their mostly liberal values are shared by everyone. They know that sex is controversial, and they tend to restrict themselves to some of the more clinical and sometimes boring aspects of sexuality. We rarely hear people speaking of abortion as a good thing (something that was a common part of rhetoric in the 1970s and 1980s); we hear it spoken of as a necessary evil, even by militant feminists. And sexual liberals now reluctantly concede that abstinence is the best choice for teenagers, something that was not part of their thinking even two decades ago.

I've spent a lot of time talking informally to young men and women, and my sense is that they too are worried about a world that seems to be coming undone. But it seems to me that some young women may use the rhetoric of abstinence to carve out a zone of sexual autonomy, a place where they have a perfectly good reason to tell young men that they are not ready for or willing to have sexual relations. And we are beginning to see from national data that young women are more likely to choose abstinence than they used to be. It also strikes me that their commitment to abstinence may not necessarily be based on a total endorsement of the values that the sexual conservatives support, and it is by no means a commitment to abstinence until marriage, but it still serves deep emotional and social needs. So what if it doesn't last until marriage? I believe that abstinence and sexual autonomy—the ability to make choices, including the choice not to be sexually active—can and do go together.

So what to think? I don't know. But I do have some ideas about what to *do*. First, when communities confront the issue of sex education, the educational authorities should consult parents with children in the affected schools more assiduously than they consult people who want to use the school to make a larger political or moral point. While it is perfectly acceptable for those who do not have children in the school that is debating sex education to share their thoughts and wishes with the local school board (schools are, after all, public institutions), special pains should be taken to find out what the parents of the school's children want. At a minimum, these parents need to know where everyone stands.

Yet in none of the four communities in which I watched the process unfold did any school board member ever ask speakers the simple questions: How many children do you have? How old are they? What schools do they attend? These questions differentiate between those who have children in the local schools and those who have no children or grown children or children in private Christian schools or children who are being home-schooled. While all of these people are entitled to have an opinion, everyone in the room should know which parents are most directly affected and which are speaking about "children" in the abstract rather than their own children.

A second option is for schools to poll all the parents, not just the activists, to register their views. Reasonably inexpensive technology makes this a possibility.

A third, and more costly, option is to provide safe places where parents (and only parents) can talk about what they want for their children when it comes to sex education. Although I have argued that the divisions in American society mean that we are unlikely as a society to come to a meeting of the minds, this does not necessarily mean that smaller groups, such as interested parents who have children attending a specific school, cannot. If these people can discuss questions such as What are the deep values at stake? What is a moral child? What problems do people see in their community and school, and how do they imagine that sex education (or the lack of it) will affect those problems? they might be able to find some common ground.[45]

Having sat through many years of interviews, I doubt that parents can navigate these issues very well on their own. Schools would have to provide facilitators acceptable to both sides, people who could help parents manage the rage and anxiety that this issue evokes. Finding such people (and getting parents to agree that they are acceptable) is a time-consuming and expensive task. However, my observations suggest that it just might be worth it, since once the issue has been ignited, very few teachers, administrators, or committed parents can do much until it is resolved one way or another.

Finally, and most radically, schools can do what at least one school district has already done: provide both a sexually conservative (abstinence-only) and a sexually liberal (comprehensive) curriculum, side by side, and let parents and students choose between them.[46]

On a larger plane, we as a society can do at least two other things. First, we can remember that what is really being debated here are the meanings of sex, gender, and family, as embodied most clearly in the institution of marriage. We live in a society that is becoming two-tier in several ways. The notion of class is becoming muddled as we move into a global economy, but we do have some evidence that the "middling classes," as the Victorians called them, are "hollowing out," as some people become much wealthier and others move down into the lower middle class.[47] There is also some evidence that marriage and family are becoming two-tier as well, with some people opting for marriage (and first birth) before investing in extended education and others delaying. In short, some are "privileging" family over career, while others are— at least for a time—privileging career over family.

In the end, much of the fight over sex education is a fight about the moral worth of two different trajectories of human life. Abstinence-until-marriage sex education presumes that people will marry relatively young and enhances the status of marriage by marking it as the only socially legitimate place to have sex. Comprehensive sex education, on the other hand, presumes that marriage will happen later in life, after people have prepared for a career.

Scholarly advocates of marriage argue that marriage has many unique benefits for its participants. As someone who has been happily married for more than two decades, I couldn't agree more. But these same advocates implicitly and sometimes explicitly argue that marriage can work its magic only when it is socially defined as the single acceptable place for sexual activity.[48]

This flies in the face of the fact that all over Europe and the United States, marriage is fading in prominence. Half of all babies conceived in the United States today are conceived by unmarried parents, and this figure is actually lower than the figure in many other countries, including those that we don't think of as particularly liberal, such as England. Also, I see no confirming evidence (except, of course, for the looming presence of Emile Durkheim, who argues that social forms have their own power over social behavior) that marriage can be socially productive only when other forms of relationships are stigmatized. So rather than arguing about sex, and adolescent sex at that, perhaps we would find it more profitable to talk about marriage—what we think about it, who should enter it, and when in the life cycle it should take place.

The other thing we can do on the grand scale is to try to articulate an affirmative vision of sexual morality. Conservative parents are clear that moral sex is married sex. It's obvious that the equation runs one way—unmarried sex is by definition immoral sex—but does it run the other way? Is all married sex a priori moral sex? What would moral sex within marriage look like?[49]

In contrast, as we've seen, sexual liberals do not think that marriage is the boundary between moral and immoral sex. But what makes sex moral for them? Some of the parents I spoke with had a very hard time articulating an answer, using very general terms about nonexploitative and mutually pleasurable sex, and seemed to think that children would just understand what was and was not moral behavior in the sexual realm.

Given our earlier discussion of how unpredictable social life is, none of us can predict the outcome of defining sexual morality more clearly. But at a minimum, it meets the needs of some parents and some young people, and it certainly enlarges the field for interesting dialogue.

This strategy may not be very popular with sexually conservative parents, as it is clearly based on the liberal idea that students can profitably use information once parents have instilled the proper moral guidelines. (This is the pattern vis-à-vis information that I earlier called programmer parents.) Sexually conservative parents, who believe that false information, or information at odds with what they believe, can lead children astray (the pattern I called gatekeeper parents), are going to worry that their children may hear things that are at odds with what they hear at home.

But the reality appears to be that parents who want young people to hear only about abstinence are in a minority. While almost all parents think that abstinence is a good thing, particularly among high school students, they don't agree with the basic premise that if young people hear nothing (or only bad things) about contraception, they will be safe. On the contrary, parents believe (and limited research seems to indicate) that teaching only about abstinence tends to lower contraceptive use when students become sexually active.

Which takes us back to the Swedes and the French. It seems to me—although again, I have only the data from my interviews to make this claim—that sex in those countries is relatively unproblematic for young people because both countries, despite their very different levels of sex education, have essentially been monocultures when it comes to sexual morality. What I mean by that (and "monoculture" is a term I borrowed from the Swedish sex education curriculum) is that young people in France and Sweden have heard the same values about sex from their parents, the media, the schools, and their peers. Even the relatively few sexual conservatives in those countries accept that they are a minority and must bow to the will of the majority. Because both countries have historically been quite homogeneous, sex has not become a vehicle for drawing boundaries, as it were, between different kinds of people, between the religious and the secular or between Catholics and Protestants.[50]

But all of that is changing. Both France and Sweden have recently faced waves of immigration, and many of the immigrants have come from parts of the world where attitudes toward sex, family, and gender are still quite traditional.[51] So as France (and to a lesser extent Sweden) considers the emotionally powerful question of whether girls can wear headscarves to school, we can imagine a not-too-distant future in which sex and sexuality become, like scarves, a boundary separating "us" from "them."

And then, as odd as it may seem, the European countries may turn to the United States, once the example of what any respectable sex educator in Europe did *not* want to be, as the leader. If we are all immigrants to the future, it may turn out that America, with its commitment to diversity, may be the model.

CHAPTER NINE

Sex Education in America and Whether It Works or Doesn't—and Why That's Not the Right Question

This book argues that sex education is now and always has been about sex and its relation to marriage, and that being about sex and marriage in turn is always about gender. In the course of the preceding chapters, we've seen how sex education developed in the early 1900s as a way of dealing with a perceived crisis in marriage, and how the kind of sex education that has been dominant for much of the past thirty or so years was in turn a response to the sexual and gender revolutions of the 1960s. In the rise of the abstinence-only movement, we see the tracks of a counterrevolution, one that attempts to turn back the events of the 1960s.

Essentially, the debate about sex education right now is a debate about values, but as is often the case in America, questions about values get obscured in the public arena by questions about practicalities. The most critical one is, does sex education work? (In this context, I mean comprehensive sex education.) Does it, as its supporters claim, encourage young people to be careful in their sexuality, permitting them to explore their sexuality in ways that their grandparents and great-grandparents could never have imagined? Or does sex education have, as supporters of abstinence have claimed, a tragically perverse effect? Does the mere existence of sex education, which normalizes the idea of adolescent sexuality, encourage young people to be sexual outside marriage, leading to all the heartbreak and other consequences, from AIDS to abortion to babies born out of wedlock, that can follow in the wake of immature sex?[1]

I hope that framing the question this way clarifies that it all depends on your point of view. If you believe that sex before marriage is morally wrong, you will naturally point to the incapacity of sex education to make sex for adolescents 100 percent safe 100 percent of the time. If you think that sex between consenting partners, married or not, is a praiseworthy or at least acceptable form of sexual conduct, you will argue that sex education has made that conduct much, much safer than it used to be.

Perhaps an analogy will make the point more dramatically. Imagine that you are an ardent environmentalist, one who believes that the worst thing that ever happened was Henry Ford's devilish invention of the motorcar. You would be on firm statistical ground in arguing that cars not only pollute the environment but are one of the major causes of death and disability in our society. You would point out that injuries connected to cars caused four and a half million visits to emergency rooms and 42,000 deaths in 2000. Cars, you would say, are toxic and deadly and should be abolished.[2]

Now imagine that you are a suburban mother commuting on the highway every day. While you might well hate Henry Ford for your own reasons, mass transit for you, as for many other busy Americans, is not a practical or even a desired option, except perhaps in the abstract. You may not have access to good public transportation, and more to the point, you and your fellow Americans have proved over and over again that you prefer the comfort and convenience of the polluting, death-dealing private automobile. As you chauffeur your kids to soccer or find yourself stuck in traffic, you point to the increases in traffic safety brought about by accomplishments in highway engineering, safety belts, child safety seats, and automobile redesign over the past quarter of a century. You and the environmentalist may never agree, because at heart you are debating about *values,* not facts.

So it is with sex and teenagers. Starting somewhere in the late 1960s, as I've argued over the course of this book, sex education began to reject the double standard and move to what we might think of as an equality model of sexuality. This was a profound, indeed historic, shift in values, although a good case can be made that sex education followed changes in public opinion rather than driving them. More to the point, this shift in values was so taken for granted, so much a part of the temper of the times, that few people noticed that the terms of the debate were changing. A few, mostly on the far right, remarked on the changes, but their claims that sex education was the road to moral perdition and, worse yet, communism were mostly greeted with derision.

Now, some thirty years later, the values at the heart of the sexual revolution are being fought over again, and what is being contested is the proper relationship of sex to marriage and of men to women. But the contest is still largely being conducted in the language laid down by the terms of the 1960s. Since the sex education of that era assumed that each individual would make a choice about what form of sexual expression was best for himself or herself, the language of how to assess sex education became one of what we nowadays would call harm reduction. The key question for people who subscribed to this model was, as you might expect, how much harm was avoided by teaching people about sex? In other words, how many individuals were able to have healthy sexual relationships without becoming unexpectedly pregnant? How many were able to have sex without transmitting a sexual disease or unintentionally making each other pregnant? (Here, as in much of the rest of the book, I am restricting myself to heterosexuality, as the public discussion itself did.) From the vantage point of this harm-reduction model, the heyday of sex education paralleled spectacular rates of harm reduction, at least when it came to pregnancy. Between 1972 and 1990, the odds that a sexually active teenage girl would become pregnant dropped by more than 25 percent.[3]

Abstinence-only education, however, rejects the core principle on which the harm-reduction model is based: that each individual should decide for himself or herself what is proper sexual behavior. Instead, it substitutes a single value for everyone, namely, no sex outside (heterosexual) marriage. But abstinence supporters too continue to make their case in terms of harm reduction, perhaps because the premise that all sex before marriage is morally wrong seems to smack too much of traditional religious doctrines. Accordingly, abstinence-only educators make the unimpeachable claim that virginity before marriage and monogamy afterward are the only truly effective ways to prevent unwed pregnancy (and most sexual diseases as well).[4]

But that's not really the point. Talk to abstinence educators carefully, or to parents who support abstinence education, and it becomes clear that even if there were to be an unexpected flowering of contraceptive and prophylactic technology so that every unmarried person could have sex with no fear of pregnancy or disease, abstinence proponents wouldn't be mollified. The harms they worry about go beyond pregnancy and disease to include social, psychological, and, most important, moral harms, and these harms cannot be addressed by technology. (As we have seen, the devaluation of marriage that sexual conservatives see in comprehensive sex education strikes them as a moral harm.) To treat men and women as sexually equal, to treat sex as a pleasure rather than the reward for the duty of marriage, they argue, is to imperil individual happiness and the future of society itself.

In the end, I'm not sure how one would go about assessing such subtle social and moral harms, particularly those to the society as a whole. But abstinence advocates, much like sex educators of the comprehensive sort, find themselves making claims about whether their programs increase or decrease the likelihood of teen sex or increase or decrease teenagers' willingness to use contraceptives or condoms, but they do so against the backdrop of unexamined assumptions about values. Convincing an entire generation of young people to be abstinent before marriage, like creating an entire generation of fully educated and sexually competent decision-makers, would be a good thing in terms of the outcomes we worry about, should either outcome become, against all odds, a realistic possibility. Yet neither seems likely to happen in the near future, which leaves us to assess how effective the two kinds of programs are as second-best alternatives. However, precisely because abstinence advocates and comprehensive sex education proponents are committed to the worth of their programs, very little critical self-assessment goes into their claims about how effective their programs are.

Whether or not either kind of sex education works in some broad sense is probably the main thing that most people not directly involved in the debate want to know. That answer is precisely what the current controversy is hard pressed to deliver.

Not only is the debate about sex education based on different but unarticulated views about the relationship of sex to marriage, it also evaluates interventions in light of those values, at the same time mixing together different kinds of harm, because the harms themselves are based on different views of the proper relationship of sex to marriage.[5] Abstinence advocates, for example, argue that if we could just turn all sex education classes into abstinence-only classes, abstinence would increase among teenagers and young adults, and as a result, rates of teen pregnancies, births, and abortions, not to mention sexual diseases, would plummet. Fair enough. They then typically go on make three more crucial claims: first, that comprehensive sex education has led to an increase in the number of sexually active teenagers; second, that no contraceptive or prophylactic is 100 percent effective; and finally and most centrally, that to teach young people about contraception is to undercut the effectiveness of the abstinence message.

Advocates of comprehensive sex education dispute the claim that it increases the likelihood of teen sex and are, to say the least, extremely doubtful that abstinence programs can reduce rates of sexual activity among teenagers. They point out that unless sex education is completely effective in persuading adolescents to be abstinent all of the time, there will still be large numbers of sexually active teens, and because abstinence education withholds information about pregnancy and disease prevention, these teens who do go on to have sex will be less protected than they are now, and hence pregnancy, birth, abortion, and sexually transmitted diseases are likely to increase. Standing on firm ground in terms of logic, comprehensive sex education supporters point out that few educational programs are capable of persuading people to be 100 percent effective at *anything*, and there is little evidence to date that abstinence-only programs will be different.[6]

In the broad strokes of the debate as it is conducted in the political arena, these are hard claims to sort though. We do know, as the supporters of comprehensive sex education are happy to hear, that few programs are capable of delivering the kinds of substantial changes in human behavior that abstinence-only programs are based on—but the exact same thing can be said of some of the more optimistic claims that comprehensive sex educators sometimes make about their own programs. We also know (of comfort to the abstinence-only crowd) that there is some evidence from other realms of behavior that the safer that people think an activity is, the more likely they are to engage in it.

Although sex education advocates of all stripes are really concerned with values, the problem of assessing practical harms is complicated by the fact that both sides mix together different kinds of practical harms. When the abstinence people argue that by making adolescent and unmarried sex seem safer than it really is, comprehensive sex education serves to increase the number of teens who have sex, they are making an argument about how common, or *prevalent,* a behavior is. When they claim that there is no such thing as "safe" sex, that no contraceptive is 100 percent effective in preventing pregnancy, they are making a claim about *individual* risk. Implicit but unexamined, therefore, are assumptions about total risk, or the level of individual risk multiplied by the prevalence, yielding the total number of people engaging in a given level of risk.

Likewise, when comprehensive sex educators say that there is little or no evidence that abstinence programs actually produce abstinence, they too are making a claim about prevalence, this time that abstinence will not reduce the numbers of sexually active teens in any significant way. When they worry that abstinence-only pro-grams stress abstinence as a moral value while withholding infor-mation about pregnancy and disease prevention, they are making a claim about an increase in individual risk. (Specifically, they worry that abstinence education will increase rates of individual risk by making individuals less likely to use effective contracep-tion and/or condoms, because their abstinence training has left them ashamed to use these strategies and because it has withheld information on where to get them and how effective they really are.) Implicitly, advocates of comprehensive sex education are making a claim about total risk as well.

The debate about sex education both in the public arena and in the four communities that I studied is muddled in a number of ways. Over and over again I heard the same kinds of confusion that my reading of the public debate reveals.[7] It implicitly com-pares moral harms (which are very hard to define, much less to measure) to practical harms. On the level of practical harms, it confounds claims about prevalence with claims about individual risk. And finally, advocates selectively showcase data on either prevalence or individual risk to make the claim that the program of the other side will lead to increased overall risks for teens and other unmarried people.

Thinking through the claims of the two sides, however, means sorting out as best we can what we know about adolescent sexual-ity, now and in the recent past, and the effects of a range of inter-ventions, both abstinence-only and comprehensive, on shaping and changing that sexuality.

I am going to forgo the classic academic cautions about how lit-tle we know and how skimpy and inadequate the data are. Let's just stipulate that when it comes to sex and especially sex among young people, we have very little unimpeachable information. Sex and all the behaviors that surround it are intimate and, as the psy-chologists would say, overdetermined social behaviors, in that a great many things affect them at the same time. They are almost impossible to measure accurately. Unless we look at things like pregnancies and births, which are themselves surprisingly difficult to measure accurately, we have to depend on self-reports, and self-reports are notoriously unreliable.

For example, we have to ask people if they have (a) engaged in sex and, if so, (b) used birth control and/or (c) used condoms to prevent disease. The problem here is that the content of these programs may affect the accurate reporting of what young people are actually doing. For example, it is reasonable to think that young people who have taken a fairly directive sex education course, whether of the abstinence kind ("You shouldn't have sex before marriage") or the comprehensive kind ("You shouldn't have sex without protecting yourself and your partner"), may well perceive social pressure to underreport how much sex they are actually having, or, conversely, to overreport how safe that sex was. Worse yet, it's not entirely clear that teenagers as a group think about sex in the same categories used by the people who design the questions. Many teenagers, for example, don't think that oral sex is sex.[8]

Also, we are trying to assess the effects of a single factor—exposure to sex education—at a time when many other things are impinging on sexual behavior as well. A well-researched body of literature, for example, suggests that the economy has an effect on adolescent risk-taking across a range of behaviors, and surely HIV/AIDS has had a powerful effect on how all of us think and act in the sexual realm.[9]

Finally, "sex education" is an incredibly motley grab bag of experiences. Although we don't have anything like the kinds of good data we would like about sex education of either variety, we do know that there is tremendous variation. In contrast to France, where the minister of education reportedly once pointed to his watch and claimed that he knew exactly what every public school student in the country was doing at that very moment, the United States has a remarkably decentralized school system. There are good historical reasons for that, but the result is that American schools enjoy wide latitude in what they teach and how they teach it. Especially with something like sex education, schools have tremendous freedom in choosing whether to teach the subject at all, and if so, what curriculum, if any, to use. By default, much of what we know about sex education in America is the product of research done by either advocacy or philanthropic organizations of various kinds. (The federal government does collect some statistics on sex education, but more commonly in its health capacity than in its education capacity.)

Although sex education is pretty close to universal for young people these days, what "sex education" actually covers varies tremendously. As of the year 2000, for example, three quarters of all states had come to mandate sex education, AIDS education, or both, and somewhere between 95 and 97 percent of teenagers reported that they had had some sex education.[10] The key word here may be "some." A 1999 Kaiser Family Foundation survey of teachers found that three out of four of those actually charged with teaching sex said that in their schools, the subject was covered in only a few class periods, sometimes as few as one. Fewer than one sex educator in ten reported teaching a course that lasted even an entire semester.[11]

To put the matter baldly, we are looking at an outcome, teenage sexual behavior, that is affected by many forces, only one of which is sex education, during a period of tremendous social change, which has surely had some independent impact on such behavior, and we are looking at everything from one classroom period to a semester's worth of classes, all in the service of trying to see if they affected the outcome.

All of this would be incredibly depressing if not for the fact that the news about teenagers and their sexuality gives room for self-congratulation to advocates on both sides of the debate, and all of the outcomes are good ones. Rates of teenage sexual activity seem to have plateaued after a very long period of increase, and may actually be declining. (Sexual activity here means not how

often teens have sex but how many teens have ever had sexual relations at all.) Of those teens who are sexually active, more seem to
be more successful at protecting themselves from pregnancy.
(They may also be more successful at protecting themselves from
disease, but this is much more difficult to ascertain.)

Almost every parent in America probably knows that unmarried sex among American teenagers has increased enormously over
the past half-century; one of the more reliable surveys shows rates
among women doubling between the late 1960s and the late
1980s, from roughly 17 percent to 40 percent of all 17-year-olds.
(Because of the history of these surveys and the deep conviction
that reproduction is something relevant only to women, most surveys about sexual and reproductive behavior are based on
women.)[12] Similar rates hold for men, although the data are less
extensive. Comparing the period between 1979 and 1988, for
example, the number of young men who had premarital sex
jumped from two thirds to three quarters.[13]

It less well known that this rate of increase seems to have flat-
tened out. Caution is due, because we have so few data, but
between 1988 and 1995 the proportion of teenage women who
were sexually active remained essentially unchanged, and between
1995 and the present it seems to have declined. Some data seem
to suggest that the same is true for men.[14]

It also seems to be clear from a variety of sources that sexually
active teenagers got better over time at protecting themselves from
pregnancy, with the risk of pregnancy for a sexually active young
woman dropping from 25 percent to 20 percent between 1972 and
1990 and to 19.7 percent in 1995. While these figures are still high
by the standards of other countries, they represent a substantial
improvement.[15] At least part of the reduction is explained by the
fact that the rate of condom use has increased exponentially over
the past two decades, going from just over half of all males using
condoms the last time they had sex to almost 70 percent, with girls
reporting a similar increase with respect to their male partners.[16]

There are clear trends that both boys and girls are reporting more willingness to use contraception, both the first time they have sex and during their most recent sexual experience.[17]

These figures suggest but do not prove that teenagers are also getting better at protecting themselves from disease. Because reporting rates for many sexually transmitted diseases apart from HIV/AIDS are notoriously unreliable, and for HIV/AIDS the lag time between exposure and diagnosis is such a long one, it's very hard to assess this trend with any certainty. Although sexual diseases, in particular HIV/AIDS, play such a central and emotive role in the sex education debate, it seems foolhardy (or dishonest) to try to settle the debate with data about them, given how bad the data are.

This brings us back to the debate over sex education, with its curious mix of values and pragmatism. People like Jenny Letterman claim that sex education increases the probability that teens will have sex while subjecting them to risky and failure-prone contraceptives and condoms. People like Melanie Stevens, in contrast, deny that claim, and argue that abstinence-only programs show no proof of reducing the prevalence of teen sex but increase the level of individual risk by lowering teenagers' use of contraceptives and condoms. How tenable are any of these claims?

To begin with the assertion that modern sex education caused the sexual revolution, at least among teenagers, the available evidence suggests that this is mostly wishful thinking (wishful in the sense that if traditional sex education caused it, then presumably substituting abstinence education would soon reduce the numbers of sexually active teens). It is true that if we were to chart rates of premarital sex along with the spread of sex education, we would find both lines increasing in rough harmony. Thus Jenny Letterman is not willfully manipulating the data when she argues that when she was a girl, sex education was far less common, but the problems sex education was designed to address were also far less common.

The logical response, of course, is that the relationship went the other way: first there was a vast expansion in the numbers of sexually active teenagers and then there was more sex education. Sex education in this view was a response not a cause.

Several pieces of evidence support this claim. First, as we have seen, the period between 1964 and 1972 saw an unprecedented change in public attitudes about sex. During those eight years— a time, by the way, before the Supreme Court's decision on *Roe v. Wade*—the American public substantially changed its mind about premarital sex, contraception, and abortion. There really was a sexual revolution, in attitudes at least, and it happened among people of all ages, although at different rates. I find it hard to imagine how sex education courses could have caused these changes in people who were long out of school by the time the 1960s came along. More likely, people taking sex education in school during those years found themselves in a setting in which a fairly sizable proportion of the population agreed that sex before marriage was acceptable as long as you cared about the person you were having sex with. Their sex education, whatever it was, merely reflected what much of the culture as a whole had come to believe.

At the same time, we know that rates of premarital sex for women of all ages, not just those who were in school during those tumultuous years, increased as well. Again, it is hard to imagine how the sex education being taught to adolescents in the 1960s would have affected the sexual behaviors of women in their twenties and thirties.

Although the data are again problematic, most European countries also saw a substantial increase in premarital sex among women of all ages. Europe presents something of a natural experiment for the claim that sex education caused the sexual revolution. Despite American stereotypes, based often on the Scandinavian countries, European countries have great disparities in what kinds of sex education they make available to young people and when they instituted such programs. France, for example, began school sex education in the late 1980s, but French teens too seem to have increased their propensity to have premarital sex come twenty years earlier.

Finally, several meta-analyses of studies conducted in this country, comparing people who take comprehensive sex education courses to those who do not, have found little evidence that taking sex education increases the likelihood of having sex. In fact, this finding is one of the more verifiable in the realm of research on sex education, which suggests that it is very robust indeed, given all the problems involved in evaluating sex education programs.[18]

So the preponderance of the evidence, as my legal colleagues would say, points against the claim that comprehensive sex education in some way increases the prevalence of teenage sex. But that finding in turn raises another, more vexing question, on the effects of sex education at reducing individual levels of risk. One way of reading the finding that sex education doesn't encourage teenagers to have more sex or to have it sooner is that sex education doesn't affect teenage sexual behavior much at all, for better or for worse.

In fact, it is surprisingly difficult to show that sex education programs do in fact increase teenagers' willingness to protect themselves from pregnancy and/or disease. Perhaps this is not surprising, in that few social programs show verifiable effects in changing individual behavior, particularly something as socially, politically, and emotionally complex as sex. And the outcome variables, as noted, are extremely difficult to measure. Finally, the wide range of "doses" of sex education available complicates the matter. Put these all together, and it should be obvious that an evaluation of specific programs cautiously concludes that clear benefits of a modest sort can be displayed only by labor-intensive (and hence expensive), long-term comprehensive courses with clearly defined teaching goals, and that even those results are open to question.[19]

Although it is reasonably difficult to show that actual programs reduce individual risk very much, the good news is that teens are in fact getting better at using contraception. All the data we've explored show that in the aggregate (as opposed to a study of participants in a single program), teenagers are using contraceptives more often, using condoms more often, and generally engaging in fewer risky sexual behaviors. So while the jury is still out, it seems reasonable to conclude that comprehensive sex education did not increase the propensity of teenagers to have sex and may have had a modest role in reducing the level of individual risk.

By the same token, rates of teenage sexual activity plateaued in the 1990s, when abstinence-only programs became more popular. Can abstinence education take credit for this change in sexual behavior? Again, keep in mind that the same processes that affect our ability to assess the effects of comprehensive sex education affect any attempt to assess abstinence education as well. Many other things were changing in the society at large, including a growing awareness of HIV/AIDS, and they may have had more effect on teenagers than sex education courses.

Evaluation of abstinence-only courses to date shows little clear evidence that they affect teen sexual behavior. While it is true, as their advocates claim, that students are more likely to endorse the *idea* of abstinence after such a course, no evaluation so far shows that students have changed their *behavior* in any significant ways.[20]

Given what we know about programs designed to change individual behavior and the lessons learned from evaluation of comprehensive programs, however, it may turn out that abstinence advocates can take some credit for delaying sexual initiation for some students. (Of course, this presumes that there is not a powerful selection effect here—that the kinds of students, or their parents, who select abstinence-only programs in the first place may well be the kinds who would to delay sexual initiation anyway.) This might be a deeply disappointing outcome to abstinence advocates, but it would be a triumph from the point of view of the larger society. From a policy point of view, in contrast to a values point of view, if teaching abstinence encourages young people to delay sexual activity by even a few months, those few months multiplied by the approximately 10 million teenagers in our society represents a sizable reduction in risk, of a magnitude that very few policy interventions of any sort can claim.

I am prepared to be openminded about abstinence programs. My own hunch—and it's not very popular among those who support comprehensive sex education programs—is that abstinence programs may in fact provide valuable social support for the idea that young people (young women in particular) don't have to be sexually active if they don't want to be. In my interviews with both parents and the few young people who were active on the issue in their schools, I was struck by the level of peer pressure surrounding sexual activity that many reported. Most comprehensive sex education programs include units that teach students how to reject sexual advances they are not comfortable with, but the passion and fervor that abstinence advocates bring to their cause puts some real muscle into those teachings.

Let's assume that the plateauing and then declining of the rates of sexual activity (which account, according to one estimate, for about 25 percent of the recently observed decline in teen birthrates) is entirely due to abstinence education, although the timing of the decline seems to predate the wide acceptance of these programs. Let's also assume that the generally improved ability of adolescents to avoid pregnancy (which accounts by this same estimate for three quarters of the decline) is entirely due to comprehensive education, although, as noted, it's hard to show much of a relationship between individual programs and actual behavioral change. If our generous assumptions were true, abstinence education and comprehensive education could both take at least some credit for declining birthrates among teens.

But what about the most worrisome claim made about abstinence programs, that such programs reduce the propensity to use contraception when and if students become sexually active?

Again, the data are very preliminary, but there are just enough studies to suggest that this may be a problem. We know from other domains of human life that programs that try to abolish a given behavior (drinking and drug use, for example) often have the paradoxical effect of persuading some people to abstain from the behavior entirely but leaving the majority equally likely to engage in the behavior but less likely to manage its risks.[21]

One recent study, for example, found that students who took a "virginity pledge" did in fact delay sexual activity longer than students who did not, but once they were sexually active, they were equally likely to contract a sexually transmitted disease and less likely than students who had not taken such a pledge to know their STD status.[22] While a virginity pledge is not exactly the same thing as abstinence-only education, the association is troubling, although there is the very real likelihood of a selection effect.

Which brings us once again to the intersection of values and data and the complex policy issues that surround teaching young people about sexuality. I noted earlier that based only on anecdotal evidence from my research in this area, I am prepared to be openminded about the idea that abstinence-only programs might offer something of value to young people, and to young women in particular.

This chapter starts with the assertion that the debate over sex education is really a debate about sex and marriage, and that debates about sex and marriage are also debates about gender, about how men and women (and boys and girls) should relate to one another, sexually and otherwise. This brings me to my immodest proposal, bound to offend both sides. Since the debate about sex education gets its passion from deeply felt ideas about gender, and women's roles in particular, *why not tell young people that?* Why not put the hidden agenda on the table and tell young people and their parents that Americans today hold two very different views about sexuality, views rooted in very different notions of the relationship of sexuality to marriage? Bringing marriage back into the conversation means addressing different views about the nature of gender and about women's roles. Young women—and men—coming of age need to know that one of the most profound and historical changes in the past century was the rise of the second women's movement of the 1960s and 1970s. They also need to know that the women's movement has not delivered on all of its promises and that men and women rarely share full equality in all realms of life.

In the end, the debate about sex education is a debate about whether the gender and sexual revolutions of the 1960s and 1970s have not entirely fulfilled their promises or were based on empty promises to begin with. Where you stand on this issue marks you as what I have called a sexual liberal or a sexual conservative, and just as liberals and conservatives in other domains of life have yet to agree on whether or not the French Revolution increased the net sum of human happiness, sexual liberals and conservatives will surely continue to differ as to whether treating women as fundamentally equal to men or treating them as fundamentally different contributes more to social and personal flourishing.

I suspect that sexual liberals and conservatives, like their counterparts in the larger political world, will never agree because each side gives priority to something different. It's a cliché, but as other researchers have found, political conservatives tend to value stability and liberty while political liberals tend to value equality, and this finding applies to the sexual realm as well.

So why not tell adolescents this? Why not acquaint them with the very real fact that Americans have a deep conflict about sex and gender, and that there is increasing evidence that this kind of conservative-liberal debate is driving political elections, not just sex education?

If we realize that the fight about sex is both a moral and a political one, we can provide students—and their parents—with the kinds of information that they need to make choices.

Appendices

A Note on Voice and Method

It seems that anthropologists have a joke these days, a version of the silly jokes everyone remembers from fifth grade: What does the postmodern anthropologist say to the indigenous person? "Enough about you, let's talk about me." Even though it isn't really that funny, it gets told a lot, and not only by anthropologists. In fact, a graduate student in sociology first told it to me, and I've retold it numberless times since then. The reason that it keeps making the rounds is explained by the late folklorist Alan Dundes, who theorized that we joke about what we feel anxious about. (Actually, I think Freud said it first, but Dundes had the world's largest collection of jokes as proof.)[1]

It turns out that "postmodern" is, like a lot of things examined in this book, an imprecise label covering a motley crew of characters and ideas. Whatever the logical troubles with the term, the idea caught on, mostly in the humanities. Drawing on certain currents of European philosophy, academics in the humanities took to using the term "postmodernism" to call attention to language and the way in which the language we use to discuss things shapes our experience of them.

Implicit in the idea of postmodernism is the concept that categories are not stable, not "out there" in some predictable way. Each individual observer brings his or her unique history and experiences to the process, so that even as mundane a concept as "family" or "parents" will be shaped by our own experiences of those words—happily married, unhappily married, happily divorced, unhappily divorced, widowed, gay or lesbian, childless or with children. From this it follows that there are real problems with what the postmodernists call, somewhat pretentiously, "intersubjectivity," meaning I can never be sure you and I are talking about the same things, given the odds we have had very different histories and experiences.

It was only a question of time before postmodernism migrated to the social sciences, washing up first, as the joke implies, on the shores of anthropology. A much-cited 1986 book titled *Writing Culture* called attention to the fact anthropologists were not merely objective observers of the colorful and exotic "other" but were themselves social beings embedded in a culture of their own.[2] More troubling, the culture of anthropology—its notions of objectivity, its sense of itself as a social "science"—was itself susceptible to the same kinds of analysis that anthropologists brought to the Kalahari Bushmen in Africa. The title of the book pointed to the fact anthropologists were not simply "discovering" or "describing" a culture that existed "out there" but were, in some very real sense, making it up as they went along.[3]

Sociologists have been resistant to the concepts of postmodernism, clutching objectivity and science to their collective chests more tightly than any other social scientists except economists. My hunch is it's because we sociologists sense ourselves to be a vulnerable discipline. History (which in the traditional division of the university is usually considered a humanity, not a social science) has the special expertise of the "then," and anthropology has the lure of the "there." So those two disciplines fend off carping outsiders by denying them any legitimacy unless they have spent time in the dusty archives (the historians) or somewhere exotic without running water (the anthropologists).

But sociologists study the here-and-now, which means that our "expertise" is much more accessible to outsiders than the expertise of historians or anthropologists. It makes a certain kind of sense to speak of someone as an "amateur historian" or even an "amateur anthropologist," but never in my life have I heard anyone described as an "amateur sociologist." It's not so much that people don't want to be amateur sociologists as that they think they already *are*. Not to put too fine a point on it, most people think that what professional sociologists do is just a gussied-up version of what everyone already knows.

As I write this, I imagine some readers wincing, figuring that this is just one more example of how politically correct sociologists have become, how we worry about the feelings of women and gay people and disabled people and the like. But what almost all social scientists understand, even if they aren't particularly willing to talk about it, is that what gets denigrated in some quarters as "PC" is actually a very deep—maybe the deepest—problem in the social sciences. It's the same one that my mentors were grappling with when I was in graduate school, and the postmodernist critique has simply put it, like some shameful family secret, squarely on the table for all to see. When push comes to shove, what the postmodernist critique is all about is questioning how sociologists (and anthropologists and historians and practitioners of the other human sciences) can presume to make claims about social reality, given that we are embedded within that reality ourselves. In terms of the old cliché, how can fish talk with any degree of expertise about water?

It is a serious and intractable problem. Some people take for granted that making sense of our culture can't be done, while other people go to the opposite lengths, assuming that there is nothing special about doing it and anyone can. This latter group assumes that any reasonably smart fish is as well equipped as any other to describe water.

The worst part of it is, if we do our work carefully and well and come up with an important social finding, many people around us will proclaim in patronizing tones, "I knew that." But they didn't, not until some social scientist spent years of effort and care getting it right.

I believe that sociology as a discipline has several things going for it, things that bring these books and others together in a recognizable way of looking at the world. More to the point, I would argue that I have been fundamentally shaped by my training as a sociologist and that this book would have been written very differently without that training.

One of the things that postmodernists love is the notion of "irony"—the concept that the medium and the message are at odds with each other much of the time. The postmodernists have gotten to me to the extent that this book is "ironic" in the following way: I am claiming in this section (conveniently positioned at the end of the book) this is a book that only a sociologist could have written and it is fundamentally an enterprise that grows out of many years of training. But the book you hold breaks the cardinal rule of sociology, because it uses the first and second persons. You and I are in a dialogue, and we have been since the first page. Like the postmodern anthropologist in the joke, you are learning a great deal more about me than sociology deems proper. In fact, any disclosure of self is considered taboo in conventional sociology, a faux pas of the first order. The ideal, the one I learned in graduate school, was to "let the facts speak for themselves," to present you with the illusion that the human equivalent of a video recorder went into the communities under study and simply recorded "the truth." In the service of this illusion, sociologists are trained from the beginning to erase any signs of self or personhood from the presentation, treating the presence of the observer as something embarrassing, like a thumb on the lens of a camera, which a true professional would never let happen. One of the reasons we often write so badly is that we are trying to erase all visible signs of our presence in the text. So we rely on the passive voice ("experiments were undertaken"), demote the people being studied to "subjects," and we take the capacity for action from the people involved and confer it on inanimate objects ("the data reveal," "Figure 1 shows").

These lessons are so deeply engrained that I began by swearing I would not use the first-person voice in this book. I began to hyperventilate when the "I" began to creep into the narrative—when it became clear that a flesh-and-blood, socially situated person, a person with a history, a body, a gender, a race, an ethnicity, and what Zorba the Greek called the whole catastrophe, was writing this book.

Having said that, let me explain why I think the postmodernist critique goes too far by erasing any possibility of "intersubjectivity," and with it any social science. In this book I have made the cosmic bet with you, the reader, that given all the blind spots that come with being of a certain age, gender, color, and history, I am not reduced to those variables, although I may be limited by them. I am betting that by this time you have a picture of what is at stake in the fight over sex education in Shady Grove and elsewhere, and who the people involved in these fights are, and what they believe in. I also suspect that you have a more systematic, more disciplined, and more truthful vision of the issue than you would if a literary scholar or a journalist (or a postmodern anthropologist, for that matter) had written the book. Let me tell you why I think that.

First, as a sociologist, I am heir to a history and a literature. For all that much of what we sociologists write is silly, enduring ideas that hold up for a substantial period of time still exist. People who are serious sociologists (rather than the amateur sociologists of everyday life) have studied that literature and steeped themselves in those ideas. In a more confident era, Robert Merton, one of the great men of sociology, was able to write about how we could see further because we stood on the shoulders of giants.[4] My claim is humbler: this book is richer than it would otherwise be because it draws on the work and insights of many other trained social scientists. Many minds, not just one, went into it—some as authors, some as people who have talked with me about the ideas of the book, and some as careful early readers. What we all have in common is a set of ideas and ways of thinking about the world that are rooted in a social science perspective.

Next, sociology has certain rules for how to go about gathering and analyzing evidence. All humans notice the weird and the unusual, but it takes training to notice the ordinary and obvious. And it takes still more training to observe accurately, to observe systematically, and to consider the ratio between the unusual and the obvious. Because sociologists are taught to worry about bias, to worry that we may just be finding what we want to find, we have a set of operating procedures designed to help us see things we don't want to see. (I sometimes tell my students, "There are nothing like a few data to mess up a perfectly good theory.")[5]

Journalists have always had the luxury of coming up with a good idea and then going out to talk to people in order to substantiate that idea, and these days some people who style themselves cultural critics do too. And often these observers are like your smartest, best-read friend: they originate something so insightful, so to the point, that they enduringly change how you think about a problem. Sociologists try to do something different, however, a messier and harder job. We come up with a good idea and then we go out to see whether it is true before we try to explain and persuade. (Although the postmodern critique has taken its toll here too, the best sociologists I know go into the field with the paradoxical intention of proving their pet theories false, on the grounds that a theory that holds up to systematic attempts to discredit it must be, as we like to say, robust.)

Here's how I tried to deal with the problem of bias. I chose four different communities fighting over sex education, located in three very different places in the United States—two in the West, one in the rural South, and one in the urban Northeast. (In the northeastern site, I conducted only a few interviews and mostly observed. Most of the interviews cited in this book occurred in the first three sites.) Over almost twenty years, I talked to people in these communities about their feelings about sex education. Although my sense of what I was looking for changed over those years, my method of studying it did not. My modus operandi was to find communities in the midst of noisy, active conflicts over sex education and then to interview the individuals most centrally involved.

Sociologists worry a lot about sampling, because it makes a difference to choose cases systematically rather than by whim. Whims, by conscious or unconscious design, can make a sociologist choose only those cases that support a preconceived hypothesis. It turns out that sampling among the universe of communities fighting over sex education is a lot trickier than it looks. To the best of my knowledge, there is no centralized database for conflicts over sex education, although as the issue has gained a higher profile, advocacy groups have begun tracking the conflicts they know about. Yet in order to "know about" a local controversy, such a group usually has to have been contacted by someone on the local scene. Smaller, more local controversies, where no one involved contacts a national advocacy group, are missed.

So I lacked what sociologists call a "sampling frame," a list of all the possible controversies I could choose among.[6] One alternative was to search local papers for accounts of controversies, but this too proved more difficult than it looked at first glance. If a controversy is truly local, especially in a small community, then it is most likely reported in small-town newspapers (typically published on a weekly basis) rather than in the larger urban papers. Small local papers, particularly weeklies, are usually not indexed on a regular basis and are very unlikely to show up in the kinds of electronic indexes (like Lexis-Nexis) that researchers rely on.

Moreover, to the extent that smaller newspapers are indexed, they are indexed on a "full-text" basis, which means that anything remotely pertaining to the words being searched (in this case "sex education" and its synonyms) will be indexed. The period that this study covers was a particularly active one with respect to sex education, what with AIDS and teenage pregnancy becoming an increasing part of everyone's vocabulary, and even small-town newspapers avidly reported on things happening on the national scene, such as Surgeon General C. Everett Koop's 1986 recommendation that sex education be given to children as young as was practical. Thus I had literally thousands of hits to comb through in my search for cases.

I eventually turned to an electronic clipping service, which indexed stories from local newspapers. Searching through its archives, I found one West Coast community and one in the South. By the mid-1990s, I had talked to enough people to have contacts among those who were "in the know" about sex education, on both sides of the issue. They alerted me to new controversies, another one on the West Coast and one in the Rust Belt East.

I chose these four communities on theoretical grounds. I wanted places where there was a curriculum under active discussion, so I could look at what people were arguing about. I wanted communities that were debating sex education as a set of ideas, so I avoided those places where discussions included plans for either a school-based clinic or a condom distribution program.[7] Finally, as the issue of sex education evolved over the years of my study, I chose a community where the debate was over what kind of sex education, abstinence-only or comprehensive, would be taught. In this town, the people opposing sex education opposed it because they wanted more forthright discussion of sex, not less.

In all these communities (although less systematically in the Rust Belt site), I used the following techniques to gather interviews. As the controversy over sex education heated up, the boards of education typically held a number of meetings to enable parents and other interested parties to comment, either in support of or in opposition to the proposed curriculum. In three of the four communities, the process of these meetings was the same. The board of education or its equivalent would convene a meeting, put up one or more microphones, and tell interested parties they would have to submit their names and addresses to the board if they wished to address it.[8] (There was an air both of improvisation and of the old-fashioned New England town meeting in this strategy, which was usually born of desperation when a board of education realized its normally tiny meetings would have to accommodate two hundred to four hundred people with little warning that trouble was brewing.)

My method was to obtain lists of the names submitted to the board in each community and then to call each person on the lists and ask for an interview. (I also observed many of these meetings.) I identified myself as a professor and told them that the interview would take about two hours. At the end of each tape-recorded interview, I asked for names of other people I should talk to. I kept doing this until I got no new names. My assistants and I transcribed all the interviews and sent the transcripts back to the people I had talked with, asking them to elaborate on the interviews and/or make corrections if they wished.

Over the course of more years than I care to remember, I analyzed the resulting material. In practice, this meant several things. First, along with my assistants, I entered the transcribed interviews into a database, which kept each interview separate by person interviewed and by community. By reading each transcript carefully, we developed and refined a second database, of codes that spanned individual cases, catching general sentiments and phenomena. Regularly updated, the output from this second database was our codebook.

An example of one code from the codebook is something we came to call the "red flag" code, which we used to capture the incidents that had gotten people involved in this issue in the first place. As you can perhaps see in the book, it's a particularly interesting code, in that it marks a moment when a person finds out that something she or he has taken for granted is not assumed by everyone.

So my assistants would read a transcript looking for material to code that fit this description:

Code: RED FLAG
Definition: a single incident that R recounts which animated
     his/her interest in the issue. Sometimes called a "moral shock."
When to Use: for the precipitating incident that got R involved.
When Not to Use: different from EXEMPLAR STORY in that it is
     not a narrative and is much less global than BIG PICTURE.

This methodology grew out of Anselm Strauss's "grounded theory" but is also deeply indebted to innovations developed by the Centers for Disease Control, which recently took on the task of systematically analyzing hundreds of qualitative interviews.[9]

After the final codebook was developed, independent coders recoded the interviews, and the degree of agreement between the two sets of coders was compared (and was quite high).[10]

Finally, we asked people a few key things about their backgrounds: their education, their occupation, their religious affiliation, if any, and such items as the number and timing of marriages and the birth of children.

With all of these sources of data, we could look at the complexity of opinions and their distribution. We could compare how people on the two sides felt about issues. We could link opinions to communities and/or to social features of advocates' lives. We could look at patterns within an individual interview and examine how common those patterns were across interviews.

By linking interviews to other interviews from the same community, we could also see what names came up most often, which gave us a rough indication of who the central players were and helped us make sure that we had sampled correctly.[11] We also created a multifaceted account of the conflict. In addition to conducting the interviews, I acquired and examined as many sex education curricula as I could find from the early 1900s to the present, with a special emphasis on the period after the discovery of the AIDS virus in 1981. (This includes abstinence-only curricula, as discussed above.) This too raises questions of sampling, particularly for the earlier period, as I have no way of knowing why some curricula were mimeographed and kept in the files of school libraries while others were lost to the mists of time. I was as inclusive as I could be, and missing curricula went missing for reasons that I had nothing to do with. The careful reader, of course, should keep in mind that when I write about sex education between the early 1900s and the 1980s, it is entirely possible that another, more successful archivist of sex education curricula would come to a different conclusion.

For obvious reasons, I cannot claim that the results I report here are representative of the country at large. Nor would I want you to think that people like Jenny Letterman and Melanie Stevens are simply types. (I remind readers that while these are real people, the names I call them in this book are pseudonyms.) The wonderful thing about humans living together is that we combine some significant similarities with many important differences. Each community and each person in this book is unique, and I would not dream of insulting either the people or the communities by suggesting that they are all cut from the same cloth.

Still, to a social scientist, the interesting details are the ones that are common across communities and people. Although these people and their communities are each one of a kind, certain things are common to all of them. As you have read about them, I hope you have been struck by how similarly people in the Rust Belt, the Sun Belt, and the South feel about certain issues, particularly when we consider those who broadly agree on the proper role of sex education in public schools.

I don't flatter myself that this study entirely explains (or, worse yet, explains away) why people feel the way they do about sex and education about it. All I can claim is that by talking to people in these four communities over almost twenty years, I came to see some patterns, and that understanding these patterns can give us some insight into where people who disagree with us about sex are coming from.

I think sociologists have one other advantage that literary scholars and journalists don't have. The very fact that we are bombarded with different critiques of our enterprise means that we spend a lot of time engaged in what the sociologist Pierre Bourdieu calls "reflexivity."[12] What he means is that we take seriously the dilemma of being a fish studying water, so much so that while we are studying the water, we try very hard to study ourselves studying the water.

So there is an odd kind of method to my madness here. I chose to use the first person as a way of making clear that a social person, as prone to shyness and anxiety and general angst as anyone else, wrote this book. I make no pretense to a Cartesian view from "above," detached from the world being studied. Perhaps more to the point, I'm a product of the same culture as the people I study. I grew up partly in this country (my father was in the military, so I spent about half my childhood abroad), I am of roughly the same age as the people I study, and I am sending my own children into the same world that the people quoted in this book worry about. I share all the hangups and national neuroses about sex that crop up in the towns I have called Shady Grove, Billingsley, Lincoln Township, and Las Colinas.

But I am not only that. I have a discipline, in two senses of that ambiguous word. As a member in good standing of the intellectual discipline of sociology, I am heir to a tradition, a literature, and what Karl Popper calls a community of knowers; as I was writing I was in constant dialogue, at least in my head, with members of that community. The other aspect of the discipline is the one I mentioned earlier, namely, the search to prove my own ideas wrong. I tried to gather the data as systematically as possible, in as orderly a fashion as I could, so that if they revealed patterns that contradicted what I thought I was finding, I would see them.

That is not an easy task, and it is doomed to failure, since postmodernism decrees that I can offer only an approximation of what twenty years of fieldwork and over a hundred interviews have taught me. But it's the best I have to offer.

Set Theoretic Models: Relationships Within Small Ns

Despite the intimidating title of this appendix, lurking here is an exciting and possibly paradigm-changing way of doing my discipline. (I didn't discover it, so I'm free to admire it as much as I want.)

Without inflicting any more sociology on you than I already have, let me just say that the quantification of my discipline in the years after World War II led to a world in which models of social reality were necessarily linear, because that's what the models measured best. For a long time, that didn't matter. Sociologists aspired to rigor; quantification brings with it considerable rigor; and for many of the things that sociologists studied in an earlier era, quantification worked reasonably well.

Alas, as most of us are only too aware, there are limits to what we can measure in a linear model. For the purposes of this discussion, a linear model says that every time A happens, B happens, and the more or less that A happens, the more or less B happens. But social life is much messier than that.[1] (My colleague David Nasatir says that when he transferred his intellectual interests from physics to sociology, he moved from the hard sciences to the difficult ones.) So in recent years, sociologists have turned to new methods to generate models of how the world works that don't rely on linear methods. Drawing on some of the same methodologies that originated in the first department of sociology, at the University of Chicago (where several early social hygienists lurked), sociologists tried to move away from the constraints of the quantitative method and into a qualitative, nonlinear view of the world.

For a long time, however, no matter how hard qualitative, theory-generating methods attempted to get a handle on the more contingent and complex aspects of social life, the kinds where things sometimes happen and sometimes don't, we were limited in our ability to cumulate, to build on the findings of others. Into this unhappy state of affairs came Charles Ragin, a sociologist who has opened doors that bring at least the promise of having qualitative methods be as rigorous and as theoretically bold as quantitative ones historically were. In two books, *The Comparative Method* and *Fuzzy Set Social Science,* Ragin has given us a way to find complex patterns in data that we might not otherwise be able to see.[2]

The method that Ragin has developed permits us to code whether or not an item (for the purposes of this discussion, a "cause") is present and whether or not another item (for the purposes of this discussion, an "outcome") is as well. Using Boolean algebra (a way of exploring logical connections mathematically), we can look at complex arrangements of cause and effect. (Computer algorithms developed by electrical engineers in the 1950s provide techniques for simplifying this kind of data.) This method, which Ragin calls qualitative comparative analysis, or QCA, works out an algorithm that most economically describes the patterns existing in the data, patterns that are sufficiently subtle to be invisible to the naked eye.

Using the data for this book, which consisted of transcribed and coded interviews with 105 people, a set of socioeconomic indicators, curricula, materials such as newspaper accounts, and as much advocacy material as we could find, we were able to create a metafile with items from many different sources about the same community, the same person, or the same issue.

The main results from the QCA analysis are reported in Chapter Five, "Becoming a Sexual Conservative or a Sexual Liberal." Running the QCA program on the linked data files, we found, as reported, that sexual conservatives come by their conservatism in one of two ways. Some people are what the traditional sociological literature leads us to expect of people who are conservative on social issues: they come from a lower socioeconomic group (as measured by the father's education or lack thereof) and had a mother who stayed home when they were growing up. Thus, in the first part of the algorithm, a person whose father did not graduate from college and whose mother was a homemaker was likely to be a sexual conservative. But the story gets more interesting and shows the power of this kind of analysis.

In the second pattern, sexual conservatives could come from families that were upper-income (as measured by father's education) but were themselves now members of a conservative religion and had opted for a traditional family where the wife stays home to care for the children. Thus when cross-linked to the narratives that people told us, the QCA revealed that there are two kinds of sexual conservatives. Some follow the expected (in the literature, at least) pattern of being less affluent and having had a confrontation with the modern world that produced a "moral shock."[3] In classic theoretical terms, these are people who had been sheltered from a broad set of experiences and values that sociologists call "modernity" and who didn't like it when they saw it. Alternatively, other people had been raised in modernity: they were educated, they were affluent, and they often worked very much in the modern sector. Many of the men we interviewed, for example, were in high-tech fields, and women, if they worked before marriage, worked alongside them. What was different for these people is that they experienced a period of emotional and social instability in their lives (often involving drugs or alcohol or both) and/or a period of rootlessness, and turned to evangelical religion and the strict moral code that came with it as a way of dealing with the overload of choices that life had confronted them with. It is in this sense that I call the first group "birthright" sexual conservatives and the second group "converted" or "born-again" sexual conservatives.

So this book represents a new way of using numbers to explore relationships within qualitative data, permitting us to see patterns that would otherwise be hidden to us.

Editing the Interviews

Although everyone probably knows this intuitively, it bears repeating that spoken and written English are two very different things. With few exceptions, most of us would be horrified to hear what we sound like if someone transcribed our conversations word for word, stutter for stutter, and "um" for "um." This is particularly true when the topic is sex education, about which people have very strong feelings. On top of that, many of the questions I asked people were ones that they had never before really considered, such as what influences had shaped their views when it came to morality or what their own sex education had been like.

It seems unfair to me simply to dump people's spoken language onto the page as if it were the equivalent of the words I have been writing and rewriting for several years now. It makes the people I interviewed look less smart and thoughtful than they really are, and me more so.

Therefore, in the service of basic fairness, I have edited the interviews slightly to remove those place-keeping "ums" and "ers" and "ahs" and "you knows" that we utter when we are thinking. I have not generally signaled when I have done that. To make these interviews more intelligible to the reader, I have also taken out repetitions. Likewise, when someone referred to something said earlier in the interview and presumed that both interviewer and interviewee knew what we were talking about, I have entered a summary of what the individual had in mind when she or he referred to "it," "that," and the like.

I have generally tried to give readers a feel for the individual manner of expression, and to keep in regionalisms and particular ways of expressing things. For example, in Billingsley, people would describe how "mamas and daddies set down" (or failed to) to talk about sex with their children. To the nonsoutherner, who does not call parents "mamas and daddies" and who "sits" down with children in the present and "sat" down with children in the past, this can sound a bit backwoodsy. I assure you that people of widely varying educations and income brackets used this construction, so I have kept it, trying not to squash everyone's language into a sort of homogenized Middle America-speak. Similarly, when individuals used "ain't" or similar constructions, I kept them, not only because they give the flavor of what I was hearing on a daily basis but because they serve to locate people within a social map. I have edited poor grammar only to clarify meaning, not ever to change a speaker's voice or intentions.

The legitimate question arises whether some of this editing twists the words or meanings coming out of people's mouths. I don't think it does, which is why I did it (purists are free to read the work of sociolinguists if they want every hesitation and hiccup transcribed.)

To give you an understanding of how my editing affects speech, here are examples of quotations from the book that juxtapose the raw and the edited versions. I have purposefully chosen quotes in which I did, by my standards, a great deal of editing.

For example, I quoted Sandy Ames as saying, "You know, we were created to be sexual beings, and that is God-created, and we actually think that that's a healthy thing within marriage. A lot of people think that 'Oh, Christians are prudes,' or whatever. It couldn't be further from the truth . . . We just believe it belongs in marriage, and within that, it's fine. But you just don't go around having that kind of time with just anybody."

What she actually said was "You know, we were created to be sexual beings, and that is God-created, and we actually think that that's a healthy thing within marriage. A lot of people think that 'Oh, Christians are prudes,' or whatever. It couldn't be further from the truth. [Laughs.] He's being difficult [referring to husband, who has said something in background]. That just couldn't be further from the truth. We just believe it belongs in marriage, and within that, it's fine. But you just don't go around having that kind of time with just anybody."

In another example, I quoted Steven Kingsley as saying, "So for example, even though I would be against homosexuality, I work with people who are homosexuals, and I've always liked them and I can respect them as individuals. In my job now, I've had many conversations with this woman who's a lesbian. I never confront her. She knows how I believe, I ask her a lot of questions, and I like hearing what she has to say."

What he actually said was, "So for example, I don't, even though I would be against homosexuality, I work with people who are homosexuals, I work with people that are homosexuals, and I'd always like them and I can respect them as an individual and in my job now, I mean, I've had many conversations with this woman who's a lesbian, and it's, I never confront her, she knows how I believe, I ask her a lot of questions, and I like hearing what she has to say."

I report that Debbie DeGroot said, "It wasn't a whole lot of ethics and it wasn't teaching kids how to *think*, how to evaluate whether this is the right time to have sex. They didn't talk about emotions. They did talk about contraceptives; just which ones were better than other ones, which ones were more effective . . . How to make a decision wasn't emphasized at all, and I suspect that might have been because parents might have gotten upset and seen that as encouraging kids to go out and have sex. Sex education emphasized the physical changes and what was going to happen to you, not making decisions about sex."

What she actually said was:

INTERVIEWER: And uh, so, do you remember anything about— you said it was really inadequate. What, if you had to characterize sort of the history of your sex education in and out of the school, what would it be like?

DD: Okay. Um. Fourth and fifth grade, it was segregated. All the girls were together, and all the boys were together, and it was mostly menstruation. And that was good, I mean, you need to know about it about that age. And the teachers were fairly good, honestly answering questions, and I'd say the same for sixth grade.

INTERVIEWER: Um. If you don't mind, I'd like to ask you more about it. Because I'm sort of in the place of interviewing a real native, almost. Because everybody else talks about it from the outside, but you've really gone through it, which I guess was your point when you got involved, you know, speaking before the board of education. Um, was it your regular teacher who taught this?

DD: Yes, all three years. It's very—very biological side of it. It wasn't a whole lot of ethics and, um, I mean, you can't teach ethics, but teaching kids how to think, how to evaluate whether this is the right time to do it, and what might be the things for and against it. They didn't talk about emotions.

INTERVIEWER: So they did teach sort of decision-making in that sense a little bit?

DD: No. I'd say they didn't. They talked biologically what would happen. They did talk about contraceptives, somewhat. Just which ones were better than other ones, which ones were more effective. But, um, not really decision-making. Other than it's better to not do it than to do it because you're very young and that kind of thing. But to make a decision wasn't emphasized at all, and I suspect that might have been because parents might have gotten upset and seen that as encouraging kids to go out and have sex.

There you have it—the raw and the processed data. I trust that I have not changed in any essential way what people said to me, and I am reassured that I heard the same things on both coasts and in the middle, so that minor editing does not detract from the ideas people were sharing with me.

For readers interested in more information about material in this book,
additional references and data points can be found at:

www.law.berkeley.edu/faculty/luker_sexgoestoschool

Notes

PROLOGUE: MRS. BOLAND, THE SEXUAL REVOLUTION, AND ME

1. The people mentioned in this book are all very real, but I have changed their names and a few identifying characteristics. To protect their confidentiality, since many of them told me things they wouldn't necessarily want their neighbors to know, I have placed some people in a different town from the one where they were interviewed, and I have swapped a few telling details. For more information about how they were chosen, see Appendix I, "A Note on Voice and Method."
2. For accounts of these earlier studies, see (all by Kristin Luker) *Taking Chances: Abortion and the Decision Not to Contracept* (Berkeley: University of California Press, 1975), *Abortion and the Politics of Motherhood* (Berkeley: University of California Press, 1984), and *Dubious Conceptions: The Politics of Teenage Pregnancy* (Cambridge: Harvard University Press, 1996).
3. For an overview, see: Kathryn Abrams, "Sex Wars Redux: Agency and Coercion in Feminist Legal Theory," *Columbia Law Review* 95, 2 (1995): 304–76; Carole S. Vance, *Pleasure and Danger: Exploring Female Sexuality* (Boston: Routledge & Kegan Paul, 1984); and Lisa Duggan and Nan D. Hunter, *Sex Wars: Sexual Dissent and Political Culture* (New York: Routledge, 1995).

CHAPTER ONE: SEX AND POLITICS IN AMERICAN LIFE

1. Anne Lamott, *Plan B: Further Thoughts on Faith* (New York: Riverhead Books, 2005).

2. I now know that Reverend Smithers left because the sexually liberal values (as I call them) that were taken for granted by almost everyone else on the committee were disturbing to him in ways that he could not quite put a finger on. This is a key part of the story—that people's values about sexuality are hard to articulate unless and until a fight about sex breaks out and slogans about sex ("abstinence only until marriage") get generated. Reverend Smithers, like Mrs. Boland, kept insisting that he wanted sex education in Shady Grove to be taught in the context of morality, and Melanie and Bethany could not have agreed more. But although the three of them were using the same word, they had very different things in mind. The sense of not being heard but of not being able to pinpoint where and how it was happening eventually prompted the reverend to feel that his time could be better spent elsewhere. When I interviewed him later, he had come to understand that the values held by most of the committee were not his, but he had trouble explaining why he had signed up in the first place. I could have told him that he, like Melanie and Bethany, simply assumed that his values about sex were the ones that everyone held.

3. In Freud's thought, the latency period stretched from roughly age seven to adolescence and meant that children become less sexual as they move from infantile to more adult sexuality. Sigmund Freud, *The Basic Writings of Sigmund Freud,* tr. and ed. A. A. Brill (New York: Modern Library, 1995), p. 551. This essay (one of the "Three Contributions to a Theory of Sex") discusses the concept of latency in detail.

4. People for the American Way, "Fact Sheet on Sex Education." Advocacy groups and public interest groups such as the Alan Guttmacher Institute and the Kaiser Family Foundation have recently surveyed teachers, principals, and students. My own attempts to find a wide array of communities contesting sex education (see Appendix I) suggest that a controversy comes to wider public attention under only two conditions: if the participants on one side contact a national advocacy group or if the fight gets attention from a major metropolitan newspaper. A fight in which none of the combatants decides to contact national groups and the story never shows up in major newspapers indexed in databases is likely to stay under the radar of groups such as People for the American Way and the Christian Coalition.

5. In 1988 the Republican National Platform said, "We oppose any programs in public schools which provide birth control or abortion services or referrals. Our first line of defense . . . must be abstinence education . . . We support efforts like the Adolescent Family Life Program to teach teens the traditional values of restraint and the sanctity of marriage." In 1992 the platform said, "We encourage abstinence education with proven track records in protecting youth from disease, pregnancy and drug use." By 2000 the section read, "We renew our call for replacing 'family planning' programs for teens with increased funding for abstinence education, which teaches abstinence until marriage as the responsible and expected standard of behavior." By 2003, the Republican party platforms of Alaska, Iowa, Minnesota, New Hampshire, North Carolina, Oregon, South Carolina, Texas, and Wisconsin all endorsed abstinence education and/or opposed comprehensive sex education. Congressional Quarterly, *Almanac*, "Republican Convention, Platform Text," 100th Congress, 2nd Session (1988), Appendix 46a, pp. 53a–57a; ibid, 102nd Congress, 2nd Session (1992), pp. 78a–99a; ibid, 104th Congress, 2nd Session (1996), pp. 31d–32d; ibid, 106th Congress, 2nd Session (1998), 29d–30d.

6. For people who do not know the history of sex education, the claim of overall public support is perhaps unexpected. My evidence suggests that particularly in its incarnation as "family life education," a shift that happened early in its history, sex education was often an accepted part of a public school education, although it covered many different kinds of materials, from warnings about venereal disease to discussions of nocturnal emissions to advice about how to choose a compatible mate. The very diversity of sex education, I suspect, was partly responsible for how favorably the public viewed it. As for popularity, as early as 1943, a Gallup Poll found almost seven out of ten Americans approved of sex education, with only 17 percent opposing such courses. (The remaining 15 percent had no opinion.) See Gallup Poll #295, question #QN19. Approval rose steadily throughout the 1960s and 1970s.

7. After this book was substantially complete, the historian Jeffrey Moran published the first book-length history of sex education, *Teaching Sex: The Shaping of Adolescence in the Twentieth Century* (Cambridge, Mass.: Harvard University Press, 2000). It is a model history of the

invention and diffusion of this particular part of American culture, but my own reading of the history differs somewhat from Moran's. Another book, Janice Irvine's *Talk About Sex: The Battles over Sex Education in the United States* (Berkeley: University of California Press, 2002), also came out late in the life of this study, but gave me a great deal of insight into the national dimensions of the debate over time.

8. Generally speaking, in the United States, fundamentalist Protestantism is a subset of evangelical Protestantism, but not always. Both groups accept the Bible as the word of God and Jesus as a personal savior. Fundamentalists regard the Bible as the literal word of God, while evangelicals see it as a source of God's teachings but do not necessarily subscribe to the idea that every word is literally true. Both groups tend toward theological conservatism and pietism and in principle to spreading the gospel (evangelizing.) There is a large literature on this in the sociology of religion; for an accessible view of the history of these tendencies, see George Marsden, *Fundamentalism and American Culture: The Shaping of Twentieth-Century Evangelicalism, 1870–1925.* (New York: Oxford University Press, 1980).

9. The notion of a cultural tool kit is from Ann Swidler, "Culture in Action: Symbols and Strategies," *American Sociological Review* 51, 2 (1986): 273–86. As later chapters make clear, a good number of people move from conservative views about sex into a conservative religion that supports those views, rather than vice versa.

10. In particular, I was worried that perhaps communities which had seen a recent influx of newcomers were somehow ripe for a controversy over sex education. (My research design did not permit me to find out whether such communities, lacking longstanding ties among residents, are disproportionately likely to have such a controversy. But as both Billingsley and Lincoln Township showed, an intact, relatively stable community is perfectly capable of generating a nasty confrontation over sex education.

11. See Jacqueline Darroch, Susheela Singh, and Jennifer J. Frost, "Differences in Teenage Pregnancy Rates Among Five Developed Countries: The Roles of Sexual Activity and Contraceptive Use," *Family Planning Perspectives* 33, 6 (2001): 244–50, 81, and table 3: "Percentage of Adolescent Females Who Ever Had Sexual Intercourse, by Age," 247. The relevant numbers for age at sexual debut are Sweden, 17.1; France, 18.0; Canada, 17.3; Great Britain, 17.5; and

United States, 17.2. Caution is urged, since most European countries have not, until recently, spent as much time assessing teenage sexuality as the United States has.

12. On rates of sexual experience and teen pregnancies and abortions, see Susheela Singh and Jacqueline E. Darroch, "Adolescent Pregnancy and Childbearing: Levels and Trends in Industrialized Countries," table 3, "Percentage of Adolescent Females Who Ever Had Sexual Intercourse, by Age; Percentage Who Had Intercourse in the Past Three Months; etc." and table 2, "Birth, Abortion and Pregnancy Rates and Abortion Ratio, by Country, According to Age Group, mid-1990s," *Family Planning Perspectives* 32, 1 (2000): 16–18; and Stephanie J. Ventura, "Trends in Pregnancy Rates for the United States, 1976–97: An Update," *National Vital Statistics Report* 49, 4 (2001): 1–10. For very similar data on births to teenagers, see United Nations, *Demographic Yearbook 2000*, series R, no. 31, table 11, "Live Birth Rates by Age of Mother, Rural-Urban Residence, Latest Available Year," showing that our rate of 49.4 births per 1,000 women under age twenty dwarfs the rates in Canada (20.2), Denmark (7.6), France (8.1), Germany (9.6), Ireland (19.6), Italy (6.9), Spain (8.0), Sweden (6.6), and Switzerland (5.6). On venereal diseases, see UNAIDS, *Report on the Global HIV/AIDS Epidemic* (Geneva: UNAIDS, 2000); and Christine Panchaud et al., "Sexually Transmitted Diseases among Adolescents in Developed Countries," *Family Planning Perspectives* 32, 1 (2000): 28. As a point of comparison, only the former Soviet bloc countries of Russia and Romania outpace our rates of syphilis and gonorrhea, not to mention diseases such as chlamydia and human papilloma virus.

13. Office of National AIDS Policy, "Youth and HIV/AIDS: An American Agenda" (Washington, D.C.: Department of Health and Human Services, 1996); "Healthy People 2000: National Health Promotion and Disease Prevention Objectives," DHHS Publication no. 91-50212 (Washington, D.C.: Government Printing Office, 1990); and Panchaud et al., "Sexually Transmitted Diseases."

14. I don't include the former Soviet bloc countries in this claim, as they are "industrialized" in ways that are different from what we conventionally mean by this term. For unintended pregnancy rates, see Leon Eisenberg, Sarah S. Brown, and Institute of Medicine (U.S.) Committee on Unintended Pregnancies, *The Best Intentions: Unin*

tended Pregnancy and the Well-Being of Children and Families (Washington, D.C.: National Academy Press, 1995). On abortion rates, see Stanley K. Henshaw, Susheela Singh, and Taylor Haas, "Recent Trends in Abortion Rates Worldwide," *International Family Planning Perspectives* 25, 1 (1999): 44–48.

15. For illustrative examples, see Surgeon General Everett Koop, "Surgeon General's Report on Acquired Immune Deficiency Syndrome," U.S. Public Health Service, Office of the Surgeon General, pp. 5, 31; California Senate Office of Research, "Issue Brief, California Strategies to Address Teenage Pregnancy"; U.S. House of Representatives, "Teen Pregnancy: What Is Being Done? A State-by-State Look," report of Select Committee on Children, Youth, and Families, 99th Congress, 1st session; and Dorothy Height, "What Must Be Done About Children Having Children?" *Ebony*, Mar. 1985, p. 27. See also Marjorie Mecklenburg, president, American Citizens Concerned for Life, and Karen Mulhauser, executive director, National Abortion Rights Action League, statements to the Subcommittee on Select Education, in "The Adolescent Health Services and Pregnancy Prevention and Care Act of 1978, HR 12146," pp. 114, 117. I think, by the way, that differences over the role of marriage and the meaning of sexuality were not as clear in the early 1970s as they have since become, so that a wide group of people joined a consensus because they were unclear about exactly what they were joining. Because of the history of sex education (see the following chapter), many people may not have known whether they were endorsing pre-1960s sex education (a prohibition model) or post-1960s sex education (a harm-reduction model). Thus, the consensus may have been based on misunderstandings of what was at stake. Still, it is remarkable that so many people agreed with the idea of sex education as a solution to sexual and social problems.

16. Virtually all sex education programs have a parental "opt-out" feature, where parents who object to having their children attend sex education classes may ask for them to be excused. Sex education advocates usually prefer such a system, in which it is assumed that parents have given consent for their children to attend unless there is a written request to the contrary. Opponents of comprehensive sex education, in contrast, tend to prefer a system in which parents must explicitly agree that their children may attend sex education classes,

a system sometimes known as "opt-in." At stake is what the default mode will be for children whose parents do not commit themselves one way or the other.

17. Jacqueline E. Darroch and Susheela Singh, "Why Is Teenage Pregnancy Declining? The Roles of Abstinence, Sexual Activity, and Contraceptive Use" (New York: Alan Guttmacher Institute, 1999).

18. My calculations come from the 1988, 1995, and 2002 National Survey of Family Growth (my thanks to Sarah Walchuk for her stellar help on this). Keep in mind that various surveys of teen sexual activity come up with different numbers. See Joan R. Kahn, William D. Kalsbeek, and Sandra L. Hofferth, "National Estimates of Teenage Sexual Activity: Evaluating the Comparability of Three National Surveys," *Demography* 25, 2 (1988): 189–204.

19. My calculations come from the National Survey of Family Growth (thanks again to Sarah Walchuk).

20. A fair question here might be how I know what Melanie wants if her values are as "unarticulated" as I say. The short answer is that having interviewed over a hundred people on this issue and having spent a very long time analyzing those interviews, I am now able to decode what Melanie was saying. See Appendix I for my methodology.

21. *Engel v. Vitale*, 370 U.S. 421 (1962). In this case, the state of New York had mandated that a nondenominational prayer be recited at the beginning of the school day; participation in the prayer was voluntary. The Court held that despite the fact that the prayer was both nondenominational and voluntary, it was in fact an "establishment" of religion in New York's public schools. The next year, in *Abington Township v. Schempp* and *Murray v. Curlett*, 374 U.S. 203 (1963), the Court held that saying the Lord's Prayer and reading the Bible were unconstitutional. For how some localities responded (and in some cases didn't) to these rulings at the time, see Kenneth M. Dolbeare and Phillip E. Hammond, *The School Prayer Decisions: From Court Policy to Local Practice* (Chicago: University of Chicago Press, 1971), and William Muir, *Prayer in the Public Schools: Law and Attitude Change* (Chicago: University of Chicago Press, 1967).

22. This, like other things that people said in a public setting, is taken from verbatim quotation from field notes of the meetings I attended.

23. As will become increasingly apparent, both emotions and the polit-

ical stakes are high in this fight, so the terminology of sex education has become increasingly contested and politicized. Sex educators of Melanie's persuasion argue that they too favor abstinence until marriage and say that abstinence-only sex ed is actually "fear-mongering" sex ed. Thus, they often argue that they are offering "abstinence-based" sex education. To people like Jenny Letterman, this is just one more case of a wolf in sheep's clothing.

24. Jacqueline E. Darroch, David J. Landry, and Susheela Singh, "Changing Emphases in Sexuality Education in U.S. Public Secondary Schools, 1988–1999," *Family Planning Perspectives* 32, 5 (2000): 204–12.

25. My use of "girl" and "boy" signals that we are speaking of young people. The data on what are sometimes called "shotgun" marriages are calculated from Martin O'Connell and Maurice J. Moore, "The Legitimacy Status of First Births to U.S. Women Aged 15–24, 1939–1978," *Family Planning Perspectives* 12, 1 (1980): table 1, p. 18. For African American women, the legitimation rate was much lower, on the order of about 30 percent (table 2, p. 19).

CHAPTER TWO: THE BIRTH OF SEX EDUCATION

1. Sticklers and my fellow academics will point out that when it comes to sex, it does not make sense to speak of revolutions that have anything resembling beginning and ending points. Different beliefs about the nature of sexuality and different practices around it diffuse slowly (or sometimes quickly) in social groups, until enough people have changed their opinions, their behavior, or both for things to seem suddenly very different, so a revolution is declared. The emerging literature on the history of sexuality and of the social practices around it makes clear sex can and does change over time. For illustrative examples, see Thomas Laqueur, *Making Sex: Body and Gender from the Greeks to Freud* (Cambridge, Mass.: Harvard University Press, 1990); Beth L. Bailey, *From Front Porch to Back Seat: Courtship in Twentieth-Century America* (Baltimore: Johns Hopkins University Press, 1988); Martin S. Weinberg, and Colin J. Williams, "Sexual Embourgeoisment? Social Class and Sexual Activity: 1938–1970," *American Sociological Review* 45, 1 (1980): 33–48; and Richard Godbeer, *Sexual Revolution in Early America: Gender*

Relations in the American Experience (Baltimore: Johns Hopkins University Press, 2002).

2. The meeting resulted in the creation of the American Social Hygiene Association (ASHA), the culmination of many years of attempts to reform American sexual behavior. Two groups of reformers, the anti-prostitution, or "purity," wing and the anti–venereal disease, or "sanitarian," wing, had long included some measure of education about sex in their programs, but it was only with the creation of ASHA that education moved front and center. I base this claim on a careful reading of what we would now call the mission statements of the predecessor organizations—the New York Committee for the Prevention of the State Regulation of Vice, the American Purity Alliance, the American Vigilance Association, the American Society of Sanitary and Moral Prophylaxis, and the American Federation for Sex Hygiene. See Gertrude R. Luce, "History of Social Hygiene," Social Hygiene Papers (hereafter SHP), box 1, folder 1, Apr. 1930, Social Welfare Archives, University of Minnesota (Luce was the administrative secretary of ASHA); American Social Hygiene Association, "First Annual Report, 1913–1914" (New York: American Social Hygiene Association, 1914); *Vigilance* 25, 3 (Mar. 1912); *Social Diseases*, 1, 3 (July 1910). There is no single history of the social hygiene movement, but see Allan M. Brandt, *No Magic Bullet: A Social History of Venereal Disease in the United States Since 1880*, expanded ed. (New York: Oxford University Press, 1987), and Jeffrey P. Moran, *Teaching Sex: The Shaping of Adolescence in the 20th Century* (Cambridge, Mass.: Harvard University Press, 2000), both of which have excellent accounts. For unpublished material on the social hygiene movement, see Irving Kassoy, "A History of the Work of the American Social Hygiene Association in Sex Education, 1876–1930," master's thesis, City College of New York, 1931; James Gardner, "Microbes and Morality: The Social Hygiene Crusade in New York City, 1892–1917," Ph.D. dissertation, Indiana University, 1974; Wallace Maw, "Fifty Years of Sex Education in the Public Schools of the United States (1900–1950): A History of Ideas," Ph.D. dissertation, Teacher's College, University of Cincinnati, 1953; and Michael Imber, "Analysis of a Curricular Reform Movement: The American Social Hygiene Association's Campaign for Sex Education," Ph.D. Dissertation, Stanford University, 1980. For a history of Progressive

reformers, see Samuel Haber, *Efficiency and Uplift: Scientific Management in the Progressive Era, 1890–1920* (Chicago: University of Chicago Press, 1964).

3. My account of this meeting draws from Anna Garlin Spencer's memoir (see below) and the account in Maw, "Fifty Years of Sex Education." Various founding documents disagree on how many and who attended this meeting. Accordingly, I have used the entire founding membership of ASHA, whether or not I can document that they were at this particular meeting, to describe who these reformers were and what they represented.

4. Anna Garlin Spencer, "Pioneers," *Journal of Social Hygiene* (1930): 157. See also "Steps in the Development of ASHA," SHP (ca. 1922), box 1, folder 1. My account covers the first meeting, in Grace Hoadley Dodge's dining room in 1913, and the subsequent meeting at which the constitution of the American Social Hygiene Association was signed. My information comes from ASHA minute books, SHP, box 5, folder 1, 1913–1914. The full list of the first board of directors includes people who missed one or another meeting.

5. Irving Kassoy, "A History of the Work of the American Social Hygiene Association in Sex Education, 1876–1930," unpublished master's thesis, College of the City of New York, New York, 1931.

6. Charles Walter Clarke, *Taboo: The Story of the Pioneers of Social Hygiene* (Washington, D.C.: Public Affairs Press, 1961), p. 61. Note that Hepburn's task that day was to enlist Eliot into the predecessor organization of AHSA, the American Federation for Sex Hygiene.

7. I have written elsewhere about the gender dimensions of this movement. See Kristin Luker, "Sex, Social Hygiene, and the State: The Double-Edged Sword of Social Reform," *Theory and Society* 27 (1998): 601–34. For a feeling for the cultural ideals that were to be united, see Barbara Welter, "The Cult of True Womanhood: 1820–1860," *American Quarterly* 18, 2, part 1 (1966): 151–74.

8. Only Anna Garlin Spencer was a mother, but the ideology of social motherwork, also known as social (or "municipal") housekeeping, was powerful for these women. They and the Progressive reformers more generally have had rather bad press in the past few decades, having been criticized for universalizing the values of their class and race to others and for foreclosing a more genuine full citizenship for women with their "maternalist" vision. (See, for example,

Anthony M. Platt, *The Child Savers: The Invention of Delinquency*, 2d ed. (Chicago: University of Chicago Press, 1977); Estelle B. Freedman, *Their Sisters' Keepers: Women's Prison Reform in America, 1830–1930* (Ann Arbor: University of Michigan Press, 1981); and Theda Skocpol, *Protecting Soldiers and Mothers: The Political Origins of Social Policy in the United States* (Cambridge, Mass.: Belknap/Harvard University Press, 1992). It strikes me as important, however, to recognize that these women were trying to create new and female-centered ways of thinking about social policy, ways that did not simply replicate the problems that they saw in male efforts at social reform. As Joan Tronto points out, this is a very difficult task and brings with it a whole set of new pitfalls; see Tronto, *Moral Boundaries: A Political Argument for an Ethic of Care* (New York: Routledge, 1993). True, these women reformers were not entirely able to transcend their own time and place, but who among us can? And they certainly tried. Florence Kelley, for example, wrote of the need for a "working-class philanthropy" which was mutual and reciprocal, in contrast to "bourgeois" philanthropy, which was hierarchical; (see Dorothy Rose Blumberg, *Florence Kelley: The Making of a Social Pioneer* (New York: A. M. Kelley, 1966), p. 79, as well as Kathryn Kish Sklar, *Florence Kelley and the Nation's Work* (New Haven: Yale University Press, 1995). The underappreciated influence of Jane Addams on modern social science is reviewed in Mary Jo Deegan, *Jane Addams and the Men of the Chicago School, 1892–1918.* (New Brunswick, N.J.: Transaction, 1988). Grace Dodge insisted that she got as much from the working girls whose cause she adopted as she gave. Perhaps the best analysis is that of John D'Emilio and Estelle B. Freedman, who note that the Progressive movement "embodied sharply conflicting impulses—social order as well as social justice, efficiency as well as uplift, faith in the power of education as well as a determination to coerce the recalcitrant" (D'Emilio and Freedman, *Intimate Matters: A History of Sexuality in America* [New York: Harper & Row, 1988], p. 203).

9. SHP, box 5, folder 3. For backgrounds on these benefactors of the American Social Hygiene Association and where their fortunes came from, see: Michael Patrick Allen, *The Founding Fortunes: A New Anatomy of the Super-Rich Families in America* (New York: Dutton, 1989). For the estimate of current values, I have turned to Samuel H.

Williamson, "What Is the Relative Value?" *Economic History Services,* April 16, 2003, http://www.eh.net/hmit/compare/.

10. Ibid.

11. National PTA, "Jubilee History—50th Anniversary 1897–1947," p. 100. On the role of social hygiene in World War I, see below, and Brandt, *No Magic Bullet,* pp. 52–95.

12. To be sure, the social hygienists attracted their share of controversy, particularly at first. See Jeffrey P. Moran, " 'Modernism Gone Mad': Sex Education Comes to Chicago, 1913," *Journal of American History* 83, 2 (1996): 481–513. Yet in contrast to the current debate, those opposed to the movement felt that sex should not be mentioned in public and did not fight over what should be taught to young people.

13. A 1902 survey found thirty-two cities with de facto legal prostitution and thirty-three more with "segregated" or "tolerated" red-light districts. See E. R. A. Seligman, *The Social Evil of Protected Prostitution: Three Investigations* (New York: G.P. Putnam's Sons, 1902).

14. Only one locality—St. Louis, Missouri—ever established a formal, "regulated" red-light district, and then only for a short period. See John C. Burnham, "The Medical Inspection of Prostitutes in the Nineteenth Century: The St. Louis Experiment and Its Sequel," *Bulletin of the History of Medicine* 45 (1971): 203–18. See also the canonical work of David Pivar, *Purity Crusade: Sexual Morality and Social Control, 1868–1900* (Westport, Conn.: Greenwood, 1973), pp. 131–203. See also Ruth Rosen, *The Lost Sisterhood: Prostitution in America, 1900–1918* (Baltimore: Johns Hopkins University Press, 1982), and Barbara Meil Hobson, *Uneasy Virtue: The Politics of Prostitution and the American Reform Tradition* (New York: Basic, 1987). A classic—inded *the* classic—community study of the 1930's descibed Muncie, Indiana, as a "wide-open" town. See Robert and Helen Merrell Lynd, *Middletown: A Study in Modern American Culture* (New York: Harcourt Brace, 1929), p. 113.

15. See Prince Albert Morrow, *Social Diseases and Marriage: Social Prophylaxis* (New York: Lea, 1904), and William P. Snow, "Clinics for Venereal Diseases: Why We Need Them, How to Develop Them," *Social Hygiene* 3, 1 (Jan. 1916): 11–25. For a more contemporary view, see Harry F. Dowling, *Fighting Infection: Conquests of the Twentieth Century* (Cambridge, Mass.: Harvard University Press, 1977), pp. 18, 91–95.

16. As the renowned classicist Keith Thomas notes, the double standard is the view that "unchastity, in the sense of sexual relations before marriage or outside of marriage, is for man if an offense, none the less a mild and pardonable one, but for a woman the matter of utmost gravity" (Thomas, "The Double Standard," *Journal of the History of Ideas* 20, 2 [Apr. 1959]: 195). The term "tolerated" actually meant "legalized" for the social hygienists, but can be understood to cover the de facto acceptance of red-light districts as well as proposals to legalize them. Such districts were so open and commercialized that guides to them were published in the larger cities.

17. Physical necessity was also known as sexual necessity. See William H. Howell, *The So-Called Sexual Necessity in Man* (Baltimore: Maryland Society of Social Hygiene, 1912); Prince Albert Morrow, *The Young Man's Problem* (New York: American Society of Sanitary and Moral Prophylaxis, 1900); and Max Joseph Exner, *The Physician's Answer: Medical Authority and the Prevailing Misconceptions About Sex* (New York: Association Press, 1913). For a more complete view of this vision of sexuality in turn-of-the century America, see Allan Brandt's *No Magic Bullet*, 25–27.

18. One feminist social hygienist put her thoughts on the matter this way: "The dogma of sexual necessity exonerated men from public resentment, but served, of course, to perpetuate the social evil by preventing the operation of the law against those who financed prostitution. By a curious lapse of reason men were excused for indulging in illicit sexual relations on the ground of their naturally promiscuous instincts, but the necessary association of women in such congress was overlooked and the individual prostitute came under the ban of public opinion" (Edith Houghton Hooker, *The Laws of Sex* [Boston: Richard G. Badger/Gorham, 1921], p. 67). Keep in mind that under the ancient doctrine of coverture, a married man could not be legally prosecuted for raping his wife. The "marital exemption" passed out of family law in all fifty states only in 1993.

19. Lavinia Dock, *Hygiene and Morality: A Manual for Nurses and Others, Giving an Outline of the Medical, Social, and Legal Aspects of the Venereal Diseases* (New York: Putnam, 1910), pp. 60–62.

20. Anna Garlin Spencer, "The Double Standard of Morals: The Last Refuge of Human Slavery," *Vigilance* 25 (Sept. 1912): 9.

21. The critique of the double standard had a long history among Amer-

ican women reformers. See Mary Ryan, "The Power of Women's Networks: A Case Study of Female Moral Reform in Ante-bellum America," *Feminist Studies* 5 (Spring 1979): 82–104, and Carroll Smith-Rosenberg, "Beauty, the Beast, and the Militant Woman: A Case Study of Sex Roles and Social Stress in Jacksonian America," *American Quarterly* 23 (1971): 562–84. For an eloquent statement of the feminist position, see Antoinette Blackwell, "The Immorality of the Regulation System," *The National Purity Congress: Its Papers, Addresses, Portraits* (New York, American Purity Alliance, 1896), p. 26. For the Maine Federation of Women's Clubs, see Karen Blair, "The Clubwoman as Feminist," Ph.D. dissertation, State University of New York at Buffalo, 1976. Chapter 4 of Ruth Rosen's *The Lost Sisterhood* offers an excellent overview of the commitment to the single standard on the part of female reformers.

22. See Steven Seidman, *Romantic Longings: Love in America, 1830–1980* (New York: Routledge, 1991), pp. 122–24, and Phillips Cutright, "The Teenage Sexual Revolution and the Myth of an Abstinent Past," *Family Planning Perspectives* 4, 1 (Jan. 1972): 25–29.

23. Frederick Jackson Turner, *The Frontier in American History* (New York: Holt, 1920).

24. Kenneth Warren, *Big Steel: The First Century of the United States Steel Corporation, 1901–2001* (Pittsburgh: University of Pittsburgh Press, 2001), p. 7. As Warren notes, much of the nominal capital was represented by physical plant. Still, at the time, it was the "largest industrial organization of any kind worldwide."

25. U.S. Census, *Historical Statistics of the United States, Colonial Times to 1970*, bicentennial ed., Part 2, Series c-228-295, "Foreign-Born Population by Country of Birth, 1850–1970" (Washington, D.C.: Government Printing Office, 1975).

26. To give a sense of how this cultural and technological shift changed everyday life, see Robert Wiebe, *The Search for Order, 1877–1920* (New York: Hill and Wang, 1967).

27. There are many fine books on this period, including the classics: J. Stanley Lemons, *The Woman Citizen: Social Feminism in the 1920s* (Urbana: University of Illinois Press, 1973), and William L. O'Neill, *Everyone Was Brave: The Rise and Fall of Feminism in America* (Chicago: Quadrangle, 1969).

28. The exact causes and mechanisms of the decline are still being

debated. Clearly, in the United States, as elsewhere, a new industrial economy led families to invest more resources in fewer children. (The classic book on the process, though it applies to England, is Joseph Banks and Olive Banks, *Feminism and Family Planning in Victorian England* [Liverpool: University Press, 1964]). Several excellent histories trace both the motivations for and the mechanisms by which birth limitation was accomplished: Linda Gordon, *Woman's Body, Woman's Right: A Social History of Birth Control in America* (New York: Grossman, 1976); James Reed, *From Private Vice to Public Virtue: The Birth Control Movement and American Society since 1830* (New York: Basic, 1978); and James C. Mohr, *Abortion in America: The Origins and Evolution of National Policy, 1800–1900* (New York: Oxford University Press, 1978). Both Reed and Gordon have published substantially revised versions of their books as the historiography of birth limitation has expanded in recent years: James Reed, *The Birth Control Movement and American Society: From Private Vice to Public Virtue* (Princeton, N.J.: Princeton University Press, 1984), and Linda Gordon, *The Moral Property of Women: A History of Birth Control Politics in America*, 3d ed. (Urbana: University of Illinois Press, 2002). In addition, farming had become massively more productive in this period; more land became farmland in the thirty years before 1900 than in all of the time since the founding of the colonies. But the mechanization of farming—the birth of agribusiness—drove down the price of farm products and led to mortgages and the transformation of independent farmers into tenants. See F. A. Shannon, *The Farmer's Last Frontier: Agriculture, 1860–1897* (New York: Farrar & Rinehart, 1945).

29. For a flavor of the concern, see Theodore Roosevelt, *The Foes of Our Own Household* (New York: George H. Doran, 1917), p. 257; Lydia Commander, *The American Idea* (New York: Barnes, 1907), p. 198; Charles Richmond Henderson (also a social hygienist of some note), "Are Modern Industry and City Life Unfavorable to the Family?" *American Journal of Sociology* 14, 5 (1909): 668–80; and Frederick L. Hoffman, "Decline in the Birth Rate," *North American Review* (1909): 675–87. It should be noted that although casual observers sometimes denounced sewing machines and their effects on female fertility, more thoughtful critics pointed out that the sewing machines they were worried about were located in sweatshops, where overwork may well have had an effect on fertility.

30. "Annual Reports of the President and Treasurer of Harvard College, 1901–1902," Harvard Archives.

31. Paul H. Jacobson, "Tables of Absolute Divorces and Annulments, and Rates, United States, 1860–1956," in *American Marriage and Divorce* (New York: Rinehart and Jacobsen, 1959), table 42, p. 90. The ratio (not rate) moved from 3 divorces per 1,000 marriages to 4, and then to 7.7. For contemporary reports that fueled the flames of anxiety, see Carroll D. Wright, *Marriage and Divorce in the United States, 1867–1886*, First Special Report of the Commissioner of Labor (Washington, D.C.: Government Printing Office, 1889), and S. N. D. North, *Marriage and Divorce*, Special Reports (Washington, D.C.: Government Printing Office, 1909). Along the same lines, see Samuel W. Dike, *Perils to the Family: An Address Delivered Before the Evangelical Alliance Conference at Washington, D.C., Dec. 8, 1897* (New York: Evangelical Alliance for the United States, 1888).

32. G. Stanley Hall, *Adolescence: Its Psychology and Its Relations to Physiology, Anthropology, Sociology, Sex, Crime, Religion, and Education* (New York: Appleton, 1904).

33. This line of analysis draws on the work of historians such as Philippe Aries, *Centuries of Childhood: A Social History of Family Life* (New York: Knopf, 1962), and John R. Gillis, *Youth and History: Tradition and Change in European Age Relations, 1770–Present* (New York: Academic, 1974). More specifically in the American context, I have drawn on the work of Howard P. Chudacoff, *How Old Are You?: Age Consciousness in American Culture* (Princeton, N.J.: Princeton University Press, 1989).

34. Kathy Lee Peiss, *Cheap Amusements: Working Women and Leisure in New York City, 1880 to 1920* (Philadelphia: Temple University Press, 1985).

35. Amos G. Warner, *American Charities.* 1894 edition, pp. 66–71.

36. Peiss, *Cheap Amusements;* Mary Odem, *Delinquent Daughters: Protecting and Policing Adolescent Female Sexuality in the United States, 1885–1920* (Chapel Hill: University of North Carolina Press, 1995); Annie Allen, "How to Save Girls Who Have Fallen," *The Survey* 24, 1 (1910): 692; and Joan Brumberg, "Ruined Girls: Changing Community Responses to Illegitimacy in Upstate New York, 1890–1920," *Journal of Social History* 18 (1984): 247–72.

37. Frances A. Kellor, *Out of Work* (New York: Putnam, 1904), p. 77. The rest of the chapter ("Responsibility for Immorality and Vice")

shows how employment bureaus and hungry young women conspired to send "girls," often immigrants, to "disorderly houses."

38. Margaret Dreir Robbin, "One Aspect of the Menace of Low Wages," *Social Hygiene* 1, 3 (June 1915).

39. David B. Tyack and Elisabeth Hansot, *Learning Together: A History of Coeducation in American Schools* (New Haven: Yale University Press/ Russell Sage Foundation, 1990), and Barbara Miller Solomon, *In the Company of Educated Women: A History of Women and Higher Education in America* (New Haven: Yale University Press, 1985).

40. Beth Bailey, *From Front Porch to Back Seat.*

41. Reformers were divided among themselves as to whether early sexuality within marriage, i.e., getting married young, was harmful. Then, as now, part of the disagreement depended on what observers imagined to be the real alternatives to early marriage—that is, licentiousness or repression.

42. G. Stanley Hall, "Education and the Social Hygiene Movement," *Social Hygiene* 1, 1 (Dec. 1914): 32–33. *Social Hygiene* was the official publication of ASHA, renamed *The Journal of Social Hygiene* in 1922.

43. Mabel MacCoy Irwin, letter to Mary S. Cobb, Mar. 4, 1909. SHP box 1, folder 4.

44. The term is the journalist Frederick Lewis Allen's; see Allen, *Only Yesterday: An Informal History of the Nineteen-Twenties* (New York: Harper and Brothers, 1931). William Leuchtenburg makes much the same point, calling it "the Revolution in Morals"; see Leuchtenburg, *The Perils of Prosperity, 1914–32* (Chicago: University of Chicago Press, 1958). Samuel Eliot Morrison, in his *Oxford History of the American People* (New York: Oxford University Press, 1965), speaks of a "revolution in morals." Actually dating the beginning and ending of something as imprecise as the first sexual revolution (or the second one, for that matter, or even the French Revolution, the archetypical revolution) is problematic. For an overview of the debate vis-à-vis the first sexual revolution, see James R. McGovern, "The American Woman's Pre–World War I Freedom in Manners and Morals," *Journal of American History*, 55, 2 (1968): 315–33.

45. Lewis Madison Terman, *Psychological Factors in Marital Happiness* (New York: McGraw-Hill, 1938), p. 321.

46. Alfred Kinsey, *Sexual Behavior in the Human Female*, table 83, "Accumulative Incidence: Pre-Marital Coitus By Decade of Birth," p. 339.

47. "Sex O'Clock in America," *Current Opinion* (Aug. 1913): 113–14;

Agnes Repplier, "The Repeal of Reticence," *Atlantic Monthly* (Mar. 1914): 297–304.

48. *Recent Social Trends in the United States: Report of the President's Research Committee on Social Trends* (New York: McGraw-Hill, 1933), vol. 1, p. 414.

49. Bailey, *From Front Porch to Back Seat*. Strictly speaking, Bailey is interested in the period just after the one examined here, the 1920s. However, her analysis indicates that an old order of sexual courtship was undergoing profound transformation.

50. Clark W. Hetherington, "Play Leadership in Sex Education," *Social Hygiene* 1, 1 (1914): 36–43.

51. Rachel Yarros, *Modern Woman and Sex* (New York: Vanguard, 1933), pp. 11–12.

52. The National Fertility Survey of 1965 found that 34 percent of poor families had unwanted fertility, compared to only 15 percent of the nonpoor. Arthur Campbell, "The Role of Family Planning in the Reduction of Poverty," *Journal of Marriage and the Family* 31 (1969): 236–45; Reed, *From Private Vice to Public Virtue*, p. 379.

53. The social hygiene movement was something of a "mother" movement to the larger group that would to try to help Americans have happier and more erotically pleasurable marriages, from sexologists to marriage counselors to the National Council on Family Relations.

54. Early social hygienists, with the emphasis on venereal disease inherited from the anti-VD physicians in their ranks, could dwell on the symptoms and consequences of diseased sexuality, something that might well distract people from "wholesome" sexuality. See George R. Dodson, "Composite Appeal," *Social Hygiene* 2, no. 1.

55. I've used the awkward word "companionable" to distinguish this model from what contemporaries of the social hygienists, people like Judge Ben Lindsey, were calling for: "companionate" marriage, which we might call "trial marriage." As Lindsey saw it, young people would marry each other to see if they were compatible, with the expectation that they would break up if they were not and if no children had been born. Ben B. Lindsey and Wainwright Evans, *Companionate Marriage* (New York: Boni & Liveright, 1927).

56. American Federation for Sex Education, "Report of the Special Committee on the Matter and Methods of Sex Education, Presented Before the Subcommittee on Sex Hygiene of the Fifteenth International Con-

gress on Hygiene and Demography" (New York: American Federation for Sex Hygiene, Dec. 1912), p. 2.

57. Benjamin Gruenberg, *Parents and Sex Education: For Parents of Young Children* (New York: American Social Hygiene Association, 1928), pp. 1–2.

58. Spencer, "The Double Standard of Morals," pp. 5–6.

59. See, among other classic works, Elaine Tyler May, *Great Expectations: Marriage and Divorce in Post-Victorian America* (Chicago: University of Chicago Press, 1980), and Seidman, *Romantic Longings*.

60. Michel Foucault, *The History of Sexuality* (New York: Pantheon, 1978). Foucault argues that in the nineteenth century, "calling sex by its name . . . became more difficult and costly" (p. 17) and that "sexuality was carefully confined; it moved into the home. The conjugal family took custody of it and absorbed it into the serious function of reproduction. The legitimate and procreative couple laid down the law" (p. 3). I find myself agreeing with Steven Seidman when he says, "Contemporary observers [e.g., people like the social hygienists] may have been wrong to juxtapose Victorian silence and prudishness about sex to their own modern frankness and freedom. They were not mistaken, however, in believing that the current public discussion of sex was something new and that it pointed to changes in the conventions of intimate life" (Seidman, *Romantic Longings*, p. 65).

61. Maurice Alpheus Bigelow, *Sex Instruction as a Phase of Social Education* (New York: American Federation for Sex Hygiene, 1913), p.7.

62. Mosher et al., *The Mosher Survey*, pp. 11, 23–24, 43–44, 67, 113.

63. Michael Gordon, "From Unfortunate Necessity to a Cult of Mutual Orgasm: Sex in American Marital Education Literature, 1830–1940," in James M. Henslen, ed., *Studies in the Sociology of Sex* (New York: Appleton-Century-Crofts, 1971), pp. 53–77.

64. I'm not prepared to argue that premarital sex was a new development on the sexual scene in the Progressive era, as there is some evidence that our founding fathers (and mothers) knew quite a bit about it: the high rates of babies born quite soon after marriage in the eighteenth century suggest that premarital sex was quite common in earlier times. For more information, see Godbeer, *Sexual Revolution in Early America*, and Michael Hindus, "Premarital Pregnancy in America, 1640–1871: An Overview and an Interpretation." *Journal of Interdisciplinary History* 5 (July 1975): 537–70.

65. Despite the fact that social hygienists were viewed by some as daring, even radical, reformers, in fact they were liberal at best. Just a few short miles from the red dining room where Grace Dodge and her friends were hatching the outlines of social hygiene, much more radical sexual ideals were being bruited about by the Greenwich Village bohemians. People such as Crystal Eastman and Emma Goldman denounced marriage as an institution that enslaved women and sought what they saw as true sexual and gender equality; see Christine Stansell, *American Moderns: Bohemian New York and the Creation of a New Century* (New York: Metropolitan, 2000). And quietly, around the edges, a homosexual subculture had begun to grow up in the Village and elsewhere. While the definition of exactly what constituted homosexuality was still in flux, the love that dared not speak its name was beginning to whisper, at least to those who were listening. See, for example, George Chauncey, *Gay New York: Gender, Urban Culture, and the Makings of the Gay Male World, 1890–1940* (New York: Basic, 1994).

66. When the United States entered World War I in April 1917, Secretary of War Newton Baker set up a Commission on Training Camp Activities, and most of the leadership of the social hygiene movement was enlisted as the organizational infrastructure of the new commission. In July of that year, Congress created the Division of Venereal Disease of the U.S. Public Health Service and an Interdepartmental Social Hygiene Board, which sought to take the message of social hygiene to the troops (Clarke, *Taboo*, p. 80, and Brandt, *No Magic Bullet*, pp. 59–95).

67. Brandt, *No Magic Bullet*, pp. 283–85. For the number of draftees, see U.S. Department of Commerce, Bureau of the Census, *Historical Statistics of the United States, Colonial Times to 1970*, "Selected Characteristics of the Armed Forces, by War," Series Y-856-903, 1140; Keeping Fit: An Exhibit for Older Boys and Young Men (Washington, D.C.: U.S. Public Health Service, 1919). There was a deep ambivalence in practice about the single standard (the military condoned visits to prostitutes by insisting upon "prophylaxis," or treatment for VD immediately after exposure, rather than outlawing such visits entirely); see Luker, "Sex, Social Hygiene, and the State" and Edith Houghton Hooker, "A Criticism of Venereal Prophylaxis," *Social Hygiene*, 4, 2 (March 1918): 179–95.

68. Such pamphlets included *When They Come Home* (Washington, D.C.:

U.S. Public Health Service, 1918). For an overview of these publications, see Newell Edson, *The Status of Sex Education in High School*
(Washington, D.C.: U.S. Public Health Service, 1922).

69. In New Jersey, which seems to have the best-documented history of
sex education, we can discern some traces of what this kind of sex
education looked like in the first half of the twentieth century. In
1919, for example, the New Jersey Department of Health, under the
venereal disease division, began giving talks to high school students
about sex, and eight years later, an "industrial city" of 130,000 people, alarmed by its burgeoning out-of-wedlock birth rates, hired a
woman physician with training from ASHA to provide educational
services for high school girls and clinical services for both girls and
boys. In 1934, Temple University began doing in-service sex education training for school nurses and teachers, and five years later
Rutgers University began doing the same. In 1939, the New Jersey
social hygiene association set up an education committee, and in 1934
it became the Advisory Committee on Social Hygiene Education to
the New Jersey State Department of Education. In 1941 this group
published its statement of goals, *An Approach to Sex Education in
Schools*. See State of New Jersey, "Education for Family Life in the
Primary Grades," bulletin 13 (1948); Mabel Grier Lesher, "Education for Family Life (New Jersey)," *Journal of Educational Sociology* 22
(1949): 440–49; and New Jersey Social Hygiene Association, Education Committee, *An Approach to Sex Education in Schools* (New York:
American Social Hygiene Association, 1941).

70. Maw, "Fifty Years of Sex Education."

71. G. G. Wetherill, *Human Relations Education: A Program Developing in
the San Diego City Schools* (New York: American Social Hygiene Association, 1946), pp. 16–24.

72. See, for example, *Strengthening Family Life Education in Our Schools:
Report of the Midwest Project on in-Service Education of Teachers* (New
York: American Social Hygiene Association, 1955).

CHAPTER THREE: SEX EDUCATION,
THE SEXUAL REVOLUTION, AND THE SIXTIES

1. The U.S. Supreme Court ended the practice, common in many
schools, of forcing teachers to take mandatory pregnancy leave
whether they wanted to or not, in its 1974 decision, *Cleveland Board*

of *Education v. Lafleur,* 414 U.S. 632. The federal government did not protect pregnant workers until the Pregnancy Discrimination Act of 1978. For more on Jo Carol Lafleur, see Peter Irons, *The Courage of Their Convictions: Sixteen Americans Who Fought Their Way to the Supreme Court* (New York: The Free Press, 1988), pp. 305–29.

2. Sam Howe Verhovek, "Ban on Pregnant Cheerleaders Lifted," *New York Times,* Nov. 3, 1993, p. B-15.

3. Sandra L. Hofferth, Joan Kahn, and Wendy Baldwin, "Premarital Sexual Activity among U.S. Teenage Women over the Past Three Decades," *Family Planning Perspectives* 19 (1987): 46–53; see also James Trussell and Barbara Vaughn, "Selected Results Concerning Sexual Behavior and Contraceptive Use from the 1988 National Survey of Family Growth and the 1988 National Survey of Adolescent Males," Working Paper No. 91–12, Princeton, N.J.: Office of Population Research, 1991.

4. See Susheela Singh and Jacqueline E. Darroch, "Trends in Sexual Activity Among Adolescent American Women: 1982–1995," *Family Planning Perspectives* 31, 5 (1999): tables 3 and 4. In the end, "convergence" is a judgment call, since estimates of adolescent sexual activity vary significantly depending on the database used. See Joyce Abma, Clea Sucoff McNeely, and Michael Resnick, "Adolescent Sexual Behavior: Estimates and Trends from Four Nationally Representative Surveys," *Family Planning Perspectives* 32, 4 (2000). But even a cursory examination of the various data indicates that white adolescents and girls have increasingly begun to engage in behavior that was once much more common among African Americans and boys.

5. For the history of homes for unwed mothers and the different racial patterns of who kept and who gave up babies, see Rickie Solinger, *Wake Up, Little Susie: Single Pregnancy and Race before Roe v. Wade* (New York: Routledge, 1992), and Regina Kunzel, *Fallen Women, Problem Girls: Unmarried Mothers and the Professionalization of Social Work, 1890–1945* (New Haven: Yale University Press, 1993).

6. James Davison Hunter, *Culture Wars: The Struggle to Define America* (New York: Basic, 1991).

7. See Jon C. Pennington, "It's Not a Revolution But It Sure Looks Like One: A Statistical Accounting of the Post-Sixties Sexual Revolution," *Radical Statistics* 83 (2003): 104–16.

8. Arlene S. Skolnick compares these changes to an earthquake; see Skol-

nick, *Embattled Paradise: The American Family in an Age of Uncertainty* (New York: Basic, 1991). I particularly like Skolnick's point that while earthquakes are unpredictable, they happen along preexisting fault lines.

9. Kerner Commission, "Report of the National Advisory Commission on Civil Disorders" (Washington, D.C.: Government Printing Office, 1968).

10. "Jackson Police Fire on Students: Two Killed and 12 Injured at Women's Dormitory," *New York Times*, May 15, 1970, p. 1; "Violence on Campus," *New York Times*, May 3, 1970, p. 5.

11. The two states were Massachusetts and Connecticut. See Mary Dudziak, "Just Say No: Birth Control in the Connecticut Supreme Court before *Griswold v. Connecticut*," *Iowa Law Review* 75, 4 (1990): 915–39, and David J. Garrow, *Liberty and Sexuality: The Right to Privacy and the Making of Roe v. Wade* (New York: Macmillan, 1994).

12. U.S. Bureau of the Census, "Fertility Indicators, 1970," *Current Population Reports*, Series P-23, no. 36, table 32, p. 53. Charles Goodyear vulcanized rubber in 1839 and obtained a patent for the process in 1841. Vulcanized rubber is stronger and more durable than unvulcanized rubber and relatively impervious to heat and cold. Within a decade, this new material was being used for contraceptive devices in the form of inexpensive condoms, diaphragms, and bulb syringes for douching. In addition, Americans used withdrawal and the rhythm method (periodic abstinence). The latter method was hampered by the fact that scientists did not ascertain until the 1930s that women's fertile period was in the middle of the cycle rather than during the menses, as is the case with other mammals.

13. Researchers began asking unmarried women in select subpopulations what contraceptives they were using in the mid-1970s. But except for women who had already borne a child out of wedlock, the only national survey (the National Survey of Family Growth) did not ask unmarried women about their sexuality until 1982. Data on premarital sex are from Singh and Darroch, "Trends in Sexual Activity Among Adolescent American Women," pp. 212–19. For an overview of surveys on sex, see Julia A. Ericksen, *Kill and Tell: Surveying Sex in the Twentieth Century* (Cambridge: Harvard University Press, 1999).

14. To get a sense of this other world, one needs only to read any of the

gay coming-of-age novels that have appeared since then, such as
Edmund White, *A Boy's Own Story* (New York: Dutton, 1982), and
Farewell Symphony (New York: Knopf, 1997).

15. John D'Emilio, *Sexual Politics, Sexual Communities: The Making of a
Homosexual Minority in the United States, 1940–1970* (Chicago: University of Chicago Press, 1983), pp. 57–91. Though radical in inspi-
ration, the first homophile organizations were forced into a more
"respectable" civil rights stance.

16. Kunzel, *Fallen Women, Problem Girls*, and Solinger, *Wake Up, Little
Susie*.

17. Jane Harriman, "In Trouble: The Story of an Unwed Woman's Decision to Keep Her Child," *Atlantic Monthly* (Mar. 1970): 94–98. Along
the same lines, see "Single Motherhood," *Time*, Sept. 6, 1971, and
"Unmarried Parent: Is Martha Doing Right?" *Senior Scholastic*, Oct.
9, 1972, p. 13. Interview with Fred Mayer, 1984. Mayer was active
in this period in trying to change the attitudes of pharmacists.

18. What was new about the abortion decision is that the Supreme Court
expanded the right to privacy they had found in *Griswold v. Connecticut* (381 U.S. 479) to cover both "bearing" and "begetting" a
child. Privacy in these cases, moreover, is a "fundamental" one, that
is, one that can only be overcome by a "compelling" state interest.
Cf. *Roe v. Wade*, 410 U.S. 113 (1973).

19. Raymond Williams, *Keywords: A Vocabulary of Culture and Society*, rev.
ed. (New York: Oxford University Press, 1983), pp. 270–74. See
also Norberto Bobbio and Allan Cameron, *Left and Right: The Significance of a Political Distinction* (Chicago: University of Chicago Press,
1996).

20. Lynn Avery Hunt, *Politics, Culture, and Class in the French Revolution;
Studies on the History of Society and Culture* (Berkeley: University of
California Press, 1984).

21. See, for example, Ruth Rosen's chapter on "The Hidden Injuries of
Sex" in her powerful history of the women's movement, *The World
Split Open: How the Modern Women's Movement Changed America* (New
York: Viking, 2000), pp. 143–95.

22. Arlie Russell Hochschild and Anne Machung, *The Second Shift:
Working Parents and the Revolution at Home* (New York: Viking, 1989),
speaks of a "stalled revolution" in gender roles.

23. This is not to say that the double standard has entirely disappeared,

of course, because there is a considerable amount of evidence to the contrary. What has changed, however, are its sharp edges. In terms of the argument I make, both the gradual decline of the (heterosexual) double standard and the rise of more open homosexuality were products of new definitions of intimate relationships. Keep in mind that what I'm talking about here is cultural ideals, not necessarily actual practices. Before the sexual revolution, many men agreed, at least in principle, that premarital sex was wrong. See Ira L. Reiss, "The Double Standard in Premarital Sexual Intercourse: A Neglected Concept," *Social Forces* 34, 3 (1956): 224–30; Erwin O. Smigel, and Rita Seiden, "The Decline and Fall of the Double Standard," *Annals of the American Academy of Political and Social Science* 376, Sex and the Contemporary American Scene (March 1968): 6–17. But see Susan Sprecher, Kathleen McKinney, and Terri L. Orbuch, "Has the Double Standard Disappeared? An Experimental Test," *Social Psychology Quarterly* 50, 1 (1987): 24–31, which suggests a double standard exists on the unconscious level.

24. Charles F. Turner, Heather G. Miller, and Lincoln E. Moses, *AIDS: Sexual Behavior and Intravenous Drug Use* (Washington, D.C.: National Academy Press, 1989); Melvin Zelnik and John F. Kantner, "The Probability of Premarital Intercourse." *Social Science Research* 1 (1972): 335–41; Melvin Zelnik and John F. Kantner, "Sexual and Contraceptive Experience of Young Unmarried Women in the United States, 1976 and 1971," *Family Planning Perspectives* 9, 2 (1977): 55–56, 58–63, 67–71.

25. Zelnik and Kantner, "Sexual and Contraceptive Experience of Young Unmarried Women"; A. F. Saluter, "Marital Status and Living Arrangements," *Current Population Reports*, Series P-20, no. 461 (Mar. 1991).

26. Jacqueline D. Forrest and Susheela Singh, "The Sexual and Reproductive Behavior of American Women, 1982–1988," *Family Planning Perspectives* 22, 5 (1990): 206–14.

27. Susan Moller Okin, *Women in Western Political Thought* (Princeton, N.J.: Princeton University Press, 1979). On social context defining biological "reality," see Kristin Luker, *Taking Chances: Abortion and the Decision Not to Contracept* (Berkeley: University of California Press, 1975), and Reva Siegel, "Reasoning from the Body: A Historical Perspective on Abortion Regulation and Questions of Equal Protection," *Stanford Law Review* 44 (Jan. 1992): 261. Siegel argues that

motherhood and its attendant expectations grow out of specific social and historical conditions rather than biology.

28. Claudia Goldin and Lawrence F. Katz, "The Power of the Pill: Oral Contraceptives and Women's Career and Marriage Decisions," *Journal of Political Economy* 110, 4 (2002): 730–70.

29. Simone de Beauvoir, *The Second Sex* (New York: Knopf, 1953), and Mary Ryan in Craig J. Calhoun, *Habermas and the Public Sphere, Studies in Contemporary German Social Thought* (Cambridge, Mass.: MIT Press, 1992).

30. On the diffusion of changing norms about sexuality and family, see Arland Thornton, Duane F. Alwin, and Donald Camburn, "Causes and Consequences of Sex-Role Attitudes and Attitude Change," *American Sociological Review* 48, 2 (1983): 211–27. Daniel Yankelovitch, *The New Morality: A Profile of American Youth in the 1970s* (New York: McGraw-Hill, 1974) tracks how these "new values" moved from college-educated youth to those with less education.

31. Yankelovitch, *The New Morality,* p. 3.

32. *The Group* was actually published in 1953 but follows the fortunes of "the group" of friends who graduated in the Vassar class of 1933. See also Beth Bailey, *From Front Porch to Back Seat* (Baltimore: Johns Hopkins University Press, 1988).

33. See Gallup Polls 780, 874. For an overview, see Benjamin I. Page and Robert Y. Shapiro, *The Rational Public: Fifty Years of Trends in Americans' Policy Preferences* (Chicago: University of Chicago Press, 1992). Once again, the expansion of sexual liberties to people of the same sex did not seem to be on the minds of most heterosexuals.

34. Ibid., pp. 104–5.

35. The General Social Survey and the Gallup Poll asked questions about abortion from the early 1960s to the eve of *Roe v. Wade* and beyond. These questions asked whether women should have abortions under different specified conditions ("Please tell me whether or not it should be possible for a pregnant woman to obtain a legal abortion if there is a strong chance of a defect in the baby . . . if she is married and does not want any more children . . . if the woman's own health is seriously endangered by the pregnancy . . . if the family has a very low income and cannot afford any more children"). There was and continues to be a discrepancy between those who favor abortion for health reasons and birth defects (the "hard" reasons) and those who

accept it for economic reasons and because a family has all the children the parents want. Still, all categories showed increases from 1962 to 1972, and a plateau (or some decrease of support) afterward. See Page and Shapiro, *Rational Public*, pp. 64, 104–10, and 400. In the ten years between 1962 and 1972 there was a change of thirty percentage points in the numbers of Americans who thought that poverty was a legitimate reason for having an abortion; between 1965 and 1972 there was a twenty-point change in people who thought that a potentially serious birth defect was. These are, needless to say, extraordinary levels of change in a very short time.

36. Yankelovitch, *The New Morality*, p. 24.
37. National Center for Health Statistics, *National Vital Statistics Reports* 50, 10 (June 6, 2002).
38. In earlier research, I asked teen mothers about events leading up to their pregnancies, and virtually all of them described the pregnancy as having happened "accidentally." Yet for most of them, the pregnancy happened after having had sex without using contraception; the fact that they had actively chosen not to have an abortion suggested that while cultural forces shape how poor, young women describe their pregnancies, their actions tell another story. In this context, see James Trussell, Barbara Vaughan, and Joseph Stanford, "Are All Contraceptive Failures Unintended Pregnancies? Evidence from the 1995 National Survey of Family Growth (a Research Note)," *Family Planning Perspectives* 31, 5 (1999): 246–47, 60.
39. The survey that asked this question (in 1974, 1979, and 1985) was the Virginia Slims Poll. Percentages approving the statement rose from 30.7 in 1974 to 47.0 in 1985, which, while still far short of a majority, is an astonishing change from the practices of just a few years earlier. See Deanna L. Pagnini and Ronald R. Rindfuss, "The Divorce of Marriage and Childbearing: Changing Attitudes and Behavior in the United States," *Population and Development Review* 19, 2 (1993): 331–47.
40. For the diffusion of these values from a small group of highly educated youth to a wider population, see Yankelovitch, *The New Morality*. For changes within the larger population, see Page and Shapiro, *Rational Public*, pp. 104–10, and Richard G. Niemi, John Muller, and Tom W. Smith, *Trends in Public Opinion: A Compendium of Survey Data* (New York: Greenwood Press, 1989), pp. 187–214.

41. Jane Mauldon and Kristin Luker, "Does Liberalism Cause Sex?" *American Prospect* 24 (1996): 80.

42. George Akerlof, Janet Yellen, and Michael Katz, "An Analysis of Out-of-Wedlock Childbearing in the United States," *Quarterly Journal of Economics* 111, 2 (1996).

43. See Ira L. Reiss, *Premarital Sexual Standards in America: A Sociological Investigation of the Relative Social and Cultural Integration of American Sexual Standards* (New York: Free Press, 1966). For an interesting perspective on these issues, see Reiss's dialogue with the sexologist Albert Ellis: Ira L. Reiss and Albert Ellis, *At the Dawn of the Sexual Revolution: Reflections on a Dialogue* (Walnut Creek, Calif.: Altamira, 2002).

44. Mary S. Calderone, M.D., "Time: The Present," *SIECUS Newsletter* 3, 5 (June 1968): 2.

45. The SEAB reported to the Division of Sex Education within the Office of the State Superintendent and was made up of five representatives of state agencies and four members of the general public. See "Illinois Policy Statement on Family Life and Sex Education, 1967," in Beatrice M. Gudridge and American Association for Health, Physical Education, and Recreation, *Sex Education in Schools: A Review of Current Policies and Programs for the Guidance of School Board Members, Administrators, Teachers, and Parents* (Washington: National School Public Relations Association, 1969).

46. Before the AIDS epidemic, there was something of a mini-panic over herpes. Between 1960 and 1970 there were only twenty-two references to the disease in the *Readers' Guide to Periodic Literature*, and most of these were of a scientific nature. Between 1971 and 1980, there were forty-eight, and most were still of a scientific nature (e.g., J. G. Stevens et al., "Latent Herpes Simplex Virus in Spinal Ganglia of Mice," *Science*, 173 [Aug. 27, 1971]: 843–45). But starting in the 1970s, then accelerating in the 1980s, the sexual dimension moved to the front as in "Herpes: The New Sexual Leprosy," *Time* 116 (July 28, 1980): 76; "Venereal Disease of the New Morality," *Today's Health* 53 (Mar. 1975): 42–43; and "The Herpes Epidemic: Has It Destroyed the Sexual Revolution?" *Glamour* 80 (Dec. 1982): 36. Oddly enough, by the 1990s, the nation's media, perhaps preoccupied with HIV/AIDS, stopped reporting on herpes almost entirely.

47. Ulrich Beck, *Risk Society: Towards a New Modernity* (Newbury Park, Calif.: Sage, 1992).

CHAPTER FOUR: SEXUAL LIBERALS AND SEXUAL CONSERVATIVES

1. The terms "left" and "right" date back to the French Revolution. In an attempt to stave off the Revolution, King Louis called a meeting of parliament. Individuals there were seated on the basis of their rank; nobility and clergy sat in the place of honor at the king's right, and commoners made do with the seats on his left. The decision of how to seat people embodied social relations, and as such was extremely fraught. When dissidents bolted from the meeting and declared themselves a new National Assembly empowered to govern France, they maintained the distinction between left and right ordained by custom, but this time with a new twist: where people sat now represented a political rather than a social position. Those seated on the left were the radicals, the defenders of the less privileged, those in favor of quick and decisive action. Those on the right were the conservatives, more cautious, more respectful of tradition, more concerned about stability. (Marcel Gauchet, however, argues that the left/right distinction only became fully consolidated during the Restoration; Guachet, *La Droite et la Gauche* [Paris: Gallimard, 1992].)

2. There were certain asymmetries in how people used these terms. For example, those supporting comprehensive sex education often called their opponents "right-wingers" and laughingly referred to themselves as "left-wingers" or even "flaming liberals." No one who supported abstinence education called himself or herself a "right-winger," perhaps because the term connotes a level of extremism that is implicitly denigrating. Meanwhile, although these people were happy to call themselves "conservative" and often enough "conservative Christians," they rarely joked about either their stance or the stance of their opponents.

3. Some of the younger people, like Mary Kay Malone, experienced the 1960s in their teenage years, but even they recall their early sex education as what I'm calling sexually conservative.

4. Compare, for example, the number of books with the idea "beyond left and right" in their titles, written by people traditionally identified with both the left and the right. Anthony Giddens, *Beyond Left and Right: The Future of Radical Politics* (Palo Alto, Calif.: Stanford University Press, 1995); David A. Horowitz, *Beyond Left and Right: The Insurgency and the Establishment* (Champaign, Ill.: University of Illinois Press, 1996); Frank Furedi, *Politics of Fear: Beyond Left and*

Right (New York: Continuum International, 2003); and Jim Wallis, *The Soul of Politics: Beyond "Religious Right" and "Secular Left"* (New York: New Press, 1995).

5. For example, see John H. Hallowell, *Main Currents in Modern Political Thought* (New York: Holt, 1950); Richard M. Weaver, "Up from Liberalism," *Modern Age* (Winter 1958–59): 29; and above all Leo Strauss, *Natural Right and History*, Charles R. Walgreen Foundation Lectures (Chicago: University of Chicago Press, 1953). Norberto Bobbio (*Left and Right: The Significance of a Political Distinction* [Chicago: University of Chicago Press, 1996]) suggests that a longing for hierarchy is the only thing that separates the right from the left.

6. In essence, I was asking people to fill in the "elements," as the cognitive linguist Eleanor Rosch calls them, of the category of sexual liberal and sexual conservative. See Eleanor Rosch, *Basic Objects in Natural Categories,* working paper no. 43 (Berkeley: Language Behavior Research Laboratory, University of California, 1975); as well as Eleanor Rosch, Barbara Bloom Lloyd, and the Social Science Research Council, *Cognition and Categorization* (Hillsdale, N.J.: L. Erlbaum Associates, 1978).

7. For example, Arland Thornton and his colleagues have found that very religious teens are less likely to have sex, but having sex makes an adolescent less religious. Likewise, very religiously observant people are less likely to live together ("cohabit," in demographic jargon), but if they do, they tend to become less religiously observant. See Arland Thornton, William G. Axinn, and Daniel H. Hill, "Reciprocal Effects of Religiosity, Cohabitation, and Marriage," *American Journal of Sociology* 98, 3 (1992): 628–61; Arland Thornton and Donald Camburn, "Religious Participation and Adolescent Sexual Behavior and Attitudes," *Journal of Marriage and the Family* 51, 3 (1989): 641–53.

8. William F. Snow, "Progress 1900–1914," *Social Hygiene* 2, 1 (1916).

9. Briefly, this is the doctrine of coverture, in which a woman was "covered" by her husband. It was classically expressed in Anglo-American law by the great commentator William Blackstone in the eighteenth century; see Blackstone, *Commentaries on the Laws of England* (Chicago: University of Chicago Press, 1979). For a lucid exposition of the history and functioning of the doctrine, see Norma Basch, *In the Eyes of the Law: Women, Marriage, and Property in Nineteenth-Century New York* (Ithaca, N.Y.: Cornell University Press, 1982).

10. *Borelli v. Bruseau*, 12 Cal. App. 4th 647 (Cal. App. 1 Dist. 1993).

11. "Current changes [in matrimonial property systems] . . . are related to changes in the ideology of marriage and in the economic and social roles of women, especially of married women, which are having an impact on this, as well as many other areas of the law. The peculiar difficulty with which all systems of marital property are presently struggling arises from the fact that the idea of the independent and equal individuality of each spouse coexists in modern industrialized and urbanized societies with the idea that marriage is somehow a community of interest of those independent and equal individuals. The coexistence is uneasy because these two ideas are always in tension." Mary Ann Glendon, "Matrimonial Property: A Comparative Study of Law and Social Change," *Tulane Law Review* 49 (1974): 21.

12. Surprisingly, most of the people I interviewed did not think that abortion was a red flag, perhaps because schools are exquisitely aware these days that abortion is controversial and treat it gingerly. Alternatively, people who oppose abortion may see that it has been legal for three decades and despair of changing the situation.

13. Similarly, Susan Shelly, who is not opposed to the use of contraception, is opposed to giving young people information about it on the grounds that to tell them how to avoid pregnancy is to accept non-marital sex. As she says, "By teaching about prophylactics and other methods of birth control, you are by giving that information saying it's okay to use it. Whereas we don't feel it is. We don't feel it's okay for teenagers to have these readily available to them. You're giving them a double message, like, 'Well, maybe you shouldn't be doing this, but just in case you do, here it is.' And that, first of all, is insulting their intelligence, because they can figure it out for themselves, you know they can find out what to do if they so choose, but they see the double message . . . And because they're still immature, I don't think they really understand how to handle that, and I think many kids go into a sexual relationship not just out of peer pressure but because the parents have made it available to them as an option."

14. This hits at the core of why the two sides disagree about homosexuality. To the sexual conservatives, homosexuality is a learned behavior, and a morally suspect one. To the liberals, it is an inborn trait, and discrimination against homosexuals is as morally problematic as discrimination against any other group with inborn traits, such

as race or gender. Supreme Court Justice Antonin Scalia weighed in on the side of sexual conservatives in *Romer v. Evans*, a case finding Colorado's Amendment 2, which defined gay rights as "special rights," unconstitutional. Scalia wrote, "The Court has mistaken a Kulturkampf for a fit of spite. The constitutional amendment before us here is not the manifestation of a 'bare . . . desire to harm' homosexuals . . . but is rather a modest attempt by seemingly tolerant Coloradans to preserve traditional sexual mores against the efforts of a politically powerful minority to revise those mores through use of the laws." Insert "African American" for "homosexual" and "traditional voting patterns" for "sexual mores" and you get a sense of how liberals feel about the fight. To conservatives, of course, homosexuals are more properly compared to bigamists and practitioners of incest than they are to African Americans.

15. Debbie is quite young and may change her views when she has children. But even as an ideal, the calm acceptance of homosexuality that she revealed in this interview and that other sexually liberal young people also revealed was striking. Even the most liberal of sexually liberal parents did not express calm indifference to their children's sexual orientation.

16. On the history of attitudes towards masturbation, see Thomas Laqueur, *Solitary Sex: A Cultural History of Masturbation* (New York: Zone Books, 2003).

17. The deep confusion about female genitalia is commented on by my friend Harriet Lerner, who notes that most parents tell their daughters about the vagina (internal genitals) when they should properly teach them about the vulva (the external genitals). The association of the word "vulva" with sexuality is probably why Americans insist upon confusion in this realm. See Harriet Lerner, "Parental Mislabeling of Female Genitals as a Determinant of Penis Envy and Learning Inhibitions in Women," *Journal of the American Psychoanalytic Association* 24, 5 (1976): 269–83.

18. Janice Irvine theorizes that this particular way of thinking about homosexuality is so powerful to many opponents of sex education because it resonates with their own sudden and powerful conversion to Christianity—to being "born again"—and makes real the idea that people can change their fundamental identities in a moment (Janice M. Irvine, *Talk About Sex: The Battles over Sex Education in the United*

States [Berkeley: University of California Press, 2002], pp. 171–240). This position echoes what Gayle Rubin calls "compulsory heterosexuality"; see Rubin, "The Traffic of Women: Notes on the Political Economy of Sex," in *Toward an Anthropology of Women*, Rayna Reiter, ed. (New York: Monthly Review Press, 1975), pp. 157–210.

19. John Bunyan, *Life and Death of Mr. Badman* (London: Oxford University Press, 1929), p. 154. I am, of course, paraphrasing.

CHAPTER FIVE: BECOMING A SEXUAL LIBERAL
OR A SEXUAL CONSERVATIVE

1. As far as I can tell, the story of Hitler's vegetarianism may be apocryphal; but see Robert Proctor, *Racial Hygiene: Medicine under the Nazis* (Cambridge, Mass.: Harvard University Press, 1988).

2. As Samuel Popkin points out in his book, *The Reasoning Voter: Communication and Persuasion in Presidential Campaigns* (Chicago: University of Chicago Press, 1991), we all use "cognitive shortcuts" to infer a larger picture from small bits of data. This is a phenomenon that other cognitive scientists refer to. For an accessible overview, see Timothy D. Wilson, *Strangers to Ourselves: Discovering the Adaptive Unconscious* (Cambridge, Mass.: Belknap/Harvard University Press, 2002).

3. Robert Wuthnow, *The Restructuring of American Religion: Society and Faith Since World War II* (Princeton, N.J.: Princeton University Press, 1988).

4. These days the term "Christian," which earlier meant simply a member of a Christian denomination, has come to mean "conservative Christian." See Michael Hout and Claude S. Fischer, "Why More Americans Have No Religious Preference: Politics and Generations," *American Sociological Review* 67, 2 (2002): 165–90. They conclude that political liberals who hold conventional (and vaguely liberal) Christian views are increasingly likely to list themselves as having no religious preference because they want to distinguish themselves from more conservative Christians.

5. Keep in mind my disclaimer that the sexual revolution made men and women *more* equal but not truly equal. As I argue later in this paragraph, the sexual revolution did not eliminate sexual exploitation but challenged the belief that I see in these interviews: that sex

was inherently sexually exploitative and that the heart of sexuality was a contest to see if a man could wrest a woman's "virtue" away from her before marriage.

6. Carole S. Vance, *Pleasure and Danger: Exploring Female Sexuality* (Boston: Routledge & Kegan Paul, 1984).

7. The sexual revolution in this respect made heterosexual sex more like homosexual sex. In any intimate relationship, there is always the risk that one party will care more—love more—than the other; that is an inherent risk of intimacy. But what changed in the sexual revolution was the cultural belief that the party who had more to lose was always and forever the woman.

8. For reasons having to do with the protection of human subjects, I did not interview people under eighteen. When I was doing this research, there was a great deal of controversy over studying the sexuality of teenagers. See Anne Simon Moffat, "Another Sex Survey Bites the Dust," *Science* 253, 5027 (Sept. 1991): 1483.

9. I use Noreen's comment here to illustrate the belief among sexual conservatives that there are limits on what children want to know at a specific time. Honesty compels me to note that when my own son was younger, he asked me a similar question, and when I began to deliver a Berkeley professor–style lecture, he quickly made clear to me that I was giving him *much* more information than he wanted.

10. The most accessible overview that I know of is Steven M. Tipton's *Getting Saved from the Sixties: Moral Meaning in Conversion and Cultural Change* (Berkeley: University of California Press, 1982), pp. 1–30.

11. Ibid., p. 1. For this same argument from another vantage point, see George Lakoff, *Moral Politics: What Conservatives Know That Liberals Don't* (Chicago: University of Chicago Press, 1996).

12. When this distinction shows up in tomes on moral philosophy, it typically divides a "deontological" style of moral reasoning from a "consequentialist" view.

13. This is what Robert Wuthnow argues in his *Restructuring of American Religion*. See also James Davidison Hunter, *Culture Wars: The Struggle to Define America* (New York: Basic, 1991). For more on the theme, see Gertrude Himmelfarb, *The De-Moralization of Society: From Victorian Virtues to Modern Values* (New York: Knopf, 1995), and William J. Bennett, *The De-Valuing of America: The Fight for Our Culture and Our Children* (New York: Summit, 1992).

14. See Ronald Inglehart, *Culture Shift in Advanced Industrial Society* (Princeton, N.J.: Princeton University Press, 1990).

15. The thesis is most associated with Inglehart but is also part of an active debate among secularization scholars in the United States. See Steve Bruce, *God Is Dead: Secularization in the West* (Oxford, Eng.: Blackwell, 2002), chap. 1, for an overview. Bruce is a proponent of the "secularization paradigm" but gives a reasonably balanced view of the debate. The data on education are calculated from U.S. National Center for Education Statistics, *1900–1985. 120 Years of Education: A Statistical Portrait* and *Digest of Education Statistics*, table 24, "Enrollment in institutions of higher education, by sex, attendance status, and type and control of institution: 1869–70 to Fall, 1991," pp. 76–78, and table 4, "Years of school completed by persons 25 years old and over, by race and sex: April 1940 to March 1991," pp. 18–20. The figures for men as a percentage of the population were 8.6 for one to three years of education (1960) and 15.6 (1980); for women, 9.0 and 14.2.

16. Wuthnow, *The Restructuring of American Religion*, pp.168–69.

17. Onalee McGraw, *The Family, Feminism and the Therapeutic State* (Washington, D.C.: Heritage Foundation, 1980).

CHAPTER SIX: BOUNDARIES, LIFE,
AND THE WHOLE DARN THING

1. John R. Alford, Carolyn L. Funk, and John Hibbing, "Are Political Orientations Genetically Transmitted?" *American Political Science Review* 99, 2 (May 2005): 153–69.

2. This is what Gresham Sykes and David Matza call "techniques of neutralization." See Sykes and Matza, "Techniques of Neutralization: A Theory of Delinquency," *American Sociological Review* 22 (1957).

3. Diana L. Eck, *A New Religious America: How a "Christian Country" Has Become the World's Most Religiously Diverse Nation* (San Francisco: Harper, 2001).

4. My data on religious preference come from the American Religious Identification Survey. This view of the social order is one often held by political conservatives as well. James Q. Wilson has sparked a transformation in policing by arguing, in his classic essay "Broken Windows," that by ignoring small infractions of public space (bro-

ken windows, graffiti), a society signals that it will stand passively by when large infractions of public space such as crime take place. James Q. Wilson and George L. Kelling, "Broken Windows," *Atlantic Monthly,* March 1982.

5. In English, the word originally applied to different kinds of angels and then came to mean ecclesiastic orders. Only in the sixteenth and seventeenth centuries did it take on its modern meaning of ranks in which some have more value or power than others.

6. This was expressed most classically in the work of Arthur Lovejoy, *The Great Chain of Being: A Study of the History of an Idea* (Cambridge, Mass.: Harvard University Press, 1948). Classical views of this were more static than modern views, which hold that people can attain greater rank by their achievements.

7. Simone de Beauvoir, *The Second Sex* (New York: Knopf, 1953), xxxv.

8. Compare this to the sexually conservative worry that children will have information that even their parents don't have.

9. This discussion of classrooms and how they are organized calls to mind Foucault's famous example of the invention of the kind of classroom that sexually conservative parents prefer, that is, with chairs facing the teacher, in a set of hierarchical rows. See Michel Foucault, *Discipline and Punish: The Birth of the Prison* (New York: Vintage, 1995), 172–74.

10. Twelve students were killed at Columbine High School in April 1999, when two students, Eric Harris and Dylan Klebold, opened fire on their classmates in what was at the time the worst school shooting in American history. See William H. Erickson, "Report of Governor Bill Owens' Columbine Review Commission" (State of Colorado, May 2001). For more on the larger phenomenon, see Katherine S. Newman, *Rampage: The Social Roots of School Shootings* (New York: Basic, 2004).

11. My children were in kindergarten and learning the whole-language approach when this chapter was being written. My daughter wrote me a note during this period that said, "go to ofis and brin home lablr," a request that I go to the office and bring home a label machine. I don't recall writing notes at all in kindergarten, and she has since progressed to a fluent command of standard written English.

12. Strictly speaking, "federalism" refers to the notion that states, not the federal government, should set policies for entities such as schools and other social institutions. Yet it is just the next step up

from the notion that local and smaller groups are more representative than are larger and more national groups. For an illustration of this view, see, for example, Douglas W. Kmiec, "The Court Rediscovers Federalism," *Policy Review* 85 (September–October 1997).

13. Appealing as this might sound in principle, the modern welfare state developed, as historians such as Michael Katz have shown, because such individual, personalized charity can be both unpredictable and patronizing. See Michael B. Katz, *In the Shadow of the Poorhouse: A Social History of Welfare in America* (New York: Basic, 1986).

14. An excellent overview of new class theory can be found in Steven G. Brint, *In an Age of Experts: The Changing Role of Professionals in Politics and Public Life* (Princeton, N.J.: Princeton University Press, 1994).

CHAPTER SEVEN: MORALITY AND SEX

1. Gertrude Himmelfarb, *The De-Moralization of Society: From Victorian Virtues to Modern Values* (New York: Knopf, 1995); Joan Tronto, *Moral Boundaries: A Political Argument for an Ethic of Care* (New York: Routledge, 1993); Anita L. Allen and Milton C. Regan, *Debating Democracy's Discontent: Essays on American Politics, Law, and Public Philosophy* (New York: Oxford University Press, 1998).

2. There is a large literature on this, some of it descriptive (what these two values systems look like) and some of it prescriptive (which of the two is better). For the former, I recommend (again) Steven Tipton's *Getting Saved from the Sixties: The Transformation of Moral Meaning in American Culture by Alternative Religious Movements* (Berkeley: University of California Press, 1977), pp. 1–30. For the latter, the literature that has grown up around (and is often critical of) Lawrence Kohlberg's view of morality is instructive, although people in this school actively deny that their model is normative—that is, describing what people *should* do rather than what they *do* do. See Kohlberg, *The Philosophy of Moral Development: Moral Stages and the Idea of Justice* (San Francisco: Harper & Row, 1981), and *The Psychology of Moral Development: The Nature and Validity of Moral Stages* (San Francisco: Harper & Row, 1984). For the flavor of the debate over Kohlberg's views, see *Lawrence Kohlberg, Consensus and Controversy* ed. Sohan Modgil and Celia Modgil (Philadelphia: Falmer, 1986).

3. For an overview, see Deborah Rhode, *The Politics of Pregnancy: Ado-*

lescent Sexuality and Public Policy (New Haven: Yale University Press, 1993).

4. In fact, as liberals will be happy to know, analysis of national data suggests that parents who talk a lot about contraception with their daughters are more likely to have daughters who use contraceptives than parents who do not talk with their children. It's not clear whether open-minded parents have daughters who obtain effective contraception or daughters who want to use effective contraception talk to their parents in order to get it. Either way, the finding seems to substantiate the liberal point that families with open communication have daughters (and presumably sons, who were not surveyed in this study) who are more likely to exercise the cherished liberal value of responsibility.

5. Much has been made of Philippe Aries's landmark study of children, and in particular his analysis of the ribald, lusty, frankly sexual atmosphere that surrounded the young Louis XVI, which Aries provocatively compares to the sheltered lives of children later, after the "invention" of childhood. But even young Louis was permitted such "liberties" only as a very young child; when he became older, he was expected to be more circumspect. See Philippe Aries, *Centuries of Childhood: A Social History of Family Life* (New York: Knopf, 1962).

6. Erving Goffman, *The Presentation of Self in Everyday Life* (Garden City, N.Y.: Doubleday, 1959).

7. See, for example, Joan Williams, *Unbending Gender: Why Family and Work Conflict and What to Do About It* (New York: Oxford University Press, 2000), and Alice Echols, *Daring to Be Bad: Radical Feminism in America, 1967–1975* (Minneapolis: University of Minnesota Press, 1989).

8. I think that the first sex educators favored a single standard based on female behavior because there was still enough residue of the separate-spheres ideology that women, assigned the role of moral guardian, could be confident that theirs was the higher standard of sexual behavior. By the 1960s, the quintessentially male standard of full-time employment in the paid labor force had become the ideal, so this time feminists argued for the sexual autonomy that men enjoyed.

9. The notion is of course Lasch's. See Christopher Lasch, *Haven in a Heartless World: The Family Besieged* (New York: Basic, 1977).

10. Barbara Ehrenreich and Arlie Russell Hochschild, eds., *Global Woman: Nannies, Maids, and Sex Workers in the New Economy* (New York: Holt, 2004).

CHAPTER EIGHT: THE POLITICS OF SEX

1. Carl Gustaf Boethius, "Sex Education in Swedish Schools: The Facts and the Fiction," *Family Planning Perspectives* 17, 6 (1986): 276–79.
2. I don't think that there has been a genuine conversion among comprehensive sex educators. Rather, they have pragmatically accepted that most parents don't want their children to be sexually active in high school or, worse yet, before, and they are happy to second this view so long as students also get the message (and the information) that if they are not abstinent, then they must take precautions against both pregnancy and disease. Public opinion polls suggest that this is exactly what the majority of parents want: a message of abstinence and a contingency plan should abstinence fail.
3. This has been documented by Michele Fine in "Sexuality, Schooling, and Adolescent Females: The Missing Discourse of Desire," *Harvard Educational Review* 58, 1 (1988): 1–29.
4. I use the term "Christian" here to include conservative Mormons and Catholics as well as fundamentalist Christians.
5. Children in Billingsley, where many people were self-described Southern Baptists, were much more modest than in the other three settings, but even these girls and boys wore outfits to school that would have gotten them sent home to change twenty years ago.
6. Guy Coq, "Scarves and Symbols," *New York Times*, Jan. 30, 2004, p. 25; Elaine Sciolino, "Hostages Urge France to Repeal Its Scarf Ban," *New York Times*, Aug. 31, 2004, p. 8.
7. See Philip Meredith, *Sex Education: Political Issues in Britain and Europe* (New York: Routledge, 1989), pp. 100–104. Again, this is something of a gloss on the historical development of sex education in Sweden, as Meredith's discussion indicates.
8. Schalet points out that the Dutch, like Americans, have strong sexual standards, but their standard is not staying chaste but avoiding promiscuity. Her argument is that Dutch parents coopt teenage sex into the family orbit, domesticating it, as it were. See Amy Townsend Schalet, "Raging Hormones, Regulated Love: Adolescent Sexuality

and the Constitution of the Modern Individual in the United States and the Netherlands," Ph.D. dissertation, University of California, Berkeley, 2003.

9. Richard Godbeer, *Sexual Revolution in Early America: Gender Relations in the American Experience* (Baltimore: Johns Hopkins University Press, 2002); Merril D. Smith, *Sex and Sexuality in Early America* (New York: New York University Press, 1998); and, of course, the classic book on the matter, John Demos, *A Little Commonwealth: Family Life in Plymouth Colony* (New York: Oxford University Press, 1970).

10. Steven Skowronek, *Building a New American State: The Expansion of National Administrative Capacities, 1877–1920* (New York: Cambridge University Press, 1982).

11. The classic citation here is Murray J. Edelman, *The Symbolic Uses of Politics* (Urbana: University of Illinois Press, 1985). The classic case study is Joseph R Gusfield, *Symbolic Crusade: Status Politics and the American Temperance Movement* (Urbana: University of Illinois Press, 1963). The idea that morality serves as a way for groups in America to distinguish themselves from others is from Michèle Lamont, *Money, Morals, and Manners: The Culture of the French and American Upper-Middle Class, Morality and Society* (Chicago: University of Chicago Press, 1992). I'm inclined to think that movements about sex are not symbolic as these authors mean it but reflect real interests, albeit in the intangible realm.

12. For an exception, see Arthur B. Spingarn, "The War and Venereal Diseases Among Negroes," *Social Hygiene* 4, 3 (1916): 333–46. Spingarn was both an active social hygienist and a member of the board of directors of the NAACP. Spingarn believed that Negroes had higher rates of VD and attributed the rates to "race discrimination and the indifference of the white communities." He moreover pointed out that "the colored girl [sic] has less education, less legal protection . . . she is the prey of men of both races. For every safeguard there is placed around the white girl, there is a corresponding obstacle placed in the path of the colored girl" (p. 335).

13. See, for example, Timothy A. Byrnes, *Catholic Bishops in American Politics* (Princeton, N.J.: Princeton University Press, 1993), and Timothy A. Byrnes and Mary C. Segers, eds., *The Catholic Church and the Politics of Abortion: A View from the States* (Boulder, Colo.: Westview, 1992).

14. There are many treatments of the emergence of fundamentalism (named after a series of manifestos, "The Fundamentals of the Faith," published between 1910 and 1912), but perhaps the most accessible is George M. Marsden, *Fundamentalism and American Culture: The Shaping of Twentieth-Century Evangelicalism, 1870–1925* (New York: Oxford University Press, 1980).

15. For analyses along these same lines, see Theodore Caplow, *Middletown Families: Fifty Years of Change and Continuity* (Minneapolis: University of Minnesota Press, 1982), and Nicholas J. Demerath III and Rhys H. Williams, *A Bridging of Faiths: Religion and Politics in a New England City* (Princeton, N.J.: Princeton University Press, 1992). On the argument that the intrusion of national (i.e., big-city, urban) values in smaller communities is at the heart of social upset, see Robert H. Wiebe, *The Search for Order, 1877–1920* (New York: Hill and Wang, 1967). This same argument is at the heart of Steven Bruce, *The Rise and Fall of the New Christian Right: Conservative Protestant Politics in America, 1978–1988.* (New York: Oxford University Press, 1988). One might say that accounts of the fall of the New Christian Right are greatly exaggerated, as Mark Twain said in another context.

16. James Davidson Hunter, *Evangelicalism: The Coming Generation* (Chicago: University of Chicago Press, 1987), p. 6.

17. For the background on these cases, see *Bob Jones University v. United States*, 461 U.S. 574 (1983).

18. Jeffrey P. Moran, "Modernism Gone Mad": Sex Education Comes to Chicago, 1913," *Journal of American History* 83, 2 (1996): 481–513.

19. A journalistic but closely observed account of this controversy can be found in Mary Breasted, *Oh! Sex Education!* (New York: Praeger, 1970).

20. *John Birch Society Newsletter*, 1964, p. 5.

21. The social hygienists reported brief flurries of local opposition to sex education in the period after World War I, but I can find no evidence of national opposition prior to MOTOREDE.

22. Commenting on the 1964 controversy, John Steinbacher said, "The people of Anaheim discovered that the Socialist school system could not teach sex instruction in a moral setting" (*The Child Seducers* [Fullerton, Calif.: Educator, 1971], p. 149).

23. The analysis of the pro-family movement comes from a content analysis of references to it in the major media and tracks connections

between and among groups. The 1977 International Women's Year Conference in Houston played a central role in providing a place where counterfeminists could mobilize.

24. Paul Scott, "Schlafly Forms New Group to Defend Family," *Human Events*, Sept. 6, 1975, p. 4; "The Pro-Family Movement," *Conservative Digest*, May-June 1980.

25. "A Righteous Indignation," *U.S. News & World Report* 124, 17 (May 1998): 20.

26. Connaught Marshner, "The Growth of Sex Respect: Saying Yes to Saying No," *Conservative Digest* 14, 11 (Dec. 1988): 46. See also Michele McKeegan, *Abortion Politics: Mutiny in the Ranks of the Right* (New York: Free Press, 1992), pp. 23–27.

27. Rosalind Petchesky, *Abortion and Woman's Choice: The State, Sexuality, and the Conditions of Reproductive Freedom* (New York: Longman, 1983).

28. See Mary Dudziak, "Just Say No: Birth Control in the Connecticut Supreme Court before Griswold v. Connecticut," *Iowa Law Review* 75, 4 (1990); Timothy Burns, *Catholic Bishops in American Politics*; Gene Burns, *The Moral Veto* (Cambridge: Cambridge University Press, 2005); and Ellen Chesler, *Woman of Valor: Margaret Sanger and the Birth Control Movement in America* (New York: Simon & Schuster, 1992).

29. On the changing American electorate, see Jeff Manza and Clem Brooks, *Social Cleavages and Political Change: Voter Alignments and U.S. Party Coalitions* (New York: Oxford University Press, 1999), and "The Gender Gap in U.S. Presidential Elections: When? Why? Implications?" *American Journal of Sociology* 103, 5 (1998): 1235–66.

30. Greg D. Adams, "Abortion: Evidence of an Issue Evolution," *American Journal of Political Science* 41, 3 (1997): 718–37.

31. The term "issue evolution" refers to the reciprocal action of issues and constituencies in democratic politics where politicians must mobilize a base; it comes from a book by the same name, namely Edward G. Carmines and James A. Stimson, *Issue Evolution: Race and the Transformation of American Politics* (Princeton, N.J.: Princeton University Press, 1989). On "Reagan Democrats," see Stanley B. Greenberg, *Middle-Class Dreams: The Politics and Power of the New American Majority* (New York: Times Books, 1995).

32. Kevin P. Phillips, *The Emerging Republican Majority* (New Rochelle, N.Y.: Arlington House, 1969).

33. Race is not a key part of my story, although perhaps it should be. For more on race and partisan realignment, see Carmines and Stimson, *Issue Evolution: Race and the Transformation of American Politics*. Interestingly, many of those active in the early mobilization of the New Right suggest that race is very much at the heart of their mobilization, even though morality, specifically sexual morality, is the center of their concern. For example, William Bennett tells in his memoir of his nomination to the National Endowment for the Humanities and his sponsors' disbelief that he could be a "real" conservative, since he kept a picture of Martin Luther King on his wall. Similarly, Richard Viguerie, one of the founders of the New Right, describes Paul Weyrich, another founder, as mobilized by a fair housing bill in the Nixon Administration; see Viguerie, *The New Right: We're Ready to Lead* (Falls Church, Va.: Viguerie, 1980), p. 54.

34. Adams, "Abortion: Evidence of Issue Evolution."

35. Duane Murray Oldfield, *The Right and the Righteous: The Christian Right Confronts the Republican Party, Religious Forces in the Modern Political World* (Lanham, Md.: Rowman & Littlefield, 1996); Manza and Brooks, *Social Cleavages*.

36. Adams, "Abortions: Evidence of Issue Evolution"

37. Gary L. Bauer, "Ideology, Politics, and the American Family: Setting the Agenda for the 1990s," Heritage Lectures, no. 212 (Washington, D.C.: Heritage Foundation, May 17, 1989).

38. David Brock, not an entirely reliable source, suggests that Republicans after the fall of the Berlin Wall discerned that sexuality and pro-family issues generally could serve the party as anticommunism had done in an earlier era. See, *Blinded by the Right: The Conscience of an Ex-Conservative* (New York: Crown, 2002). Cf.: "Alone in the [first] Bush White House, [William] Kristol presciently identified perceived moral collapse and a reassertion of sexual traditionalism as issues through which Republican politics might be revived after the Cold War" (p. 52). But if that is so, Kristol's insight drew on the hard work of tacticians such as Richard Viguerie and Paul Weyrich, who in turn drew on the work of mostly unheralded (except perhaps within the inner circle) theorists such as Onalee McGraw and Connaught Marshner.

39. I hope the historical overview of sex education has revealed that the relationship between contraception, abortion, and gender equity is

a historically contingent one. By that I mean that twentieth-century social hygienists took for granted that men could be encouraged to act more like women sexually, thus making issues such as birth control and abortion less central to gender equity. Further, many nineteenth-century feminists actively opposed birth control, fearing that it would enable men to take sexual advantage of their wives without fear of pregnancy. See Linda Gordon, "Why Nineteenth-Century Feminists Did Not Support Birth Control," in Barrie Thorne and Marilyn Yalom, eds. *Rethinking the Family: Some Feminist Questions* (New York: Longman, 1982).

40. Fred L. Block, *Postindustrial Possibilities: A Critique of Economic Discourse* (Berkeley: University of California Press, 1990). Robert Wiebe writes convincingly of the cultural upheavals during the Progressive era, as regional communities became merged into a new, national culture, see Wiebe, *The Search for Order.*

41. Ronald Inglehart and Pippa Norris, *Rising Tide: Gender Equality and Cultural Change Around the World* (New York: Cambridge University Press, 2003), and Samuel P. Huntington, *The Clash of Civilizations and the Remaking of World Order* (New York: Simon & Schuster, 1996).

42. Thomas Byrne Edsall, "Blue Movie," *Atlantic Monthly* 291, 1 (2002): 36–37.

43. Karl Polanyi, *The Great Transformation* (New York: Farrar & Rinehart, 1944).

44. Zygmunt Bauman, *Modernity and the Holocaust* (Cambridge, England: Polity Press, 1989).

45. I've been very impressed with the work that the Public Conversations Project of Cambridge, Massachussetts (http://www.publicconversations .org), has been doing in this realm. PCP, founded by family therapists, comes in at the invitation of a community and provides a setting where people explore areas of agreement rather than difference.

46. See Sharon Lerner, "The Sex Ed Divide," *American Prospect*, Sept. 23, 2001, p. A15.

47. The terms come from Frank Levy and National Committee for Research on the 1980 Census, *Dollars and Dreams: The Changing American Income Distribution* (New York: Russell Sage Foundation, 1987). See also Levy's most recent book on the topic, *The New Dollars and Dreams: American Incomes and Economic Change* (New York: Russell Sage Foundation, 1998).

48. For example, see Linda J. Waite and Maggie Gallagher, *The Case for Marriage: Why Married People Are Happier, Healthier, and Better Off Financially* (New York: Doubleday, 2000).

49. Conservative Christians have their own sex manuals (cf Beverly and Tim LaHaye, *The Act of Marriage: The Beauty of Sexual Love* [Grand Rapids, Mich.: Zondervan, 1976]).

50. On the role of boundaries in human life, see Michele Lamont and Virag Molnar, "The Study of Boundaries in the Social Sciences," *Annual Review of Sociology* 28 (Aug. 2002): 167–95.

51. See Inglehart and Norris, *Rising Tides*.

CHAPTER NINE: SEX EDUCATION IN AMERICA

1. As I have pointed out that it is not so much immature sex that leads to worrisome consequences but American sex, as practiced by people of all ages, that leads to social problems. Abstinence-only backers are not likely to make the argument (although it is a tenable one) that since Americans as a group handle their sexuality less well than inhabitants of other countries, it is worthwhile to try to delay the entry of young people into what is, in the circumstances, a riskier activity here than elsewhere.

2. Mark Delucchi, "The Social Cost of Motor Vehicle Use," *Annals of the American Academy of Political and Social Science* 553 (1997): 130–42.

3. Calculated from Alan Guttmacher Institute, *Sex and America's Teenagers*, p. 41, and National Center for Health Statistics, *National Vital Statistics Reports*, vol. 53, no. 9, "Preliminary Data on Births, 2003," pp. 4, 8, 10, and vol. 52, no. 3, "Estimated Pregnancy Rates for the United States, 1990–2000, an Update," pp. 1, 3–9.

4. Keeping in mind that the category of sexually transmitted diseases is somewhat flexible, in theory some sexual diseases can be transmitted by behavior that is intimate but not usually thought of as sexual, such as kissing.

5. My thinking about these issues was given substantially more focus by the work of my colleague Rob MacCoun; see Robert MacCoun and Peter Reuter, *Drug War Heresies: Learning from Other Vices, Times, and Places* (New York: Cambridge University Press, 2001).

6. See Mark W. Lipsey and David B. Wilson, "The Efficacy of Psychological, Educational, and Behavioral Treatment: Confirmation from a Meta-Analysis," *American Psychologist* (1993): 1181–1209.

7. To make this claim, I undertook a content analysis of the claims of both abstinence-only and comprehensive advocacy organizations as well as of what advocates on this issue said in the public media.

8. Lisa Remez, "Oral Sex among Adolescents: Is It Sex or Is It Abstinence?" *Family Planning Perspectives* 32, 6 (2000): 298–304. For a summary of the effects of the economy on risk-taking behavior, see Jonathan Gruber, *Risky Behavior Among Youths: An Economic Analysis* (Chicago: University of Chicago Press, 2001).

9. Tina Hoff, Liberty Green, Mary McIntosh, Nicole Rawlings, and Jean D'Amico, *Sex Education in America: A View from Inside the Nation's Classrooms* (Menlo Park, Calif.: Kaiser Family Foundation, 2000), pp. 1–116; M. A. Schuster, R. M. Bell, and D. E. Kanouse, "The Sexual Practices of Adolescent Virgins: Sexual Activities of High School Students Who Have Never Had Vaginal Intercourse," *American Journal of Public Health* 86, 11 (1996): 1570–76; and G. J. Gates and F. L. Sonenstein, "Heterosexual Genital Activity Among Adolescent Males: 1988 and 1995," *Family Planning Perspectives* 32, 6 (2000): 295–97.

10. Since the National Survey of Family Growth started out as a fertility survey, it interviews only women of childbearing age. Joyce C. Abma, et al., *Fertility, Family Planning and Women's Health: New Data from the 1995 National Survey of Family Growth* (Hyattsville, Md.: National Center for Health Statistics, 1997), p. 110, table 91: "Number of women 18–44 years of age and percent who had formal instruction about the specified sex education topics before they were 18, by selected characteristics." See also Laura Duberstein Lindberg, Leighton Ku, and Freya Sonenstein, "Adolescents' Reports of Reproductive Health Education, 1988 and 1995," *Family Planning Perspectives* 32, 5 (2000): 220–26.

11. Hoff, et al, *Sex Education in America*.

12. I have been pointing out for more than twenty-five years that all reproductive acts, at least those of the old-fashioned sort not involving laboratories, take both a male and female to accomplish, and that focusing our attention on women only betrays the ideology of reproduction, not the biology.

13. The data are from the National Survey of Adolescent Males, which looked only at young men aged 17–19, so data are not strictly comparable to the data on women, which cover women 15–19. However, it is the trend line that is relevant here. Much as was the case

with women, more recent data seem to suggest that the proportion of young men in this age group who are sexually experienced has declined, with only 68% of these young men reporting that they have had sex. See Freya L Sonenstein, Joseph H. Pleck, and Leighton C. Ku, "Levels of Sexual Activity Among Adolescent Males in the United States," *Family Planning Perspectives* (1991) 23:162–67, and their "Sexual Activity, Condom Use and AIDS Awareness Among Adolescent Males," *Family Planning Perspectives* 21 (1989): 152–58.

14. John S. Santelli, Laura Duberstein Lindberg, Joyce Abma, Clea Sucoff McNeely, and Michael Resnick, "Adolescent Sexual Behavior: Estimates and Trends from Four Nationally Representative Surveys," *Family Planning Perspectives* 32, 4 (2000): 156–65, 194; Joyce C. Abma and Freya Sonenstein, "Sexual Activity and Contraceptive Practices Among Teenagers in the United States, 1988 and 1995," National Center for Health Statistics, *Vital Health Statistics* 23, no. 21 (2000); and Centers for Disease Control and Prevention, "Trends in Sexual Risk Behaviors among High School Students—United States, 1991–1997," pp. 1–78; *Morbidity and Mortality Weekly Review* 47, 36 (1998): 749–52. I ran my own calculations from data from the National Survey of Family Growth.

15. Alan Guttmacher Institute, *Sex and America's Teenagers*, p. 21; independent calculations by author. Keep in mind, however, that these figures for pregnancies, as opposed to births, are approximate, as all available databases underreport abortions. See Jacqueline E. Darroch and Susheela Singh, *Why is Teenage Pregnancy Declining? The Roles of Abstinence, Sexual Activity and Contraceptive Use,* Occasional Report no. 1 (New York: Alan Guttmacher Institute, 1999).

16. National Centers for Disease Control, "Youth Risk Behavior Surveillance Survey 2003," and *Morbidity & Mortality Weekly Report* 2004, 53 (SS-2): 1–29.

17. Jane Mauldon and Kristin Luker, "The Effects of Contraceptive Education on Method Use at First Intercourse," *Family Planning Perspectives* 28, 1 (1996): 19–24, 41.

18. See Douglas Kirby, *Emerging Answers: Research Findings on Programs to Reduce Teen Pregnancy* (Washington, D.C.: National Campaign to Prevent Teen Pregnancy, 2001), and Douglas Kirby, *Sexuality Education: An Evaluation of Programs and Their Effects — An Executive Summary* (Santa Cruz: Mathtech, Inc., 1984).

19. D. Kirby, *A Review of Educational Programs Designed to Reduce Sexual*

Risk-Taking Behaviors Among School-Aged Youth in the United States (Springfield, Va.: National Technical Information Service, 1995), and Douglas Kirby, Meg Korpi, Richard P. Barth, and Helen H. Cagampang, "The Impact of the Postponing Sexual Involvement Curriculum Among Youths in California," *Family Planning Perspectives* 29, 3 (1997): 100–108.

20. Lisa D. Lieberman, Heather Gray, Megan Wier, Renee Fiorentino, and Patricia Maloney, "Long-Term Outcomes of an Abstinence-Based, Small-Group Pregnancy Prevention Program in New York City Schools," *Family Planning Perspectives* 32, 5 (2000): 237–45.

21. For an overview of this literature, see MacCoun and Reuter, *Drug War Heresies,* 72–100.

22. P. S. Bearman and H. Bruckner, "Promising the Future: Virginity Pledges and First Intercourse," *American Journal of Sociology* 106, 4 (2001): 859–912; H. Bruckner and P. Bearman, "After the Promise: The STD Consequences of Adolescent Virginity Pledges," *Journal of Adolescent Health* 36, 4 (2005): 271–78; H. Bruckner, A. Martin, and P. S. Bearman, "Ambivalence and Pregnancy: Adolescents' Attitudes, Contraceptive Use and Pregnancy," *Perspectives on Sexual and Reproductive Health* 36, 6 (2004): 248–57.

APPENDIX I: A NOTE ON VOICE AND METHOD

1. Alan Dundes wrote exhaustively on this topic, so it is hard to pick out a single exemplar, but for an introduction see Dundes, *Cracking Jokes: Studies of Sick Humor Cycles and Stereotypes* (Berkeley, Calif.: Ten Speed Press, 1987).

2. James Clifford, George E. Marcus, and School of American Research, *Writing Culture: The Poetics and Politics of Ethnography* (Berkeley: University of California Press, 1986).

3. For a wonderful contribution that turns modern institutional culture (including that of scholarship) in on itself, see Annelise Riles, *The Network Inside Out* (Ann Arbor: University of Michigan Press, 2000).

4. Robert King Merton, *On the Shoulders of Giants: A Shandean Postscript* (New York: Harcourt Brace & World, 1965).

5. It turns out T. H. Huxley said this first, when he spoke of the "tragedy of a theory killed by a fact."

6. As I argue in Appendix II, I was not attempting random sampling,

that is, a statistically representative set of cases that would stand in for all the cases in the universe. Rather, I was purposively sampling, as Glaser and Strauss call it. But the question of bias is as important, if not more important, in this kind of sampling as in random sampling. Cf. Barney L. Glaser and Anselm L. Strauss, *The Discovery of Grounded Theory: Strategies for Qualitative Research* (Chicago: Aldine, 1967).

7. Only a minority of school-based clinics in fact dispense contraception on site, as opposed to referring students to outside health-care providers. Yet my reading of local newspapers convinced me that this distinction was lost on most people and was a controversy of a different kind from one over what young people should be taught.

8. I should note that many more than four meetings were involved. In two of the communities, the level of outrage was so high, and the board of education was so unprepared for the level of public response, that multiple meetings were held—three in one case, four in the other.

9. Barney G. Glaser and Anselm L. Strauss, *The Discovery of Grounded Theory: Strategies for Qualitative Research* (Chicago: Aldine, 1967); K. M. MacQueen et al., "Codebook Development for Team-Based Qualitative Analysis," *Cultural Anthropology Methods* 10, 2 (1999): 31–36; James W. Carey et al., "Intercoder Agreement in Analysis of Responses to Open-Ended Interview Questions: Examples from Tuberculosis Research," *Cultural Anthropology Methods* 8, 3 (Oct. 1996): 1–5.

10. All interviews were coded for reliability by a second coder, but given the huge number of interviews in this study, systematically comparing reliability coding would have been a prohibitively time-consuming task. The technical measure of intercoder reliability is the kappa score, and we computed kappa scores for a random sample of all interviews. They were reassuring enough that there seemed to be no need to compute kappa scores for all interviews.

11. We simply used a hypertext linking capacity to create meta-accounts of a conflict and tallies of the roster of advocates. Strictly speaking, this is a universe rather than a sample, as we tried to interview everyone whose name came up as an activist. The nonresponse rate was quite low: 5 people over 169 interviews. For the purposes of analysis, however, we used only the 105 interviews of people most directly involved.

12. Pierre Bourdieu and Loïc J. D. Wacquant, *An Invitation to Reflexive Sociology* (Chicago: University of Chicago Press, 1992).

APPENDIX II: SET THEORETIC MODELS

1. For a particularly elegant expression of this point, written by someone who is a master of the linear model, see Andrew Abbot, "Transcending Linear Reality," *Sociological Theory* (Autumn 1988): 169–86.
2. Charles Ragin, *The Comparative Method: Moving Beyond Qualitative and Quantitative Strategies* (Berkeley: University of California Press, 1987); and *Fuzzy Set Social Science* (Chicago: University of Chicago Press, 2000).
3. The term "moral shock" is James Jasper's. See Jasper, "Recruiting Strangers and Friends: Moral Shocks and Social Networks in Animal Rights and Anti-nuclear Protests," *Social Problems* 42, 4 (1995): 493–512, and *The Art of Moral Protests* (Chicago: University of Chicago Press, 1997).

Bibliography

Aberle, Sophie D., and George W. Corner, *Twenty-Five Years of Sex Research: History of the National Research Council's Committee for Research in Problems of Sex, 1922–1947.* Philadelphia: Saunders, 1953.

Abma, Joyce C., A. Chandra, W. Mosher, L. Peterson, and L. Piccinino. "Fertility, Family Planning, and Women's Health: New Data from the 1995 National Survey of Family Growth." National Center for Health Statistics, *Vital Health Statistics* 23, no. 19 (1997).

Abma, Joyce C., and Freya Sonenstein. "Sexual Activity And Contraceptive Practices Among Teenagers in the United States, 1988 and 1995." National Center for Health Statistics, *Vital Health Statistics* 23, no. 21 (2000).

Abrahamse, Allan F., Peter Morrison, and Linda Waite. *Beyond Stereotypes: Who Becomes a Single Teenage Mother?* Santa Monica, Calif.: Rand Corporation, 1988.

Aceto, Vincent J. *Explorations in Sex Education: An Annotated Bibliography of Selected Readings, Instructional Materials, and Programs of State Departments of Education, Associations, and Individual School Districts.* Albany: School of Library Science, State University of New York, 1968.

Achilles, Paul Strong. *The Effectiveness of Certain Social Hygiene Literature.* New York: American Social Hygiene Association, 1923.

Adams, Gina, Sharon Adams-Taylor, and Karen Pittman. "Adolescent Pregnancy and Parenthood: A Review of the Problem, Solutions, and Resources." *Family Relations* 38, no. 2 (1989): 223–29.

Adams, Greg. "Abortion: Evidence of an Issue Evolution." *American Journal of Political Science* 41, no. 3 (1997): 718–37.

Advisory Committee on Social Hygiene Education to the N.J. State Department of Education. *An Approach to Sex Education in School,* 1941.

Akerlof, George, and Janet Yellen. "New Mothers, Not Married." *The Brookings Review* 14, no. 4 (1996): 18–21.

Akerlof, George, Janet Yellen, and Michael Katz. "An Analysis of Out-of-Wedlock Childbearing in the United States." *Quarterly Journal of Economics* 111, no. 2 (1996): 276–317.

Aldous, Joan, and Wilfried Dumon. "Family Policy in the 1980s: Controversy and Consensus." *Journal of Marriage and the Family* 52, no. 4 (1990): 1136–51.

Alexander, Sharon J. "Implications of the White House Conference on Families for Family Life Education." *Family Relations* 30, no. 4 (1981): 643–50.

Allen, Annie. "How to Save Girls Who Have Fallen." *The Survey: A Journal of Constructive Philanthropy* 1, no. 1 (1910): 684–96.

Allen, Gary. *Sex Education Problems.* Belmont, Mass.: American Opinion, 1969.

Allyn, David. *Make Love, Not War.* Boston: Little, Brown, 2000.

Alwin, Duane. "From Obedience to Autonomy: Changes in Traits Desired in Children, 1924–1978." *Public Opinion Quarterly* 52 (1988): 33–52.

American Academy of Pediatrics. *Sex Education for Adolescents: A Bibliography of Low-Cost Materials.* Chicago: American Library Association, 1980.

American Council of Christian Churches. Laymen's Commission. *How Red Is the National Council of Churches?* Pittsburgh, 1966.

American Federation for Sex Hygiene. *Report of the Sex Education Sessions of the Fourth International Congress on School Hygiene and of the Annual Meeting of the Federation.* New York: American Federation of Sex Hygiene, 1913.

————. *Report of the Special Committee on the Matter and Methods of Sex Education, Presented before the Subsection on Sex Hygiene and Demography, Held in Washington, D.C., September Twenty-Third to Twenty-Eighth, Nineteen Hundred and Twelve.* New York: C. I. Goldmann, 1913.

American Social Hygiene Association. *The American Social Hygiene Association, 1914–1916.* New York: ASHA, 1916.

————. *The Community, Prostitution, and Venereal Diseases: A Plan for Organized Action.* New York: ASHA, 1920.

————. *Health for Girls.* New York: ASHA, 1933.

————. *Problems of Sexual Behavior: Research, Education, Community Action.* New York: ASHA, 1948.

————. *Strengthening Family Life Education in Our Schools: Report of the Midwest Project on In-service Education of Teachers.* New York: ASHA, 1955.

————. Committee on National Defense Activities. *Why Let It Burn? The Case Against the Red Light District.* Publication No. 193. New York: ASHA, 1919.

American Social Hygiene Association, E. L. Keyes, and United States Interdepartmental Social Hygiene Board. *Report of the Scientific Researches on the Venereal Diseases.* New York: ASHA, 1924.

American Social Hygiene Association and United States War Department, Civilian Medical Division. *Beyond Victory: Build Better Health, Better Homes, Better Communities.* New York: ASHA, 1946.

American Society of Sanitary and Moral Prophylaxis. *Transactions* 2, 1908.

An, Chong-Bum, Robert Haveman, and Barbara Wolfe. "Teen Out-of-Wedlock Births and Welfare Receipt: The Role of Childhood Events and Economic Circumstances." *The Review of Economics and Statistics* 75, no. 2 (1993): 195–208.

Anderson, Edna, Marjorie East, and Joan Thomson. *Definitive Themes in Home Economics and Their Impact on Families, 1909–1984.* Washington, D.C.: American Home Economics Association, 1984.

Arcus, Margaret E. *Family Life Education: Toward the 21st Century. Family Relations* 41, no. 4 (1992): 390–93.

————. "Should Family Life Education Be Required for High School Students? An Examination of the Issues." *Family Relations* 35, no. 3 (1986): 347–56.

Ariès, Philippe. "Thoughts on the History of Homosexuality." In *Western Sexuality.* Ed. P. Ariès and A. Béjin. Oxford, Eng.: Oxford University Press, 1985.

Bachrach, Christine, and Wendy Baldwin. "Abortion Underreporting." *Family Planning Perspectives* 23, no. 5 (1991): 233.

Bahr, Howard M., and Bruce A. Chadwick. "Religion and Family in Middletown, USA." *Journal of Marriage and the Family* 47, no. 2 (1985): 407–14.

Bailey, Beth. *From Front Porch to Back Seat.* Baltimore, Johns Hopkins University Press, 1988.

————. "Prescribing the Pill: Politics, Culture and the Sexual Revolution in America's Heartland." *Journal of Social History* 30, no. 4 (1997): 827–56.

————. *Sex in the Heartland.* Cambridge, Mass.: Harvard University Press, 1999.

————. "The Sexual Revolution: Was It Revolutionary?" In *The Colum-*

bia Guide to America in the 60s. Ed. David Farber and Beth Bailey. New York: Columbia University Press, 2001. pp. 134–42.

Baker, John Newton. *Sex Education in High Schools.* New York: Emerson, 1942.

Baker, Luther G. *The Rising Furor over Sex Education.* Northfield, Ill.: SIECUS Publications, 1969.

———, and James B. Darcy. "Survey of Family Life and Sex Education Programs in Washington Secondary Schools and Development of Guidelines for Statewide Coordinated Programs." *Family Coordinator* 19, no. 3 (1970): 228–33.

Ball, Howard. *The Supreme Court in the Intimate Lives of Americans: Birth, Sex, Marriage, Childrearing, and Death.* New York: New York University Press, 2002.

Balliet, Thomas M. "Introduction of Sex Education into Public Schools." *American Social Hygiene Association* (1927): 5.

Banks, Joseph Ambrose, and Olive Banks. *Feminism and Family Planning in Victorian England.* New York: Schocken, 1964.

Barber, Jennifer S., William G. Axinn, and Arland Thornton. "Unwanted Childbearing, Health, and Mother-Child Relationships." *Journal of Health and Social Behavior* 40, no. 3 (1999): 231–57.

Barnett, Jerrold, and Cynthia S. Hurst. "Abstinence Education for Rural Youth: An Evaluation of Life's Walk Program." *The Journal of School Health* 73, no. 7 (2003): 254.

Bartee, Wayne C., and Alice Fleetwood Bartee. *Litigating Morality: American Legal Thought and Its English Roots.* New York: Praeger, 1992.

Bauer, Gary L. *Ideology, Politics, and the American Family: Setting the Agenda for the 1990s.* Washington, D.C.: Heritage Foundation, 1989.

———, et al. *The Family: Preserving America's Future: A Report to the President from the White House Working Group on the Family.* Washington, D.C.: The Group, 1986.

Bauman, Karl E., and J. Richard Udry. "The Difference in Unwanted Births Between Blacks and Whites." *Demography* 10, no. 3 (1973): 315–28.

Bearman, Peter S., and Hannah Brückner. "Promising the Future: Virginity Pledges and First Intercourse." *American Journal of Sociology* 106, no. 4 (2001): 859–912.

Beatty, Willard W., Benjamin C. Gruenberg, and Herbert Winslow

Smith. *Sex Instruction in Public Schools.* New York: American Social Hygiene Association, 1936.

Bebell, Clifford F. S. *Family Life Education Contributes to the Preparation of Teachers.* New York: American Social Hygiene Association, 1959

Beck, Curtis E., and Lester F. Avery. *Sex Education and Human Heredity.* Ed. Arthur C. Hearn. Curriculum Bulletin No. 172. Eugene: University of Oregon School of Education, 1957.

Bederman, Gail. *Manliness and Civilization : A Cultural History of Gender and Race in the United States, 1880–1917.* Chicago: University of Chicago Press, 1995.

Bell, Howard. *Youth Tell Their Story.* Washington, D.C.: American Council on Education, 1938.

Bennett, William J. *The Broken Hearth: Reversing the Moral Collapse of the American Family.* New York: Doubleday, 2001.

———. *The De-Valuing of America: The Fight for Our Culture and Our Children.* New York: Summit, 1992.

———. *The Index of Leading Cultural Indicators: Facts and Figures on the State of American Society.* New York: Simon & Schuster, 1994.

Berger, David G., and Morton G. Wenger. "The Ideology of Virginity." *Journal of Marriage and the Family* 35, no. 4 (1973): 666–76.

Bersamin, Melina M., S. Walker, E. D. Waiters, D. A. Fisher, and J. W. Grube. "Promising to Wait: Virginity Pledges and Adolescent Sexual Behavior." *Journal of Adolescent Health* 36, no. 5 (2005): 428–36.

Bigelow, Maurice Alpheus. *Adolescence.* Rev. ed. New York: Funk & Wagnalls, 1937.

———. *Health Education in Relation to Venereal Disease Control Education.* New York: American Social Hygiene Association, 1941.

———. *Teachers' Manual of Biology: A Handbook to Accompany the "Applied Biology" and the "Introduction to Biology" by Maurice A. Bigelow and Anna N. Bigelow.* New York: Macmillan, 1912.

———. *Social Hygiene and Youth in Defense Communities.* Publication No. A-410. New York: American Social Hygiene Association, 1942.

Birken, Laurence. *Consuming Desire: Sexual Science and the Emergence of a Culture of Abundance, 1871–1914.* Ithaca, N.Y.: Cornell University Press, 1988.

———. "The Sexual Counterrevolution: A Critique of Cultural Conservatism." *Social Research* 53, no. 1 (1986): 22.

Blair, Karen J. *The Clubwoman as Feminist: True Womanhood Redefined, 1868–1914.* New York, Holmes & Meier, 1980.

Blanchard, Dallas A. *The Anti-Abortion Movement and the Rise of the Religious Right: From Polite to Fiery Protest.* New York: Maxwell Macmillan, 1994.

Blinn-Pike, Lynn. "Preteen Enrichment: Evaluation of a Program to Delay Sexual Activity Among Female Adolescents in Rural Appalachia." *Family Relations* 45, no. 4 (1986): 380–86.

Bobbio, Norberto. *Left and Right: The Significance of a Political Distinction.* Chicago: University of Chicago Press, 1996.

Boethius, Carl Gustaf. "Sex Education in Swedish Schools: The Facts and the Fiction." *Family Planning Perspectives* 17, no. 6 (1986): 276–79.

Bolce, Louis, and Gerald De Maio. "Religious Outlook, Culture War Politics, and Antipathy Toward Christian Fundamentalists." *Public Opinion Quarterly* 63, no. 1 (1999): 29–61.

Borell, Merriley. "Biologists and the Promotion of Birth Control Research, 1918–1938." *Journal of the History of Biology* 20, no. 1 (1987): 51–87.

Brandt, Allan M. *No Magic Bullet: A Social History of Venereal Disease in the United States Since 1880.* Expanded ed. New York: Oxford University Press, 1987.

Breasted, Mary. *Oh! Sex Education.* New York: Praeger, 1970.

———. "Saving Sex for the Back Seat." *Village Voice,* Sept. 18, 1969.

Brennan, Mary C. *Turning Right in the Sixties: The Conservative Capture of the GOP.* Chapel Hill: University of North Carolina Press, 1995.

Brewster, Karin L., Elizabeth C. Cooksey, David K. Guilkey, and Ronald R. Rindfuss. "The Changing Impact of Religion on the Sexual and Contraceptive Behavior of Adolescent Women in the United States." *Journal of Marriage and the Family* 60, no. 2 (1998): 493–504.

Brown, Sara S., and Leon Eisenberg, eds. *The Best Intentions: Unintended Pregnancy and the Well-Being of Children and Families.* Washington, D.C.: National Academy Press, 1995.

Brown, William J., et al. *Syphilis and Other Venereal Diseases.* Cambridge, Mass.: Harvard University Press, 1970.

Bruckner, Hannah, and Peter S. Bearman. "After the Promise: the STD Consequences of Adolescent Virginity Pledges." *Journal of Adolescent Health* 36 (2005): 271–78

Bumpass, Larry. "What's Happening to the Family? Interactions Between Demographic and Institutional Change," *Demography* 27, no. 4 (1990): 483–98.

Bureau of Social Hygiene. "The Problem of Sex Education in Schools." California State Board of Health, n.d., pp. 23–16.

Burnham, John C. "The Medical Inspection of Prostitutes in the Nineteenth Century: The St. Louis Experiment and Its Sequel." *Bulletin of the History of Medicine* 45 (1971): 203–18.

———. "The Progressive Era Revolution in American Attitudes Towards Sex." *Journal of American History* 59 (Mar. 1973): 885.

Cady, Bertha Louise Chapman, and Vernon Mosher Cady. *The Way Life Begins: An Introduction to Sex Education.* New York: American Social Hygiene Association, 1917.

Calderone, Mary. "Health Education for Responsible Parenthood." *American Journal of Public Health* (Jan. 1964): 1735–40.

California Department of Education. *Education for Human Sexuality: A Resource Book and Instructional Guide to Sex Education for Kindergarten Through Grade Twelve.* Sacramento, 1979.

California State Board of Health. Bureau of Social Hygiene. *The Problem of Sex Education in Schools.* San Francisco: California State Board of Health, n.d.

California State College, Los Angeles. *Sex Information and Education Bibliography.* Los Angeles, Department of Health and Safety Studies: n.d.

Caplow, Theodore. *Middletown Families: Fifty Years of Change and Continuity.* Minneapolis: University of Minnesota Press, 1982.

Carnes, Mark C., and Clyde Griffen, eds. *Meanings for Manhood: Constructions of Masculinity in Victorian America.* Chicago, University of Chicago Press, 1991.

Cavins, Harold M. *National Health Agencies: A Survey with Especial Reference to Voluntary Associations.* Washington, D.C.: Public Affairs Press, 1945.

Centers for Disease Control and Prevention. "Trends in Sexual Risk Behaviors Among High School Students—United States, 1991–1997." *Morbidity and Mortality Weekly Report* 47, no. 36 (1998): 749–52.

Chauncey, George. *Gay New York: Gender, Urban Culture, and the Makings of the Gay Male World, 1890–1940.* New York: Basic, 1994.

Chesler, Ellen. *Woman of Valor: Margaret Sanger and the Birth Control Movement in America.* New York: Simon & Schuster, 1992.

Chicago Society of Social Hygiene. *General Need for Education in Matters of Sex.* Chicago: CSSH, n.d. (1906?).

Christian Coalition. *Contract with the American Family: A Bold Plan to Strengthen the Family and Restore Common-Sense Values.* Nashville, Tenn.: Moorings, 1995.

Clarke, Alan. "Moral Protest, Status Defence, and the Anti-Abortion Campaign." *British Journal of Sociology* 38, no. 2 (1987): 235–53.

Clarke, Charles Walter. "Social Hygiene Study of Los Angeles County." Typescript, 1947.

———. *Taboo: The Story of the Pioneers of Social Hygiene.* Washington: Public Affairs Press, 1961.

Conover, Pamela Johnston. "The Mobilization of the New Right: A Test of Various Explanations." *The Western Political Quarterly* 36, no. 4 (1983): 632–49.

Corsa, Leslie. "Public Health Programs in Family Planning." *American Journal of Public Health* 56 (1966): supplement.

Cott, Nancy F. "Passionlessness: An Interpretation of Victorian Sexual Ideology, 1790–1850." *Signs* 4 (Autumn 1978): 219–36.

Courtney, Phoebe. *The Sex Education Racket: An Exposé.* New Orleans: Free Men Speak, 1969.

Craig, Barbara H., and David M. O'Brien. *Abortion and American Politics.* Chatham, N.J.: Chatham House, 1993.

Cremin, Lawrence Arthur. *American Education: The Colonial Experience, 1607–1783.* New York: Harper & Row, 1970.

Critchlow, Donald T. *Intended Consequences: Birth Control, Abortion, and the Federal Government in Modern America.* New York: Oxford University Press, 1993.

Cutright, Phillips. "The Teenage Sexual Revolution and the Myth of an Abstinent Past." *Family Planning Perspectives* 4, no. 1 (Jan. 1972): 25–29.

Darroch, Jacqueline E., David J. Landry, and Susheela Singh. "Changing Emphases in Sexuality Education in U.S. Public Secondary Schools, 1988–1999." *Family Planning Perspectives* 32, no. 5 (2000): 204–12.

Darroch, Jacqueline E., Susheela Singh, and Jennifer J. Frost. "Differences in Teenage Pregnancy Rates Among Five Developed Countries: The Roles of Sexual Activity and Contraceptive Use." *Family Planning Perspectives* 33, no. 6 (2001): 244–250, 81.

Davis, Nancy J., and Robert Robinson. "Are the Rumors of War Exag-

gerated? Religious Orthodoxy and Moral Progressivism in America."
American Journal of Sociology 102, no. 3 (1996): 756–87.

DeLamater, John. "The Social Control of Sexuality." *Annual Review of Sociology* 7 (1981): 263–90.

Demerath III, N. J. "Excepting Exceptionalism: American Religion in Comparative Relief." *Annals of the American Academy of Political and Social Science* 558 (Jul. 1998): 28–39.

————, and Rhys H. Williams. *A Bridging of Faiths: Religion and Politics in a New England City.* Princeton, N.J: Princeton University Press, 1992.

D'Emilio, John, and Estelle Freedman. *Intimate Matters: A History of Sexuality in America,* New York: Harper and Row, 1988.

Dennett, Mary Ware. *Birth Control Laws: Shall We Keep Them, Change Them, or Abolish Them?* New York: F. H. Hitchcock, 1926.

Dewey, John. *Theory of the Moral Life.* New York: Holt, Rinehart and Winston, 1908.

Dickinson, R. L., and L. Beam. *The Single Woman: A Medical Study in Sex Education.* Baltimore: Williams and Wilkens, 1934.

Dietzler, Mary Macey, and Thomas Andrew Storey. *Detention Houses and Reformatories as Protective Social Agencies in the Campaign of the United States Government Against Venereal Diseases.* Washington, D.C.: Government Printing Office, 1922.

Dock, Lavinia L. *Hygiene and Morality: A Manual for Nurses and Others, Giving an Outline of the Medical, Social, and Legal Aspects of the Venereal Diseases.* New York: Putnam, 1910.

Dorothy, Charles V. *God Speaks Out on the New Morality.* Pasadena, Calif.: Ambassador College Press, 1964.

Drake, Gordon V. *Is the Schoolhouse the Proper Place to Teach Raw Sex?* Tulsa, Okla.: Christian Crusade, 1968.

Duffy, John. *The Sanitarians: A History of American Public Health.* Urbana: University of Illinois Press, 1990.

Durkheim, Emile. "A Discussion on Sex Education." In *Durkheim: Essays on Morals and Education.* Ed. W. S. F. Pickering. London: Routledge and Kegan Paul, 1979, pp. 140–48.

Dutile, Fernand N. *Sex, Schools, and the Law.* Springfield, Ill.: C. C. Thomas, 1986.

Eckberg, Douglas L. "The Physicians' Anti-Abortion Campaign and the Social Bases of Moral Reform Participation." *Social Forces* 67, no. 2 (1988): 378–97.

Eggert, Chester Lee, and Frances Bruce Strain. *Framework for Family Life Education: A Survey of Present-Day Activities in Sex Education.* Washington, D.C.: American Association for Health, Physical Education, and Recreation, 1956.

Ehrmann, Winston W. "Changing Sexual Mores." *In Values and Ideals of American Youth.* Ed. E. Ginzberg. New York: Columbia University Press, 1961.

———. *Premarital Dating Behavior.* New York: Holt, 1959.

———. "Premarital Sexual Behavior and Sex Codes of Conduct with Acquaintances, Friends, and Lovers." *Social Forces* 38 (1959): 158–64.

Erskine, Hazel G. "Morality." *Public Opinion Quarterly* 30 (1966/1967): 669–80.

———. "More on Morality and Sex." *Public Opinion Quarterly* 31 (1967): 116–28.

———. "More on the Population Explosion and Birth Control." *Public Opinion Quarterly* 31 (1967): 303–13.

———. "The Population Explosion, Birth Control, and Sex Education." *Public Opinion Quarterly* 30 (1966): 490–501.

Ester, Peter, Loek Halman, and R. A. de Moor, eds. *The Individualizing Society: Value Change in Europe and North America.* European Values Studies. Tilburg, Netherlands: Tilburg University Press, 1993.

Evans, John H. "Worldviews or Social Groups as the Source of Moral Value Attitudes: Implications for the Culture Wars Thesis." *Sociological Forum* 12, no. 3 (1997): 371–404.

Exner, Max Joseph. *Education for Marriage.* New York: American Social Hygiene Association, 1933.

Fass, Paula S. *The Damned and the Beautiful: American Youth in the 1920s.* New York: Oxford University Press, 1977.

Felsenthal, Carol *The Sweetheart of the Silent Majority: The Biography of Phyllis Schlafly.* Garden City, N.Y.: Doubleday, 1981.

Fenton, John H. *The Catholic Vote.* New Orleans: Hauser/Galleon, 1960.

Fernald, Mabel Ruth, Beardsley Ruml, Mary Holmes Stevens Hayes, and Almena Dawley. *A Study of Women Delinquents in New York State.* New York: Century, 1920.

Fine, Michelle. "Sexuality, Schooling, and Adolecent Females: The Missing Discourse of Desire." *Harvard Educational Review* 58, no. 1 (Feb. 1988).

Flaherty, David H. "Law and the Enforcement of Morals in Early America." *Perspectives in American History* 5 (1971): 225–26.

Flegel, Dorothy. "Social Hygiene Content in Biology Classes of Oregon High Schools." Oregon State College, 1935.

Fleishman, John A. "Attitude Organization in the General Public: Evidence for a Bidimensional Structure." *Social Forces* 67 (1988): 159–84.

———. "Types of Political Attitude Structure: Results of a Cluster Analysis." *Public Opinion Quarterly* 50, no. 3 (1986): 371–86.

Folsom, Joseph K. "Changing Values in Sex and Family Relations." *American Sociological Review* 2, no. 5 (1937): 717–26.

Force, Elizabeth S. "Family Life Education 1970: A Regional Survey." *Family Coordinator* 19, no. 4 (1970): 295–300.

Foster, William Trufant, ed. *The Social Emergency: Studies in Sex Hygiene and Morals.* Boston: Houghton Mifflin, 1914.

Foucault, Michel. *The History of Sexuality.* New York: Pantheon, 1978.

Fournier, Alfred, Prince A. Morrow, and Wallace I. Terry. *Syphilis and Marriage. Lectures Delivered at the St. Louis Hospital, Paris.* New York: D. Appleton, 1881.

Freedman, Estelle. "The New Woman: Changing Views of Women in the 1920s." *Journal of American History* 61 (Sep. 1974): 372–93.

Freeman, Jo. "Feminism vs. Family Values: Women at the 1992 Democratic and Republican Conventions." *PS: Political Science and Politics* 26, no. 1 (1993): 21–28.

Galbraith, Anna M. *The Family and the New Democracy: A Study in Social Hygiene.* Philadelphia: W. B. Saunders, 1920.

Galloway, Thomas Walton. *Sex and Social Health: A Manual for the Study of Social Hygiene.* New York: American Social Hygiene Association, 1924.

Gambrell, Alan E. *Unfinished Business: A SIECUS Assessment of State Sexuality Education Programs.* New York: SIECUS, 1993.

Gardella, Peter. *Innocent Ecstasy: How Christianity Gave America an Ethic of Sexual Pleasure.* New York, Oxford University Press, 1985.

Gardner, James. "Microbes and Morality: The Social Hygiene Crusade in New York City, 1892–1917." Doctoral dissertation, Indiana University, 1974.

Gates, Gary J., and Freya L. Sonenstein. "Heterosexual Genital Activity Among Adolescent Males: 1988 and 1995." *Family Planning Perspectives* 32, 6 (2000): 295–97.

Glazer, Nathan. "Fundamentalists: A Defensive Offensive." In *Piety and*

Politics: Evangelicals and Fundamentalists Confront the World. Ed. Richard Neuhaus and John Cromartie. Washington: Ethics and Public Policy Center, 1987.

Godbeer, Richard, *Sexual Revolution in Early America*. Baltimore, Md.: John Hopkins University Press, 2002.

Goodson, Patricia, Sandy Suther, B. E. Pruitt, and Kelly Wilson. "Defining Abstinence: Views of Directors, Instructors, and Participants in Abstinence-Only-Until-Marriage Programs in Texas." *The Journal of School Health* 73, no. 3 (1987): 91–97.

Gordon, Linda. *Woman's Body, Woman's Right: A Social History of Birth Control in America*. New York: Grossman, 1976.

Gordon, Michael. "From Unfortunate Necessity to a Cult of Mutual Orgasm: Sex in American Marital Education Literature 1830–1940." In *Studies in the Sociology of Sex*. Ed. James M. Henslen. New York: Appleton-Century-Crofts, 1971, pp. 53–77.

Grossberg, Michael. *Governing the Hearth: Law and the Family in Nineteenth-Century America*. Chapel Hill: University of North Carolina Press, 1985.

Gruenberg, Benjamin C. *How Can We Teach About Sex?* New York: Public Affairs Committee, 1946.

————. *Parents and Sex Education*. New York: American Social Hygiene Association, 1923.

————, ed. *High Schools and Sex Education: A Manual of Suggestions on Education Related to Sex*. Washington, D.C.: United States Public Health Service, 1922.

Gruenberg, Benjamin, and J. L. Kaukonen. *High Schools and Sex Education*. Washington, D.C.: United States Public Health Service, 1940.

Guthe, Thorstein. *Sexually Transmitted Diseases (STD), Scope and Control Measures: Report*. Strasbourg: Council of Europe, European Health Committee, 1974.

Hadden, Jeffrey, and Anson Shupe, eds. *Secularization and Fundamentalism Reconsidered: Religion and the Political Order*. New York: Paragon, 1989.

Haider-Markel, Donald P., and Kenneth J. Meier. "The Politics of Gay and Lesbian Rights: Expanding the Scope of the Conflict." *Journal of Politics* 58, no. 2 (1996): 332–49.

Heatherly, Charles L., and B. Y. Pines, eds. *Mandate for Leadership III: Policy Strategies for the 1990s*. Washington, D.C.: Heritage Foundation, 1989.

Hertel, Bradley R., and Michael Hughes. "Religious Affiliation, Attendance, and Support for 'Pro-Family' Issues in the United States." *Social
Forces* 65, no. 3 (1987): 858–82.

Himmelfarb, Gertrude. *The De-Moralization of Society: From Victorian
Virtues to Modern Values.* New York: Knopf, 1995.

———. *Marriage and Morals Among the Victorians: Essays.* New York:
Knopf, 1986.

Himmelstein, Jerome L. *To the Right: The Transformation of American Conservatism.* Berkeley: University of California Press, 1990.

———, and James A. McRae, Jr. "Social Conservatism, New Republicans, and the 1980 Election." *Public Opinion Quarterly* 48, no. 3
(1984): 592–605.

Hindus, Michael. "Premarital Pregnancy in America, 1640–1871: An
Overview and an Interpretation." *Journal of Interdisciplinary History* 5
(July 1975): 537–70.

Hobbs, Albert Hoyt, and America's Future Inc. *Seek for Sex Education and
You Shall Find.* New Rochelle, N.Y.: America's Future, 1969.

Hoff, Tina, Liberty Green, Mary McIntosh, Nicole Rawlings, and Jean
D'Amico. *Sex Education in America: A View from Inside the Nation's Classrooms.* Menlo Park, Calif.: Kaiser Family Foundation, 2000, pp. 1–116.

Hofferth, Sandra L., Joan Kahn, and Wendy Baldwin. "Premarital Sexual Activity among U.S. Teenage Women over the Past Three
Decades." *Family Planning Perspectives* 19 (1987): 46–53.

Hofferth, Sandra L., and Kristin A. Moore. "Early Childbearing and Later
Economic Well-Being." *American Sociological Review* 44, no. 5 (Oct.
1979): 784–815.

Hofferth, Sandra L., and Lori Reid. "Early Childbearing and Children's
Achievement and Behavior over Time." *Perspectives on Sexual and Reproductive Health* 34, no. 1 (2002): 41–49.

Hogan, Dennis P., Nan Marie Astone, and Evelyn M. Kitagawa. "Social
and Environmental Factors Influencing Contraceptive Use Among
Black Adolescents." *Family Planning Perspectives* 17, no. 4 (1985):
165–69.

Hogan, Dennis P., and Evelyn M. Kitagawa. "The Impact of Social Status, Family Structure, and Neighborhood on the Fertility of Black
Adolescents." *American Journal of Sociology* 90, no. 4 (1985): 825–55.

Horn, Margo. *Before It's Too Late: The Child Guidance Movement in the United
States, 1922–1945.* Philadelphia: Temple University Press, 1989.

Hottois, James, and Neal A. Milner. *The Sex Education Controversy: A Study of Politics, Education, and Morality.* Lexington, Mass: Lexington Books, 1975.

Hout, Michael, and Claude S. Fischer. "Why More Americans Have No Religious Preference: Politics and Generations." *American Sociological Review* 67, no. 2 (2002): 165–90.

Hughes, Jane, and Ann P. McCauley. "Improving the Fit: Adolescents' Needs and Future Programs for Sexual and Reproductive Health in Developing Countries." *Studies in Family Planning* 29, no. 2 (1998): 233–45.

Hunt, Alan. *Governing Morals: A Social History of Moral Regulation.* Cambridge Studies in Law and Society. New York: Cambridge University Press, 1999.

Hunter, James Davison. *Culture Wars: The Struggle to Define America.* New York: Basic, 1991.

———. *Evangelicalism: The Coming Generation.* Chicago: University of Chicago Press, 1987.

Hyles, Jack. *Sex Education Program in Our Public Schools: What Is Behind It?* Life-Changing Pamphlet Library. Murfreesboro, Tenn.: Sword of the Lord, 1969.

Imber, Michael. "Analysis of a Curricular Reform Movement: The American Social Hygiene Association's Campaign for Sex Education." Doctoral dissertation, Stanford University, 1980.

———. "Toward a Theory of Educational Origins: A Genesis of Sex Education." *Educational Theory* 34, no. 3 (1984): 275–86.

Impact Publishers. *Pavlov's Children: They May Be Yours.* Los Angeles, Calif.: Impact Publishers, 1969.

Inglehart, Ronald. *Culture Shift in Advanced Industrial Society.* Princeton, N.J.: Princeton University Press, 1990.

———, and Pippa Norris. *Rising Tide: Gender Equality and Cultural Change Around the World.* New York: Cambridge University Press, 2003.

Irvine, Janice M. *Talk About Sex: The Battles over Sex Education in the United States.* Berkeley: University of California Press, 2002.

Jones, Elise F., ed. *Teenage Pregnancy in Industrialized Countries: A Study Sponsored by the Alan Guttmacher Institute.* New Haven, Conn.: Yale University Press, 1986.

Kahn, Joan R., William D. Kalsbeek, and Sandra L. Hofferth. "National Estimates of Teenage Sexual Activity: Evaluating the Comparability of Three National Surveys." *Demography* 25, no. 2 (1988): 189–204.

Kassoy, Irving. "A History of the Work of the American Social Hygiene Association in Sex Education, 1876–1930." Master's thesis, City College of New York, 1931.

Kellogg, Edmund Halsey, et al. "The World's Laws and Practices on Population and Sexuality Education." Medford, Mass.: Law and Population Program, Fletcher School of Law and Diplomacy, Tufts University, 1975.

Keyes, Edward Loughborough, and Charles William Eliot. *Morals and Venereal Disease.* New York: American Social Hygiene Association, 1916.

Kirby, Douglas. "A Review of Educational Programs Designed to Reduce Sexual Risk-Taking Behaviors Among School-Aged Youth in the United States." #PB96108519. Springfield, Va.: National Technical Information Service, 1995.

———. "Sex Education in the Schools." In *Sexuality and American Social Policy.* Ed. Jayne A. Garrison, M. D. Smith, and D. J. Besharov. Menlo Park, Calif.: Kaiser Family Foundation, 1994.

———, Meg Korpi, Richard P. Barth, and Helen H. Cagampang. "The Impact of the Postponing Sexual Involvement Curriculum Among Youths in California." *Family Planning Perspectives* 29, no. 3 (1997) 100–108.

Klassen, Albert D., Colin J. Williams, Eugene E. Levitt, Hubert J. O'Gorman. *Sex and Morality in the U.S.: An Empirical Enquiry Under the Auspices of the Kinsey Institute.* Middletown, Conn.: Wesleyan University Press, 1989.

Knoke, David. "Stratification and the Dimensions of American Political Orientations." *American Journal of Political Science* 23 (1979): 772–91.

Kozakiewicz, Miko. *Sex Education and Adolescence in Europe: Sexuality, Marriage, and the Family.* London: International Planned Parenthood Federation, Europe Region, 1981.

Ku, Leighton C., Freya L. Sonenstein, and Joseph H. Pleck. "The Association of AIDS Educaton and Sex Education with Sexual Behavior and Condom Use Among Teenage Men." *Family Planning Perspectives* 24 (1992). 100–106.

Kunzel, Regina. *Fallen Women, Problem Girls: Unmarried Mothers and the*

Professionalization of Social Work, 1890–1945. New Haven: Yale University Press, 1993.

LaHaye, Tim, and Beverly LaHaye. *The Act of Marriage: The Beauty of Sexual Love.* Grand Rapids, Mich.: Zondervan, 1976.

Landry, David J., Lisa Kaeser, and Cory L. Richards. "Abstinence Promotion and the Provision of Information About Contraception in Public School District Sexuality Education Policies." *Family Planning Perspectives* 31, no. 6 (1999): 280–86.

Laqueur, Thomas Walter. *Solitary Sex: A Cultural History of Masturbation.* New York: Zone, 2003.

Laumann, Edward O., et al. *The Social Organization of Sexuality: Sexual Practices in the United States.* University of Chicago Press, 1994.

Lears, T. J. Jackson. *No Place of Grace: Antimodernism and the Transformation of American Culture 1880–1920.* New York: Pantheon, 1981.

Lederer, S., and J. Parascandola. "Dr. Ehrlich's Magic Bullet." *Journal of the History of Medicine* 53, no. 4 (1998): 345–70.

Lemons, J. Stanley. *The Woman Citizen: Social Feminism in the 1920s.* Urbana: University of Illinois Press, 1973.

Lesher, Mabel Grier. "Education for Family Life (New Jersey)." *Journal of Educational Sociology, Education for Family Living* 22, no. 7 (1949): 440–49.

Lickona, Thomas. *Educating for Character.* New York: Bantam, 1991.

Lieberman, Lisa D., Heather Gray, Megan Wier, Renee Fiorentino, and Patricia Maloney. "Long-Term Outcomes of an Abstinence-Based, Small-Group Pregnancy Prevention Program in New York City Schools." *Family Planning Perspectives* 32, no. 5 (2000): 237–45.

Lienesch, Michael. "Right-Wing Religion: Christian Conservatism as a Political Movement." *Political Science Quarterly* 97, no. 3 (1982): 403–25.

Lockwood, Alan L. "Effects of Values Clarification and Moral Development Curricula on School-Age Subjects: A Critical Review of Recent Research." *Review of Educational Research* 48 (1978): 325–64.

Long, William Bayard, and Jacob Alter Goldberg, eds. *Handbook of Social Hygiene.* Philadelphia: Lea & Febiger, 1938.

Luker, Kristin. "Sex, Social Hygiene and the State: The Double-Edged Sword of Social Reform." *Theory and Society* 27 (1998): 601–34.

Manley, Helen, ed. *A Curriculum Guide in Sex Education.* St. Louis, Missouri: State Publishing Co., 1966.

Manza, Jeff, and Clem Brooks. *Social Cleavages and Political Change: Voter*

Alignments and U.S. Party Coalitions. New York: Oxford University Press, 1990.

Marsden, George M. *Fundamentalism and American Culture: The Shaping of Twentieth-Century Evangelicalism, 1870–1925.* New York: Oxford University Press, 1980.

Marshall, Susan E. "Who Speaks for American Women? The Future of Antifeminism." *Annals of the American Academy of Political and Social Science* 515 (1991): 50–62.

Martin, John Levi. "Structuring the Sexual Revolution." *Theory and Society* 25 (1996): 105–51.

Mast, Coleen Kelly. *Sex Respect: The Option of True Sexual Freedom — a Public Health Manual for Teachers.* Respect for Sexuality, 1986.

May, Elaine Tyler. *Great Expectations: Marriage and Divorce in Post-Victorian America.* Chicago: University of Chicago Press, 1980.

Mayer, William G. *The Changing American Mind: How and Why American Public Opinion Changed Between 1960 and 1988.* Ann Arbor: University of Michigan Press, 1993.

McCann, Carole R. *Birth Control Politics in the United States, 1916–1945.* Ithaca: Cornell University Press, 1994.

McGovern, James R. "The American Woman's Pre-World War I Freedom in Manners and Morals." *Journal of American History* 55, no. 2 (Sep. 1968): 315–33.

McGraw, Onalee. *Secular Humanism and the Schools: The Issue Whose Time Has Come.* "Critical Issues." Washington, D.C.: Heritage Foundation, 1976.

McLanahan, Sara. "Diverging Destinies: How Children Are Faring under the Second Demographic Transition." *Demography* 41, no. 4 (2004): 607–27.

McLanahan, Sara, and Karen Booth. "Mother-Only Families: Problems, Prospects, and Politics." *Journal of Marriage and the Family* 51, no. 3 (1989): 557–80.

Meredith, Philip. *Sex Education: Political Issues in Britain and Europe.* New York: Routledge, 1989.

Michigan Department of Education. *Guidelines for Reproductive Health, Family Planning, and Venereal Disease.* 1978.

Miller, Alan S., and John P. Hoffmann. "The Growing Divisiveness: Culture Wars or a War of Words?" *Social Forces* 78, no. 2 (1999): 721–45.

Minnesota Department of Education. *Guidelines for Family Life and Sex Eeducation, Grades K–12.* Curriculum bulletin no. 32. St. Paul: Minnesota Department of Education, 1970.

Moran, Jeffrey P. "'Modernism Gone Mad': Sex Education Comes to Chicago, 1913." *Journal of American History* 83, no. 2 (1996): 481–513.
———. *Teaching Sex: The Shaping of Adolescence in the 20th Century.* Cambridge, Mass.: Harvard University Press, 2000.

Morrow, Prince A. *Social Diseases and Marriage: Social Prophylaxis.* New York: Lea Brothers, 1904.

Mosher, Clelia Duel, James MaHood, and Kristine Wenburg. *The Mosher Survey: Sexual Attitudes of 45 Victorian Women.* New York: Arno Press. 1980.

Moxon, R. P. *White Cross Purity League.* New York: Young Men's Christian Association, 1888.

Mueller, Carol, and Thomas Dimieri. "The Structure of Belief Systems among Contending ERA Activists." *Social Forces* 60, no. 3 (1982): 657–75.

Nathanson, Constance. *Dangerous Passage: The Social Control of Adolescent Women's Sexuality,* Philadelphia: Temple University Press, 1991.

National Congress of Parents and Teachers. *The Story of the Rocky Mountain Project: PTA and ASHA Programs in Family Life Education.* Chicago: National Congress of Parents and Teachers, 1964.

National Education Association. "Sex Hygiene and Sex Morality as the Aim of Sex Education." *NEA Journal of Addresses and Proceedings* 53 (1915).

National Education Association. Commission on Professional Rights and Responsibilities. *Suggestions for Defense Against Extremist Attack: Sex Education in the Public Schools.* Washington, D.C.: National Education Association, 1970.

New Jersey Social Hygiene Association. Education Committee. *An Approach to Sex Education in Schools.* No. 1, Series of Bulletins on Education for Family Life. New York: American Social Hygiene Association, 1941.

New York Social Hygiene Society. *Origin of This Movement: Its Objects, Aims, and Methods of Work.* New York: NYSHS, 1906.

Nie, Norman H., and Kristi Andersen. "Mass Belief Systems Revisited: Political Change and Attitude Structure." *Journal of Politics* 36, no. 3 (1974): 540–91.

Nie, Norman H., Sidney Verba, and John R. Petrocik. *The Changing American Voter.* Cambridge, Mass.: Harvard University Press, 1976.

O'Connell, Martin, and Maurice J. Moore. "The Legitimacy Status of First Births to U.S. Women Aged 15–24, 1939–1978." *Family Planning Perspectives* 12, no. 1 (1980): 16–25.

Odem, Mary. *Delinquent Daughters: Protecting and Policing Adolescent Female Sexuality in the United States, 1885–1920*. Gender and American Culture. Chapel Hill: University of North Carolina Press, 1995.

Office of National AIDS Policy. "Youth and HIV/AIDS: An American Agenda." Washington, D.C.: Department of Health and Human Services, 1996.

Okin, Susan Moller. *Women in Western Political Thought*. Princeton, N.J.: Princeton University Press, 1979.

Olson, Daniel V. A., and Jackson Carroll. "Religiously Based Politics: Religious Elites and the Public." *Social Forces* 70 (1992): 765–86.

Ossowska, Maria. *Social Determinants of Moral Ideas*. Philadelphia: University of Pennsylvania Press, 1970.

Page, Benjamin I., and Robert Y. Shapiro. *The Rational Public: Fifty Years of Trends in Americans' Policy Preferences*. Chicago: University of Chicago Press, 1992.

Paget, Norman W. *A Diary of a Family Life Education Experiment*. San Bernardino, Calif.: Family Service Agency of San Bernardino, 1961.

Pagnini, Deanna L., and Ronald R. Rindfuss. "The Divorce of Marriage and Childbearing: Changing Attitudes and Behavior in the United States." *Population and Development Review* 19, no. 2 (1993): 331–47.

Panchaud, Christine, et al. "Sexually Transmitted Diseases Among Adolescents in Developed Countries." *Family Planning Perspectives* 32, 1 (2000): 24–32, 45.

Peek, Charles W., George D. Lowe, and L. Susan Williams. "Gender and God's Word: Another Look at Religious Fundamentalism and Sexism." *Social Forces* 69, no. 4 (1991): 1205–21.

Peiss, Kathy Lee. *Cheap Amusements: Working Women and Leisure in New York City, 1880 to 1920*. Philadelphia: Temple University Press, 1985.

Petchesky, Rosalind P. *Abortion and Woman's Choice: The State, Sexuality, and the Conditions of Reproductive Freedom*. Longman Series in Feminist Theory. New York: Longman, 1983.

Pines, Burton Yale. *Back to Basics: The Traditionalist Movement That Is Sweeping Grass-Roots America*. New York: Morrow, 1982.

Pivar, David. *Purity Crusade: Sexual Morality and Social Control, 1868–1900*. Westport, Conn.: Greenwood, 1973.

Pope, Hallowell, and Dean D. Knudsen. "Premarital Sexual Norms, the Family, and Social Change." *Journal of Marriage and the Family* 27 (1965): 314–23.

Popenoe, David. "The National Family Wars." *Journal of Marriage and the Family* 55, no. 3 (1993): 553–55.

Porter, Roy, and Mikulas Teich, eds. *Sexual Knowledge, Sexual Science: The History of Attitudes to Sexuality.* Cambridge, Eng.: Cambridge University Press, 1994.

Prendergast, William B. *The Catholic Voter in American Politics: The Passing of the Democratic Monolith.* Washington, D.C.: Georgetown University Press, 1999.

Pusey, William Allen. *The History and Epidemiology of Syphilis.* Gehrmann Lectures. Springfield, Ill.: Charles C. Thomas, 1933.

Rath, Louis, Merrill Harmin, and Sidney Simon. *Values and Teaching.* Columbus, Ohio: Charles E. Merrill, 1966.

Reed, James. *The Birth Control Movement and American Society: From Private Vice to Public Virtue.* Princeton, Princeton University Press, 1978.

Reiss, Ira L. 1956. "The Double Standard in Premarital Sexual Intercourse: A Neglected Concept." *Social Forces* 34: 224–30.

———. 1957. "The Treatment of Pre-Marital Coitus in 'Marriage and the Family' Texts." *Social Problems* 4: 334–38.

———. 1961. "Sexual Codes in Teen-Age Culture." *Annals of the American Academy of Political and Social Science* 338: 53–62.

———. 1964. "The Scaling of Premarital Sexual Permissiveness." *Journal of Marriage and the Family* 26: 188–98.

Repjolier, Agnes. "The Repeal of Reticence." *Atlantic Monthly* (Mar. 1914): 297–304.

Rhode, Deborah L. "Adolescent Pregnancy and Public Policy." *Political Science Quarterly* 108, no. 4 (1993): 635–69.

Rhymes, Douglas A. *No New Morality: Christian Personal Values and Sexual Morality.* Indianapolis: Bobbs-Merrill, 1964.

Ribuffo, Leo P. *The Old Christian Right: The Protestant Far Right from the Great Depression to the Cold War.* Philadelphia, Temple University Press, 1983.

Rice, Thurman B. *Those First Sex Questions.* Bureau of Health Education, Sex Education Pamphlet. Chicago: American Medical Association, 1940.

Richardson, Theresa R. *The Century of the Child: The Mental Hygiene Movement and Social Policy in the United States and Canada.* Albany: State University of New York Press, 1989.

Riley, James C. *Population Thought in the Age of the Demographic Revolution.* Durham, N.C.: Carolina Academic Press, 1985.

Rinehart, Sue Tolleson, and Jerry Perkins. "The Intersection of Gender Politics and Religious Beliefs." *Political Behavior* 11, no. 1 (1989): 33–56.

Roof, Wade Clark, and William McKinney. "Denominational America and the New Religious Pluralism." *Annals of the American Academy of Political and Social Science* 480 (Jul. 1985): 24–38.

Rose, Sonya. "Cultural Analysis and Moral Discourses: Episodes, Continuities and Transformations." In *Beyond the Cultural Turn*. Ed. Victoria Bonnell and Lynn Hunt. Berkeley: University of California Press, 1999.

Rosen, Ruth. *The Lost Sisterhood: Prostitution in America, 1900–1918.* Baltimore: Johns Hopkins University Press, 1982.

Rosenkrantz, Barbara Gutmann. *Public Health and the State: Changing Views in Massachusetts, 1842–1936.* Cambridge: Harvard University Press, 1972.

Rosoff, Jeannie I., and Asta M. Kenney. "Title X and Its Critics." *Family Planning Perspectives* 16, no. 3 (1984): 111–13, 15–16, 19.

Rossi, Alice. "A Biosocial Perspective on Parenting." *Daedalus* 106 (1977): 1–31.

Rotundo, E. Anthony. "Learning About Manhood." In *Manliness and Morality: Middle-Class Morality in Britain and America, 1800–1940.* Ed. J. A. Mangan and James Walvin. Manchester, Eng.: Manchester University Press, 1987, pp. 35–48.

Rozell, Mark J., and Clyde Wilcox. "Second Coming: The Strategies of the New Christian Right." *Political Science Quarterly* 111, no. 2 (1996): 271–94.

Ryan, Mary. "The Power of Women's Networks: A Case Study of Female Moral Reform in Ante-bellum America." *Feminist Studies* 5 (Spring 1979): 82–104.

Sacramento County, Calif. Office of the Superintendent of Schools. *Planning for Curriculum Development in Family Life and Sex Education.* Sacramento, 1968.

Sanger, William W. *The History of Prostitution: Its Extent, Causes, and Effects Throughout the World. Being an Official Report to the Board of Alms-House Governors of the City of New York.* New York: Harper, 1858.

Santelli, John S., Laura Duberstein Lindberg, Joyce Abma, Clea Sucoff McNeely, and Michael Resnick. "Adolescent Sexual Behavior: Estimates and Trends from Four Nationally Representative Surveys." *Family Planning Perspectives* 32, no. 4 (2000): 156–65, 194.

Scales, Peter. "Sex Education in the '70s and '80s: Accomplishments,

Obstacles and Emerging Issues." *Family Relations* 30, no. 4 (1981): 557–566.

Schaeffer, Francis A. *A Christian Manifesto.* Westchester, Ill.: Crossway, 1981.

———. *How Should We Then Live?: The Rise and Decline of Western Thought and Culture.* Old Tappan, N.J.: F. H. Revell, 1976.

———, and C. Everett Koop. *Whatever Happened to the Human Race?* Old Tappan, N.J.: F. H. Revell, 1979.

Schneider, William. "The Real Choices on Family Values." *National Journal,* June 27, 1992, p. 1554.

Schuster, Mark A., R. M. Bell, and D. E. Kanouse. "The Sexual Practices of Adolescent Virgins: Genital Sexual Activities of High School Students Who Have Never Had Vaginal Intercourse." *American Journal of Public Health* 86, no. 11 (1996): 1570–76.

Schvaneveldt, Jay D., and Margaret H. Young. "Strengthening Families: New Horizons in Family Life Education." *Family Relations* 41, no. 4 (1992): 385–89.

Sears, James T., ed. *Sexuality and the Curriculum: The Politics and Practices of Sexuality.* New York: Teachers College Press, 1992.

Seidman, Steven. *Embattled Eros: Sexual Politics and Ethics in Contemporary America.* New York: Routledge, 1992.

———. *Romantic Longings: Love in America, 1830–1980.* New York: Routledge, 1991.

Shah, Farida, Melvin Zelnik, and John F. Kanter. "Unprotected Intercourse Among Unwed Teenagers." *Family Planning Perspectives* 7, no. 1 (1975): 39–44.

Shibley, Mark A. "Contemporary Evangelicals: Born-Again and World Affirming." *Annals of the American Academy of Political and Social Science* 558 (1998): 67–87.

Shumsky, Neil Larry. "Tacit Acceptance: Respectable Americans and Segregated Prostitution, 1870–1910." *Journal of Social History* 19 (Fall 1986): 664–79.

Simmons, Christina. *Marriage in the Modern Manner: Sexual Radicalism and Reform in America, 1914–1941.* Providence, R.I.: Brown University Press, 1982.

Skolnick, Arlene S. *Embattled Paradise: The American Family in an Age of Uncertainty.* New York: Basic, 1991.

Smigel, Erwin O., and Rita Seiden. "The Decline and Fall of the Double Standard." *Annals of the American Academy of Political and Social Science* 376 (1968): 6–17.

Smith, Daniel Scott. "The Long Cycle in American Illegitimacy and Prenuptial Pregnancy." In *Bastardy and Its Comparative History.* Eds. Peter Laslett et al. Cambridge, Eng.: Cambridge University Press, 1980.

Smith, Tom W. "A Report: The Sexual Revolution?" *Public Opinion Quarterly* 54, no. 3 (Autumn 1990): 415–35.

Smith-Rosenberg, Carroll. "Beauty, the Beast, and the Militant Woman: A Case Study of Sex Roles and Social Stress in Jacksonian America." *American Quarterly* 23 (1971): 562–84.

Snow, William F. *Social Hygiene and the White House Conference on Child Health and Protection.* New York: American Social Hygiene Association, 1931.

———. *Social Hygiene in Schools: Report of the Subcommittee on Social Hygiene in Schools.* New York: White House Conference on Child Health and Protection, 1932.

———. *What Shall We Read?* New York: American Social Hygiene Association, 1914.

Solinger, Rickie. *Wake Up, Little Susie: Single Pregnancy and Race before Roe v. Wade.* New York: Routledge, 1992.

Southard, Marion O., and Helen Lerrigo. *Approaching Adulthood.* Sex Education Series. Washington, D.C.: Joint Committee on Health Problems in Education of the National Education Association and the American Medical Association, 1966.

Sprecher, Susan Kathleen McKinney, and Terri L. Orbuch. "Has the Double Standard Disappeared?: An Experimental Test." *Social Psychology Quarterly* 50, no. 1 (1987): 24–31.

Stolzenberg, Ross M., Mary Blair-Loy, and Linda J. Waite. "Religious Participation in Early Adulthood: Age and Family Life Cycle Effects on Church Membership." *American Sociological Review* 60, no. 1 (1995): 84–103.

Stone, Lee Alexander. *An Open Talk with Mothers and Fathers: Presenting Some Present Day Problems in Social Hygiene.* Kansas City, Mo.: Burton, 1920.

Stout, Harry S. *The New England Soul: Preaching and Religious Culture in Colonial New England.* New York: Oxford University Press, 1986.

Strong, Bryan. "Ideas of the Early Sex Education Movement in America, 1890–1920." *History of Education Quarterly* 12, 2 (Summer 1972): 129–61.

Sulloway, Alvah. *Birth Control and Catholic Doctrine.* Boston: Beacon, 1959.

Swan, George Steven. "The Political Economy of American Family Policy, 1945–85." *Population and Development Review* 12, no. 4 (1986): 739–58.

Tatalovich, Raymond, and Byron W. Daynes. *Social Regulatory Policy: Moral Controversies in American Politics.* Boulder, Colo.: Westview, 1988.

Thomas, Keith. "The Double Standard." *Journal of the History of Ideas* 20, no. 2 (1959): 195–216.

Thomas, Lois B., and Myra H. Watt. *Family Life and Sex Education: A Bibliography from the Educational Materials Center, Division of Research Training and Dissemination, Bureau of Research.* Office of Education Publication Oe-14031–39. Washington, D.C.: U.S. Department of Health, Education, and Welfare, 1966.

Thompson, Sharon. "Search for Tomorrow: On Feminism and the Reconstruction of Teen Romance." In *Pleasure and Danger: Exploring Female Sexuality.* Ed. Carole S. Vance. Boston: Routledge and Kegan Paul, 1984.

Thornton, Arland. "Changing Attitudes Toward Family Issues in the United States." *Journal of Marriage and the Family* 51 (1989): 873–93.

Tipton, Steven M. *Getting Saved from the Sixties: Moral Meaning in Conversion and Cultural Change.* Berkeley: University of California Press, 1982.

Tronto, Joan C. *Moral Boundaries: A Political Argument for an Ethic of Care.* New York: Routledge, 1993.

Trudell, Bonnie Nelson. *Doing Sex Education: Gender Politics and Schooling.* New York: Routledge, 1993.

Trussell, James. "Teenage Pregnancy in the United States." *Family Planning Perspectives* 20, no. 6 (Nov.-Dec. 1988): 262–72.

U.S. Department of Health, Education, and Welfare. *Report on Family Planning: Activities of the U.S. Department of Health, Education, and Welfare in Family Planning, Fertility, Sterility, and Population Dynamics.* Washington, D.C.: Government Printing Office, 1966.

———. Public Health Service. *The National Venereal Disease Control Program.* 2d ed. Vol. 56, Public Health Service Publications. Washington, D.C.: United States Government Printing Office, 1951.

U.S. House of Representatives. "Family Planning Services: Hearing before the Subcommittee on Public Health and Welfare of the Committee on Interstate and Foreign Commerce." Serial no. 91–70. Washington, D.C.: Government Printing Office, 1970, pp. 68–76; 190–193.

————. Select Committee on Children, Youth, and Families. "Teen Pregnancy: What Is Being Done? A State-by-State Look." A Report. Washington, D.C.: Government Printing Office, 1986

U. S. Senate. Subcommittee on Health of the Committee on Labor and Public Welfare. Hearing to Enact the National School-age Mother and Child Health Act of 1975.

Van Buskirk, Edgar Flandreau. *Sex and Character Education (A Course for Parents)*. Cincinnati: Cincinnati Social Hygiene Society, 1925.

Ventura. Stephanie J. "Trends in Pregnancy Rates for the United States, 1976–97: An Update." *National Vital Statistics Report* 49, 4 (2001): 1–10.

————, Sally C. Curtin, and T. J. Mathews. *Teenage Births in the United States: National and State Trends, 1990–96*. Hyattsville, Md.: Centers for Disease Control and Prevention/National Center for Health Statistics, 1998.

Vinovskis, Maris. *An "Epidemic" of Adolescent Pregnancy?: Some Historical and Policy Considerations*. New York: Oxford University Press, 1988.

Wayman, Frank Whelon, and Ronald R. Stockton. "The Structure and Stability of Political Attitudes: Findings from the 1974–76 Dearborn Panel Study." *Public Opinion Quarterly* 47, no. 3 (1983): 329–46.

Wells, Robert V. "Illegitimacy and Bridal Pregnancy in Colonial America." In *Bastardy and Its Comparative History*. Eds. Peter Laslett et al. Cambridge, Mass.: Harvard University Press, 1980.

Wetherill, G. G. *Human Relations Education: A Program Developing in the San Diego City Schools*. New York: American Social Hygiene Association, 1946.

Whitehead, Barbara Dafoe. *The Divorce Culture*. New York: Knopf, 1997.

Wilson, James Q. "Family Values Debate." *Commentary* 95, no. 4 (1993): 24–16.

————. "The Rediscovery of Character: Private Virtue and Public Policy." *Public Interest* 81 (Fall 1985): 3–16.

Witmer, Helen Leland, and F. Stuart Chapin. *The Attitudes of Mothers Toward Sex Education*. [Minneapolis]: University of Minnesota Press, 1929.

Wolfe, Alan. "Prospects for a Common Morality." *Hastings Center Report* 24 (1994): 44.

Wolfe, Alan. *Whose Keeper? Social Science and Moral Obligation*. Berkeley: University of California Press, 1989.

Wood, Michael, and Michael Hughes. "The Moral Basis of Moral Reform: Status Discontent Vs. Culture and Socialization as Explanations of Anti-Pornography Social Movement Adherence." *American Sociological Review* 49, no. 1 (1984): 86–99.

Woodberry, Robert D., and Christian S. Smith. "Fundamentalist Conservative Protestants in America." *Annual Review of Sociology* 24 (1998): 25–56.

Woodrow, Walter H. "Sex-Instruction as the Core of a High School Biology Course." Ph.D. dissertation, Indiana State Teachers' College, 1931.

Woodrum, Eric. "Determinants of Moral Attitudes." *Journal for the Scientific Study of Religion* 27 (1988): 553–73.

Worthington, George E., and Ruth Topping. *Specialized Courts Dealing with Sex Delinquency: A Study of the Procedure in Chicago, Boston, Philadelphia, and New York.* New York: F. H. Hitchcock, 1925.

Wuthnow, Robert. *Meaning and Moral Order: Explorations in Cultural Analysis.* Berkeley: University of California Press, 1987.

———. *The Restructuring of American Religion: Society and Faith Since World War II.* Princeton, N.J.: Princeton University Press, 1988.

Yankelovitch, Daniel. *The New Morality: A Profile of American Youth in the 1970s.* New York: McGraw-Hill, 1974.

Yarros, Rachelle. *Modern Woman and Sex.* New York: Vanguard, 1933.

Zelizer, Viviana A. *Pricing the Priceless Child: The Changing Social Value of Children.* New York: Basic, 1985.

Zimmerman, Jonathan. *Distilling Democracy: Alcohol Education in America's Public Schools, 1880–1925.* Lawrence: University Press of Kansas, 1999.

Ziporyn, Terra Marie. *Disease in the Popular American Press: The Case of Diphtheria, Typhoid Fever, and Syphilis, 1870–1920.* Contributions in Medical Studies No. 24. New York: Greenwood, 1988.

Index

abortion, 25, 30–31, 33, 69, 71, 73, 77–78,
    80–82, 85, 128, 304*n*, 311*n*
  by American adults, 23
  liberal vs. conservative views on, 92, 94,
    97–98, 188
  as necessary evil, 234
  politics and, 215, 217, 219, 221, 224–25
  pro-choice vs. pro-life positions on, 224
  public approval of, 306*n*–7*n*
  religion and, 216–17
  resignation about, 231
  sex education and, 24, 111, 231–32
  by teenagers, 23, 26, 187, 285*n*
absolutes, moral, 184–85, 193
abstinence, 103–4, 139
  as moral value, 249
  sexual autonomy and, 234
abstinence education, 22, 30–31, 159, 191, 236,
    238, 283*n*, 288*n*
  and delayed sexual initiation, 256–58
  efficacy of, 248, 253, 256–58
  federal financing of, 223
  harm reduction and, 245–48
  liberal vs. conservative views on, 92, 97, 102,
    111, 139
  politics and, 222–23
  values and, 245–47, 249
Adams, Greg, 225
Addams, Jane, 291*n*
Adolescent Family Life Act (AFLA), 222, 283*n*
adolescents, 47
  see also teenagers
advocacy groups, 282*n*
AFLA (Adolescent Family Life Act), 222, 283*n*
African Americans, 126
  and Bush/Clinton election, 230
  at Christian academies, 219

and legitimation rate for women, 288*n*
premarital sex and, 66–67, 74
sex education controversy and, 91
social hygiene movement and, 216
Spingarn's study of, 320*n*
AIDS, *see* HIV/AIDS
Akerlof, George, 82
Allen, Woody, 200
altruism, 233
American Citizens Concerned for Life, 24
American Social Hygiene Association (ASHA),
    38, 40, 61, 289*n*–90*n*
American society:
  diversity of, 214, 239
  Puritan hypothesis and, 214
  risky sexuality and, 325*n*
Ames, Sandy (pseud.), 96, 99, 106, 146–47,
    176–77, 196, 277
anatomy, 25
Anglo-American common law, 106, 310*n*
anthropology, 263–64
antiabortion movements, 215
  European, 231
anti-Communist opposition to sex education,
    220
Aries, Philippe, 318*n*
ASHA (American Social Hygiene Association),
    38, 40, 61, 289*n*–90*n*
attitudes, liberalization of, 138
authority, 147
  in sex education debate, 136
  sexual conservatives and, 158, 160, 173
  sexual liberals and, 168, 186–87

Bailey, Beth, 51
Bauer, Gary, 225–26
Bauman, Zygmunt, 232

Sweden, 207–11, 213–15, 231, 238–39
  teenage births in, 285*n*
Switzerland, teenage births in, 285*n*
symbolic politics, 216
syphilis, 41, 285*n*

talents, parable of, 158
Talk About Sex: The Battles over Sex Education in the United States (Irvine), 284*n*
teachers, 175–78, 197–98, 226–27
Teaching Sex: The Shaping of Adolescence in the Twentieth Century (Moran), 283*n*
teenagers, 22–23, 26, 47
  abortion rates of, 23, 26, 285*n*
  age and sexual activity of, 210–11
  births among, 23, 26, 257, 285*n*
  conflicting moral codes of, 188
  decision-making by, 188–90
  French, 212, 255
  in parental consent and notification laws, 188–89
  pregnancy of, 26, 29, 78, 245, 252, 257, 285*n*
  religion and sexual activity of, 310*n*
  sexual activity of, 26, 74, 81–82, 140–41, 210–12, 247–48, 251–52, 256–57, 285*n*, 310*n*, 327*n*
  sexually transmitted diseases among, 23, 253, 258, 285*n*
  sexual revolutions and, 47–48
  style and clothing of, 210, 319*n*
  Swedish, 210–11
television, 196, 198
  social change and, 218
Temple University, 301*n*
temptation, 154, 189–90, 192, 194
Ten Commandments, 184, 187, 194
Terman, Lewis, 51
Thomas, Irene (pseud.), 103–4
Thomas, Keith, 293*n*
Thomassen, Reverend Erik (pseud.), 101, 123
Thornton, Arland, 310*n*
Tipton, Steven, 136
tolerance, 185
traditional values coalition (pro-family movement), 219, 221–23, 321*n*
True Love Waits education program, 222
twelve-step groups, 145

upper-class youth, 49
upper-income families:
  marriage in, 228
  sexual conservatives in, 275

upper-middle class, 125
urbanization, 46

value neutrality, 227
values, 28, 33, 122, 183, 185, 195
  abstinence education and, 246, 249, 258
  decision-making and, 194
  democratization of, 137–38
  information and, 201
  material reality and, 126, 138
  of parents and children, 187
  religion and, 147
  of schools and teachers, 175
  sex education and, 24–25, 30, 243, 247
  sexuality and, 179, 282*n*
  shift in, 244–45
  social group determined by, 126
  see also family values
venereal diseases, *see* sexually transmitted diseases
Vietnam War, 69
Viguerie, Richard, 323*n*
virginity, 28
virginity pledge, 258
virtues, 183

Warner, Amos G., 48–49
Wasserman test, 41
Webber, Dave (pseud), 102–3, 193
welfare state, 123, 175, 317*n*
Weyrich, Paul, 323*n*
white Americans, premarital sex and, 66–67, 74
whole-language educational method, 171, 316*n*
Wilson, James Q., 314*n*
wives:
  in common law, 106–7, 203, 310*n*
  sexual conservatism and role of, 146, 200, 229
women:
  in common law, 106–7, 203, 310*n*
  globalizing culture and, 230
  poverty of, and single motherhood, 33
  professional, 75, 81
  role of, 159, 203–4, 233, 259
  sexual autonomy and, 234
  see also female and male, boundaries between; female sexuality; feminism; motherhood; wives
women's clubs, 40, 43
women's movement, *see* feminism
working-class, 47–49, 53
  and marriage, 228
World Values Survey, 229